Start Me Up!

NEW BRANDING FOR BUSINESSES

gestalten

Foreword

The things we buy and surround ourselves with are supposed to make our everyday lives easier and better. But as oodles of sprouting startups offer endless alternatives for everything we acquire—from the perfect piece of furniture to the best bottle of gin for your mini bar—we no longer simply shop, but carefully curate our belongings. Take the trivial tube of toothpaste, perhaps the most pervasive old-fashioned cliché representing marital crises. The focus nowadays lies less on the way we press out the packaging than on the chosen product itself. Snoop around the bathroom cabinet of any curator-consumer and you'll certainly see something superior to Colgate. Let's hope that brands don't break up relationships like wrongly pressed-out toothpaste packaging purportedly did. But this much seems certain: badly chosen commodities are now considered a blunder. So today's businesses buckle down for the better and strive for the best. But what makes a good brand, and who are the makers behind them? What designs do we feel drawn to? What differentiates this generation of creative entrepreneurs from the big-business players of the past?

Back in the day, when all it took to be big in business was to trade the perfect product, a few large companies built up the first brands that epitomized social status and laid the foundation for contemporary consumer culture. Only later would businesses learn to cater to the consumers of today, including the most sought-after target group—the so-called creative class whose high standards have set a new benchmark for brands. This book compiles a selection of creative branding solutions conceived to cut through today's clutter and fit into our fine-tuned taste: packaging designed to please connoisseurs, along with signets, slogans, and strategies composed to speak to consumers who approach carefully considered commodities as their capital. Current trends are more fluid and more diverse than ever before as we choose not to listen too closely to the global giants that dictated style in former decades. Instead, we turn to today's miscellaneous design directions derived from the manifold desires of our time, one of which is a genuine yearning for yesteryear's groundedness.

Companies are striving to prove that the good things in life still exist by providing their customers with a plethora of products from fairly unimposing family firms. While some may shrug at the sight of simply branded offerings, somewhat antiquated packaging, and low-key logos, many actually feel comforted by designs as discreet and endearingly awkward as the outfits of Steve Jobs or Jerry Seinfeld. It seems as though it isn't irony that makes them so likeable, but rather a smack of no-nonsense. Basic is the new beauty, along with products paired with a passion for practicality. Glaring graphics alone do not impress choosy consumers. Beyond glamorous appearances, consumers care about quality, as well as the provenance of the coffee they drink and the brands they buy.

Businesses think and trade globally these days, and small startups greatly benefit from growing markets. Confronted with immense international competition, more and more of them bet on locally sourced products and locally styled packaging. Imbued with a sincere sense of belonging, some branding solutions thwart today's tendency toward cross-country communication with folkloric forms and regionally anchored rallying cries. Both created and bought by a generation of cosmopolitan connoisseurs, such brands evoke the spirit of our present. The ubiquitous urge to go global has made us all a bit homesick. And knowing that the contemporary consumer has long lost trust in the mass communication of global giants, entrepreneurs are encouraged to return to their roots. Brands built on heritage are likely to be trusted and loved.

The general shift toward tradition has set off a new wave of authentic artisanship, especially in the realm of gastronomy and consumer goods. Bespoke services are booming, and so are shops selling small, personally packed batches of their products. Not too long ago, mass-produced packaging promised sealed freshness, but today we return to the biscuit jar, seeking the snugness of small corner shops and enjoying each cookie individually. With a preference for products that promise to accompany us for a while, we also favor styles that do not run the risk of falling out of fashion, brands that we trust to withstand the test of time. And we certainly take our time choosing them.

With the World Wide Web and its wish lists just a click away, the search for the right brand has become a science in itself. To shop sophisticatedly today is to have selective style and to trace secret tips. Big brands are responding with pop-up shops, pseudonymous sub-labels, and limited editions, but small businesses still retain the affection of the true connoisseurs who choose that which is not easy to google and get. Spurred by a romantic wish for rarity, they shun the high street and instead browse backstreets for the hot and hidden. Markets may be global, but more often than not, understatement wins against overexposure, the unique over the ubiquitous, and modesty over mass marketing. Today, effective branding is based on stories, and successful style based on substance.

To add interesting background information is to increase a brand's appeal. This strategy seems to have been widely adopted among cereal companies that fill up funny folding boxes. Indeed, breakfast brands communicate stories to their sleepy readers, sharing entertaining anecdotes about their founders' personal lives. Next to the extensive nutrition fact tables, contemporary customers are demanding another type of transparency. Brands have always been anxious to speak to us, but it seems that only recently have they started to listen to what we want. Today's best brands care about context, and communicate with sincerity and soul. While bawling out simple slogans was a supposed wonder weapon of the past, the present‘s proper panacea is personality.

The shift from simple product providers to brands with personality originated from the affluent society‘s desire for distinction. Once the market brimmed with suitable offerings, companies began to distinguish themselves through branding. Decades later, when decently designed brands became available in bulk too, consumers' attention turned to brands' behavior. The brand-client relationship continues to become more complex as consumers are granted a significant say, but brands, like humans, can surprise and delight just as easily as they can betray and disappoint. In fact, brands are increasingly being given human-like vocabulary. In the past, lauded admen would compare designs to voices and describe brands with active verbs. Loud Nike still exhorts, and soft-spoken Sony still dreams, but the visual identities of today's smaller brands have added an immense range of vocal registers and character traits. Which brings us from the brands' personalities to the people behind them.

The majority of projects showcased in this book are based on a spirit of collaboration and mutual trust between their makers. The entrepreneur's high appreciation for aesthetics and holistic creative solutions has brought about a new openness in including designers in the business development process. As a result, many modern branding agencies balance between design and business consulting, helping to define the corporate concept. The entrepreneur brings personal perspective and at times contributes creative input. Entrepreneurship has never been so closely connected to the creative industry, and it is now more than ever considered a creative project in itself. An era of entrepreneurial experimentation is ushered in with the notion that creativity is no longer just a commodity contributed by a commissioned designer, but is now seen as the core of the brand.

When it comes to corporate identity, painstaking perfection is being put aside to make room for vivid versatility. Not only has our relationship with brands become more personal, but brands themselves have become more humane. Today's brands are alive: thanks to visionary entrepreneurs and unclenched designers, we can expect the unexpected. The shift in attitude is reflected in the use of the term "corporate identity" over "corporate branding," the latter having a stolid stigma attached to it that evokes misleading marketing tricks.

Brimming with imaginative business ideas that range from a turban tailoring house to an artistically ambitious porn production studio, this book presents brands that break away from stereotypes. It features business founders and designers who work above and beyond their call of duty to come up with surprising branding solutions. These are fresh entrepreneurs who enjoy their newly gained freedom to the fullest, and creatives who play with visual clichés to challenge our preconceptions and the market's prevailing media choices. There is a sporting sense of "just do it" in contemporary branding, but we have surely come a long way from a few famous firms with snappy slogans. Today's brands do it sustainably with soul, sincerity, style, and a smile!

The Beauty Candy Apothecary

BEAUTY PARLOR

Singapore
by Bravo Company

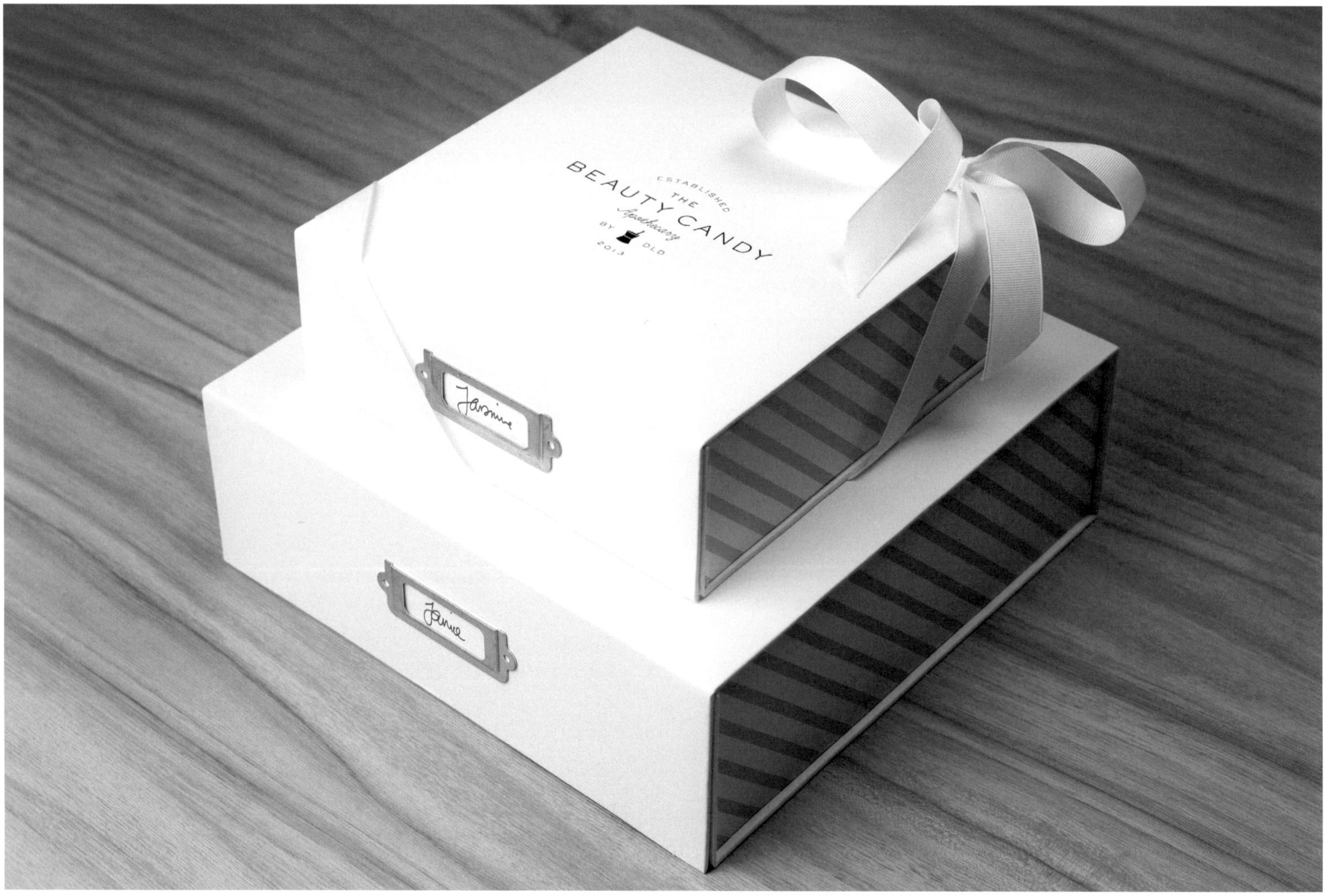

CHEMIST'S CUTIE, BELLE BOUTIQUE! THE BEAUTY CANDY APOTHECARY SUPPLIES SINGAPORE WITH ESSENTIAL LIFESTYLE REMEDIES.

The Beauty Candy Apothecary sells a sweet selection of beauty products and lifestyle accessories from around the world. Founded by fashion designer Astrie Sunindar-Ratner, the concept store was conceived as a culmination of her passion for undecking pretty products in unexpected places, and her dream of opening a shop inspired by the small boutiques in New York's Soho, London's Notting Hill, and Tokyo's Omotesando. With that in mind, Bravo Company created a boutique-like brand for Beauty Candy. The tidy typography takes cues from traditional apothecary trademarks.

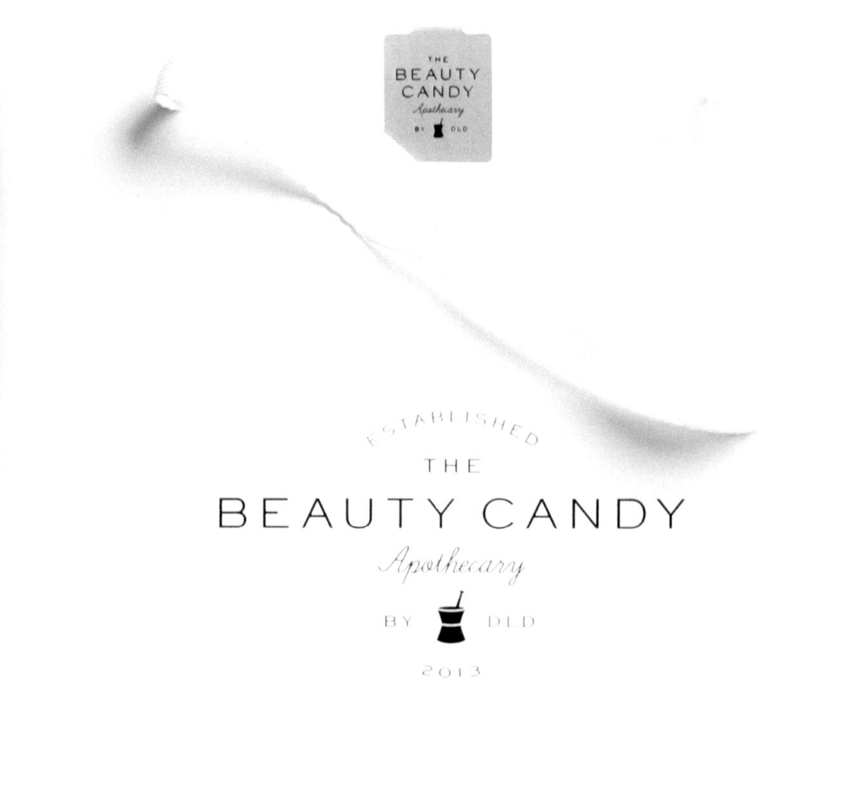

Caroline

ADDRESS—501 BUKIT TIMAH ROAD
#01-05B CLUNY COURT SINGAPORE 259760
TELEPHONE—+65 6314 3828
WEBSITE—WWW.BEAUTYCANDY.COM.SG

THE
BEAUTY CANDY
Apothecary

WWW.BEAUTYCANDY.COM.SG

With Love,

Caroline

THE
BEAUTY CANDY
Apothecary

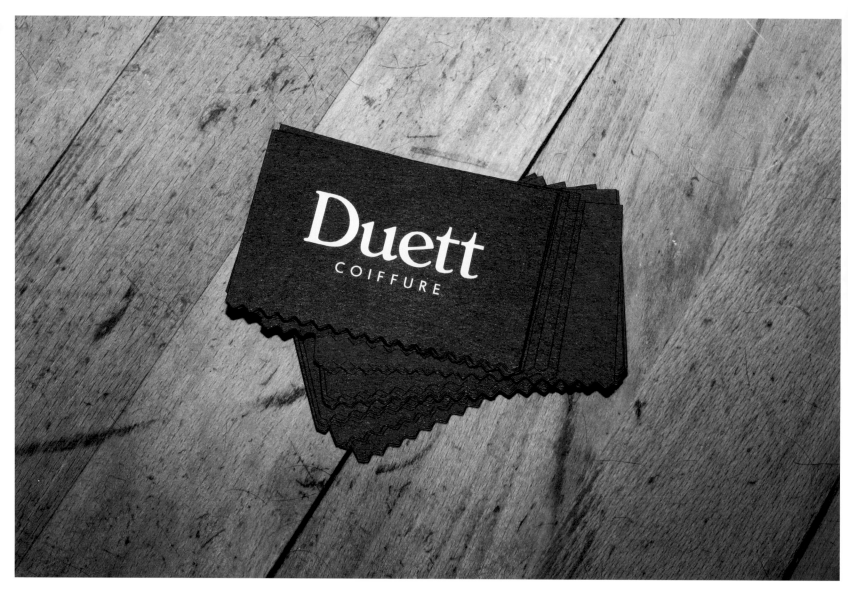

Coiffure Duett

HAIR SALON

St. Gallen, Switzerland, *by Bureau Collective*

CLEVER DIE-CUTS FOR COIFFURE DUETT: BUREAU COLLECTIVE CREATED A CLASSY CORPORATE IDENTITY FOR THE COMPANY AND TRULY CUTTING-EDGE CARDS.

The term duett denotes a musical work to be performed by two musicians. In this case, we have two hairdressers, Fabienne Meier and Nadine Loser, concertedly running their St. Gallen salon. The two like to think of their daily business as a duett, a coordinated interaction between the client and the hairdresser. Bureau Collective were brought on board for the branding, and came up with a set of sleek corporate graphics including distinct die-cut business cards for the hairdressing duo. The salon's interior was carefully composed to match both the brand's classic theme and the architectural setting.

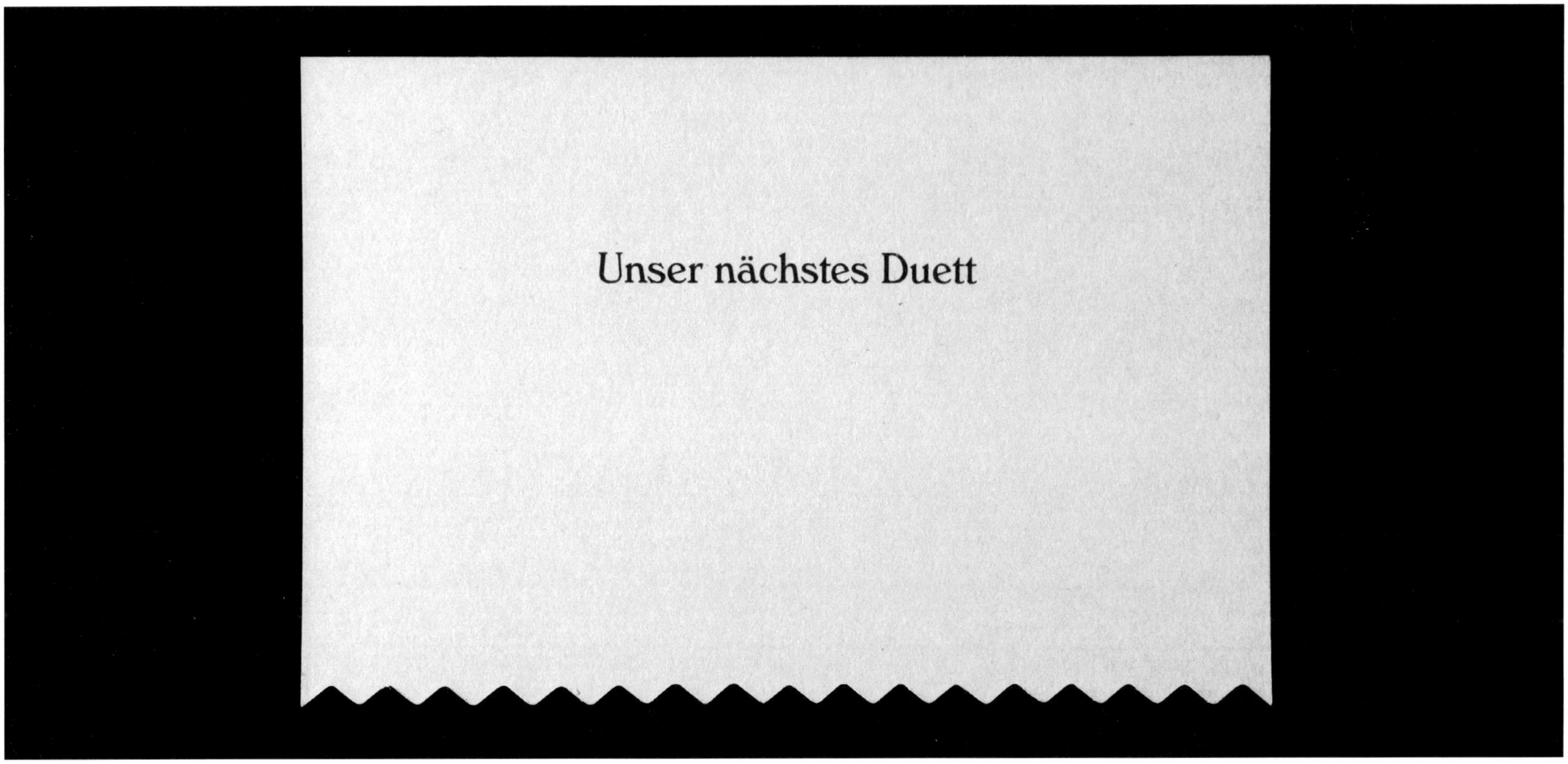

Unser nächstes Duett

Appointment Card

Glory Hazel

PORN PRODUCTION STUDIO

Basel, Switzerland
by Bureau Collective

PORN HAS NEVER BEEN THIS PRETTY. GLORY HAZEL SQUEEZES THE INDUSTRY'S POTENTIAL WITH A SUPER SEXY CORPORATE IDENTITY.

Underwhelmed by the aesthetic aspirations of popular pornographic productions, Sabine Fischer and Sandra Lichtenstern set out to satisfy the senses of the sophisticated consumer by founding Glory Hazel. Devoting body and soul to play lustfully with pornography's untapped potential, the firm counters stolid scenes and stereotypes of a fascinatingly uncreative industry with sensuously creative content and pleasant presentation. Based on their background in the creative field, Fischer and Lichtenstern see porn as a delicate design challenge, and collaborated with Bureau Collective to give Glory Hazel its luscious look.

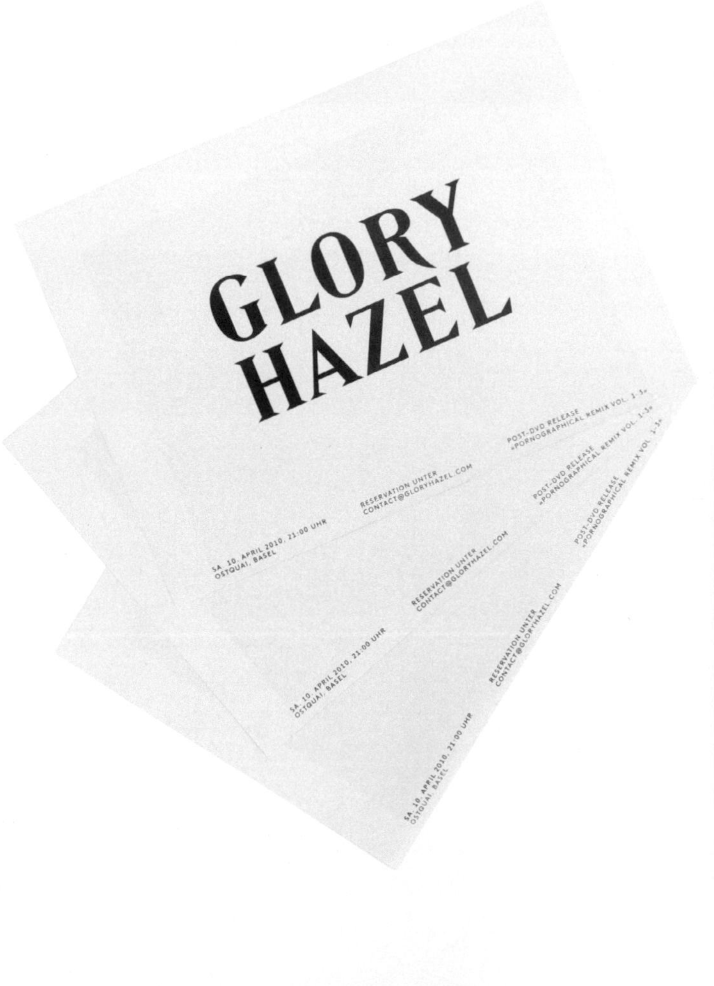

GLORY HAZEL

Pornographical
Remix

vol. : 1–3

Belle à DaDa
Clockwise From Above
Magnum, Magnum!

GLORY HAZEL hat sich mit Leib und Seele dem Darstellungsfeld der Pornografie verschrieben und spielt lustvoll mit dessen noch ungenutztem Potential. Im Fokus steht die sinnlich-kreative und innovative Auseinandersetzung mit diesem ästhetisch vernachlässigten Bereich.

Die DVD »Pornographical Remix Vol.: 1–3« ist kreatives Recycling zahlreicher Pornofilme aus den Siebzigerjahren. GLORY HAZEL ist der Meinung, dass dieses Filmmaterial Stellen von ästhetischer Qualität sexueller Darstellung enthält, wie sie heute nicht mehr zu finden ist. Zahlreiche solcher Qualitätsmomente wurden für »Pornographical Remix« herausgefiltert.

Die Filmschnipsel durchliefen ein strenges und sehr persönliches Auswahlverfahren und wurden zu einem neuen Ganzen zusammengefügt. So sind drei Porno-Remixes entstanden, welche den sexuell-visuellen Ansprüchen von GLORY HAZEL genügen. Fadenscheinige Dialoge und omnipräsentes Gestöhne wurden durch eigens dafür komponierte Musik ersetzt.

Die drei Kurzfilme verzichten ganz auf Storytelling, vielmehr handelt es sich um erregende Stimmungscollagen, die sich vom heute gängigen Brei aus nackter Haut und dumpfer Künstlichkeit abheben.

Ziel ist es, damit auch jene anzusprechen, die bis anhin einen weiten Bogen um Pornos gemacht haben.

Diese DVD darf Jugendlichen unter 18 Jahren weder gezeigt, noch in einer anderen Form zugänglich gemacht werden.

www.gloryhazel.com
contact@gloryhazel.com

Laufzeit: ca. 30 Minuten
© Magma Film

GLORY HAZEL hat sich mit Leib und Seele dem Darstellungsfeld der Pornografie verschrieben und spielt lustvoll mit dessen noch ungenutztem Potential. Im Fokus steht die sinnlich-kreative und innovative Auseinandersetzung mit diesem ästhetisch vernachlässigten Bereich.

Die DVD »Pornographical Remix Vol.: 1–3« ist kreatives Recycling zahlreicher Pornofilme aus den Siebzigerjahren. GLORY HAZEL ist der Meinung, dass dieses Filmmaterial Stellen von ästhetischer Qualität sexueller Darstellung enthält, wie sie heute nicht mehr zu finden ist. Zahlreiche solcher Qualitätsmomente wurden für »Pornographical Remix« herausgefiltert.

Die Filmschnipsel durchliefen ein strenges und sehr persönliches Auswahlverfahren und wurden zu einem neuen Ganzen zusammengefügt. So sind drei Porno-Remixes entstanden, welche den sexuell-visuellen Ansprüchen von GLORY HAZEL genügen. Fadenscheinige Dialoge und omnipräsentes Gestöhne wurden durch eigens dafür komponierte Musik ersetzt.

Die drei Kurzfilme verzichten ganz auf Storytelling, vielmehr han-

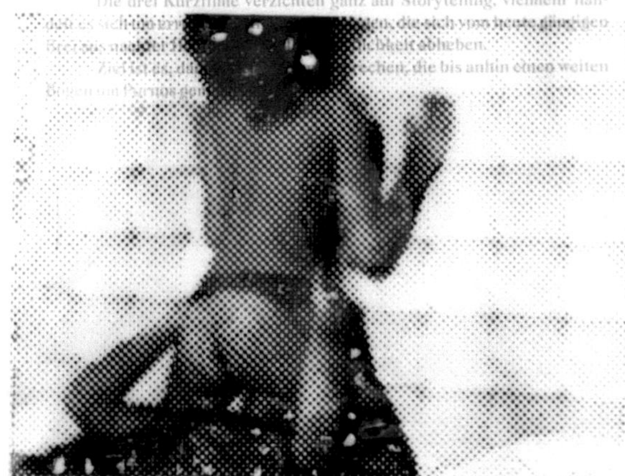

Diese DVD darf Jugendlichen unter 18 Jahren weder gezeigt, noch in einer anderen Form zugänglich gemacht werden.

www.gloryhazel.com
contact@gloryhazel.com

Laufzeit: ca. 30 Minuten
© Magma Film

MITUNTER
PORNOGRAFISCH
MUNTER

GLORY HAZEL

Allschwilerstrasse 35
CH-4055 Basel

sandra@gloryhazel.com
www.gloryhazel.com

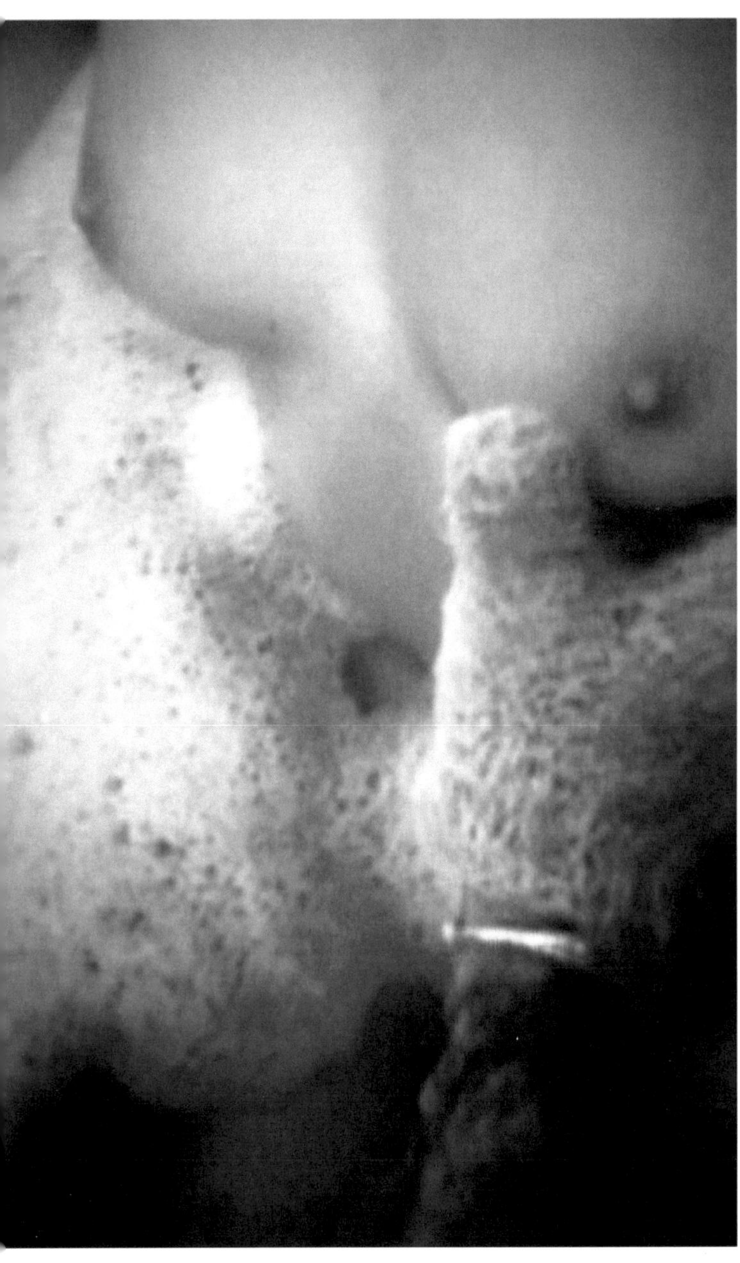

MITUNTER
PORNOGRAFISCH
MUNTER

GLORY HAZEL

Allschwilerstrasse 35
CH-4055 Basel

sabine@gloryhazel.com
www.gloryhazel.com

L'Atelier Blanc

HAIR COLORIST

Paris, France, *by Codefrisko*

L'ATELIER BLANC IS MASTER COLORIST FRÉDÉRIC MENNETRIER'S WHITE WORKSHOP. CODEFRISKO'S CAMEO COMPOSITIONS CONNOTE THE CONSCIENTIOUSNESS OF HIS CRAFT AND THE ALCHEMY OF COLORS.

L'Atelier Blanc is home to haute haircare performed by Paris's prestigious colorist Frédéric Mennetrier and his team. Having worked as a color consultant for L'Oreal Professional for 15 years, Mennetrier decided to open his own "white workshop," the salon that would serve as a superb setting for personalized pigmentation. Considering coloring a craft affiliated with the alchemy of colors, he envisioned an intimate space inspired by the concept of the classic cabinet of curiosities. Codefrisko were called on to put the plan into practice and to develop a corporate identity in accordance with the concept. Their ornamental cameo logo composition denotes the antique nobility of a chemist and his elixirs for eternal beauty. The hourglass icon within the emblem's frieze border symbolizes the standstill of time: any appointment with Mennetrier starts with a screening session that takes a minimum of three hours.

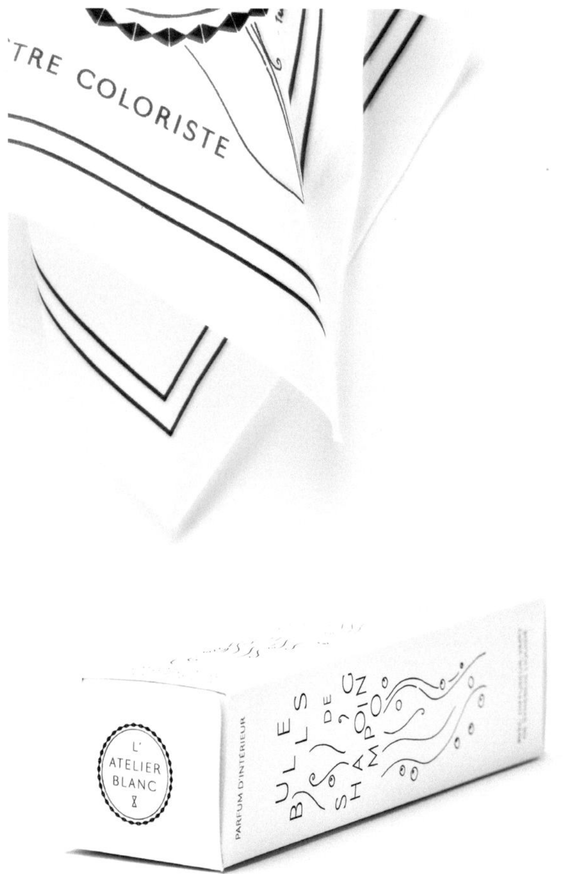

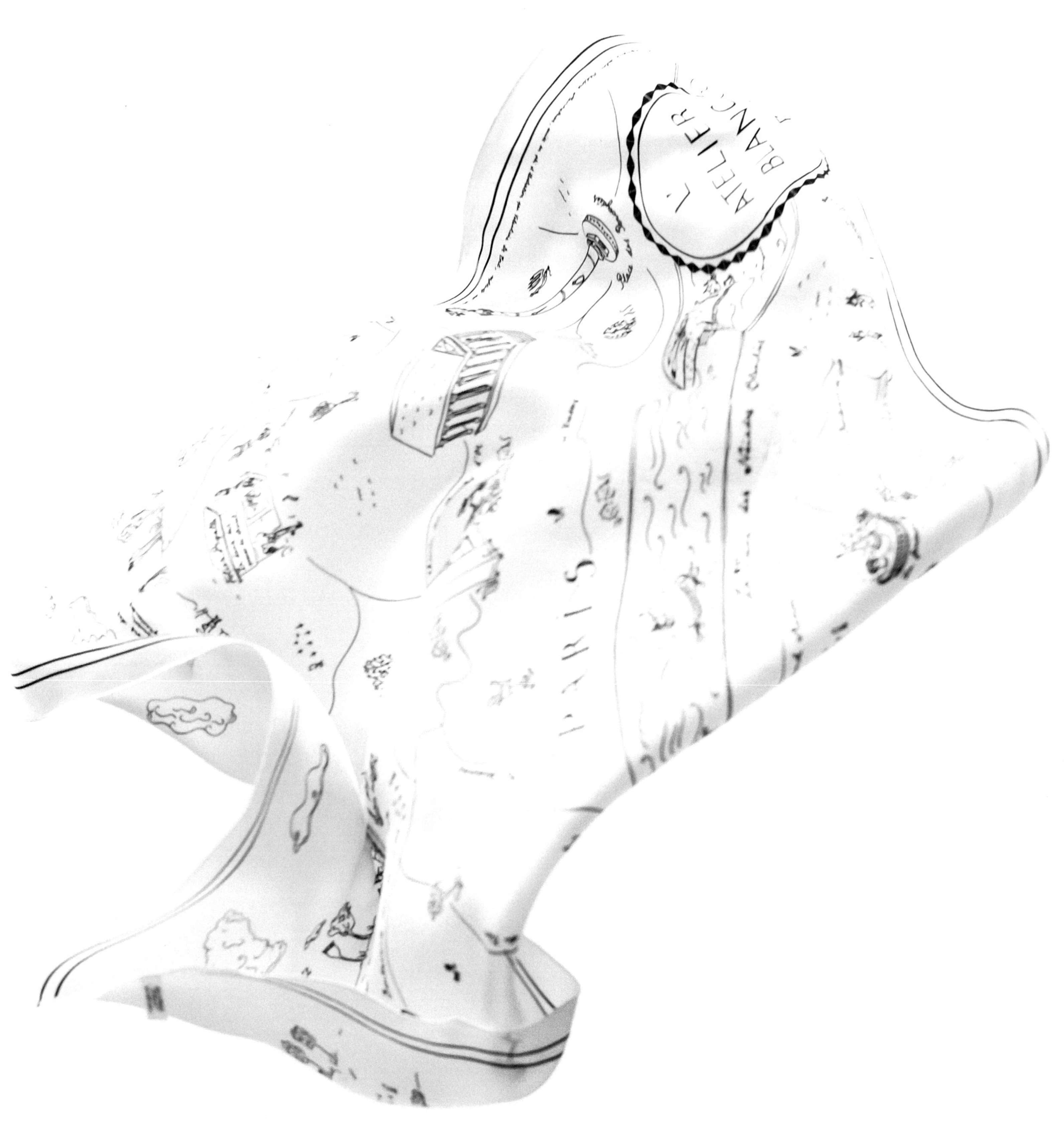

AM
DORFPLATZ
8
KÖSTLICHES
STEIRISCHES

Am Dorfplatz 8

DELICATESSEN

Weitendorf, Austria

by Moodley Brand Identity

BETTINA STOISSER-HUBMANN SHOWS A WINNING TOUCH FOR FASHIONABLE FARMING. TEAMING UP WITH MOODLEY'S DESIGNERS, SHE MANAGED TO TURN AM DORFPLATZ 8 INTO THE NUMBER ONE ADDRESS FOR STYRIAN SPECIALTIES.

Weitendorf's Am Dorfplatz 8 has long been a good address for fine farm-made delicacies and culinary delights from the countryside. Yet farmer Bettina Stoisser-Hubmann raises the bar even higher than the generations that have previously managed the Styrian farm. Her ambition led her to "redefine her yield" away from country kitsch to an authentic range of all-natural products. The solution, masterly implemented by Moodley Brand Identity, was a straightforward brand to upgrade Stoisser-Hubmann's high-quality specialties, which would be sold in beautifully wrapped limited editions. Her popular Styrian pumpkin seed oil now comes in noble clay bottles, and her chutneys in likeable little jars.

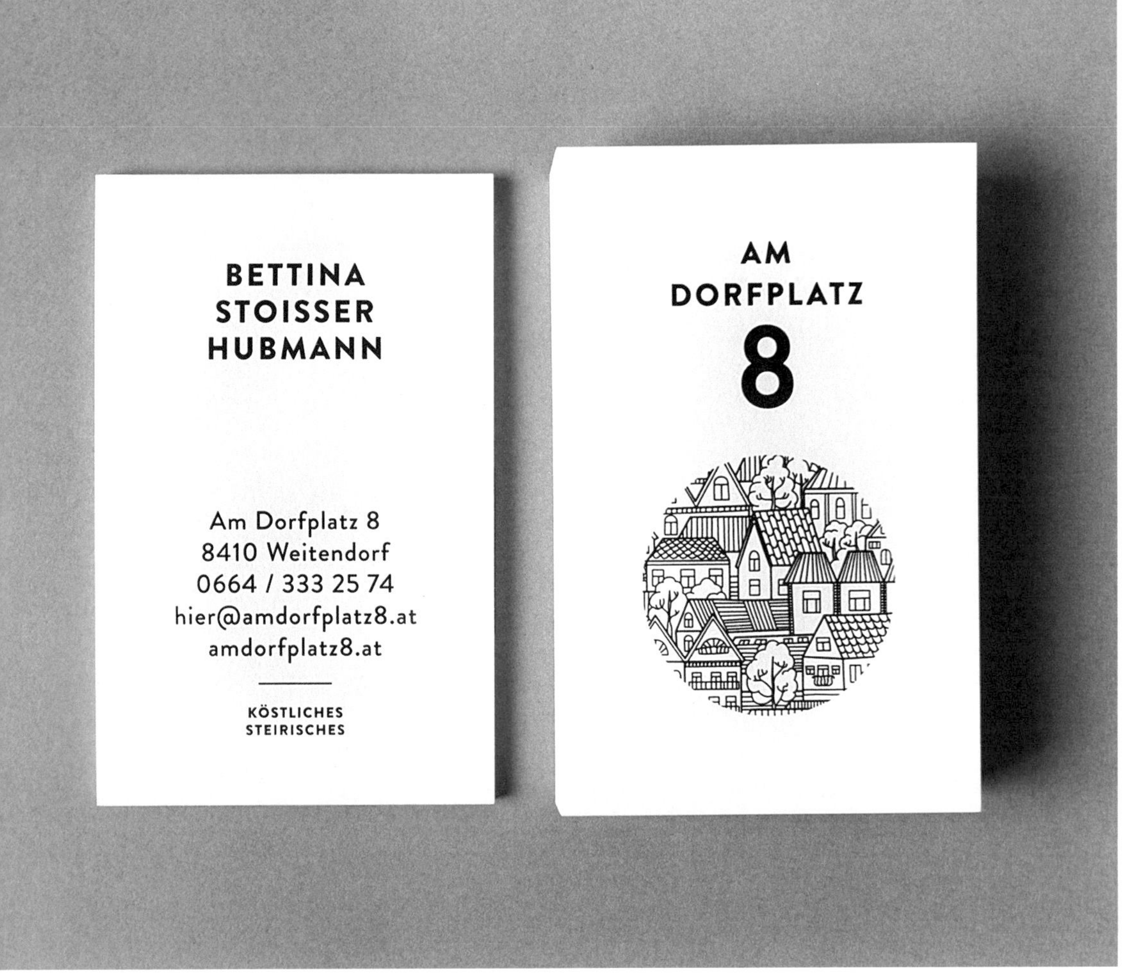

Martina Sperl

UPHOLSTERY

Graz, Austria, *by Moodley Brand Identity*

SICK OF SEDATE SETTEES?
MARTINA SPERL UPDATES UPHOLSTERING AND IMPRESSES WITH A CONCISE CORPORATE IMAGE.

Tired of the well-worn working structures and styles of her traditional trade, upholsterer Martina Sperl set herself the mission of freshening up the field with her own workshop. Set up as an antidote to the archaic stereotypes of the somewhat sleepy sector, the place serves as the perfect setting for Sperl to breathe fresh life into her furniture and add a personal touch to suit contemporary taste. Moodley Brand Identity adopted Martina Sperl's personal approach and arrived at a tangible brand as persistent as her product.

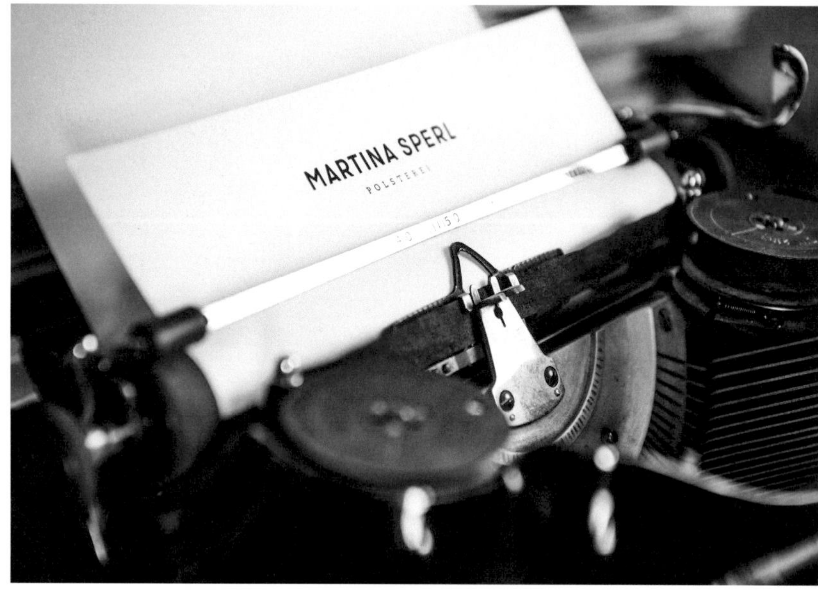

Opening Invitation

Leading Search Partners

LEADING SEARCH PARTNERS SUPPORTS FIRMS BY FINDING HIGH-PROFILE PERSONNEL IN SECRET SPOTS. THEIR CORPORATE IDENTITY TELLS THE STORY OF THEIR TREASURE HUNT FOR TOP TALENTS.

RECRUITMENT AGENCY

Vienna, Austria, *by Moodley Brand Identity*

While hundreds of headhunters are looking for talents, only few of them succeed in finding the right ones. The Austrian recruitment agency Leading Search Partners operates two offices in Austria, one in Serbia, and another in Slovenia, and communicates within a global network to assure more than mere demand analysis. To connect companies and top talents for the long term, they ask attentively and headhunt away from trodden trails. Moodley Brand Identity's cheerful corporate identity parallels the company's core competencies, linking them to those of treasure seekers, pearl divers, and gold-diggers.

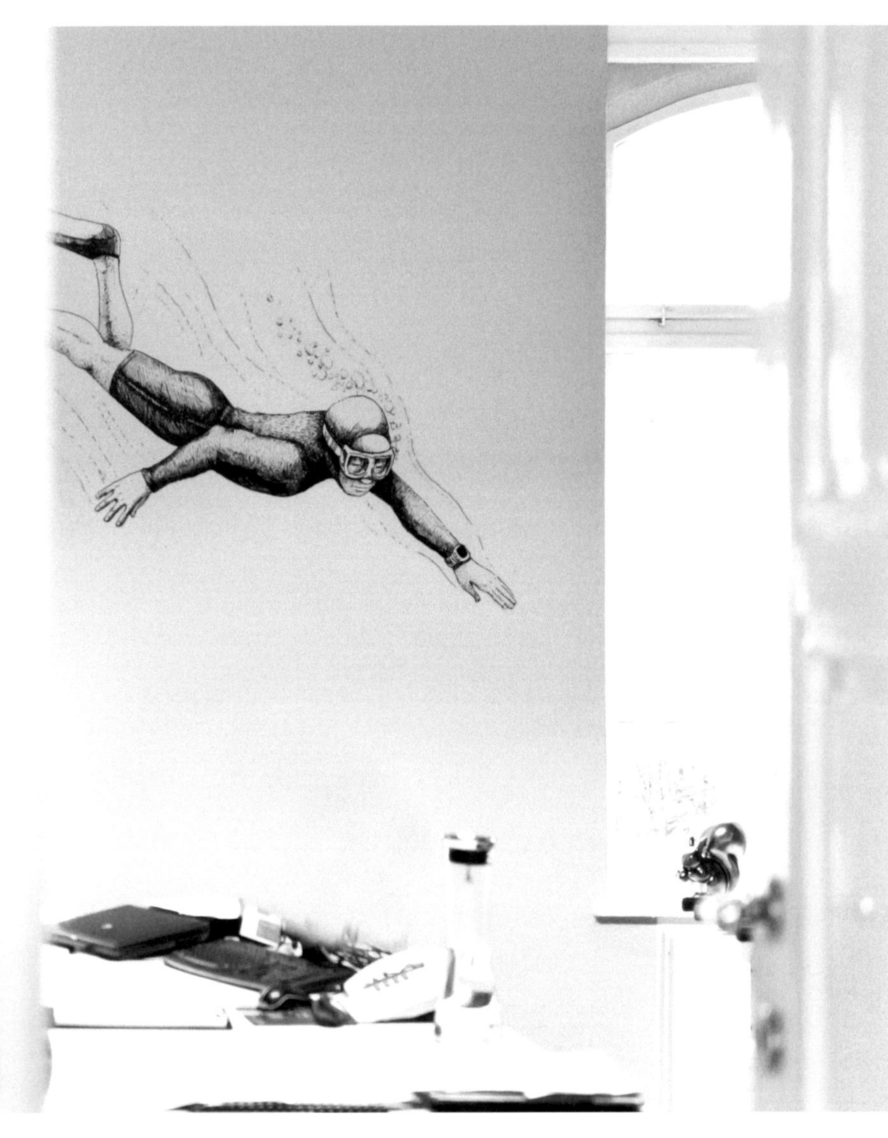
 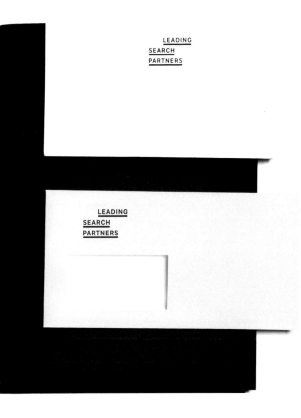
LEADING
SEARCH
PARTNERS
LEADING
SEARCH
PARTNERS
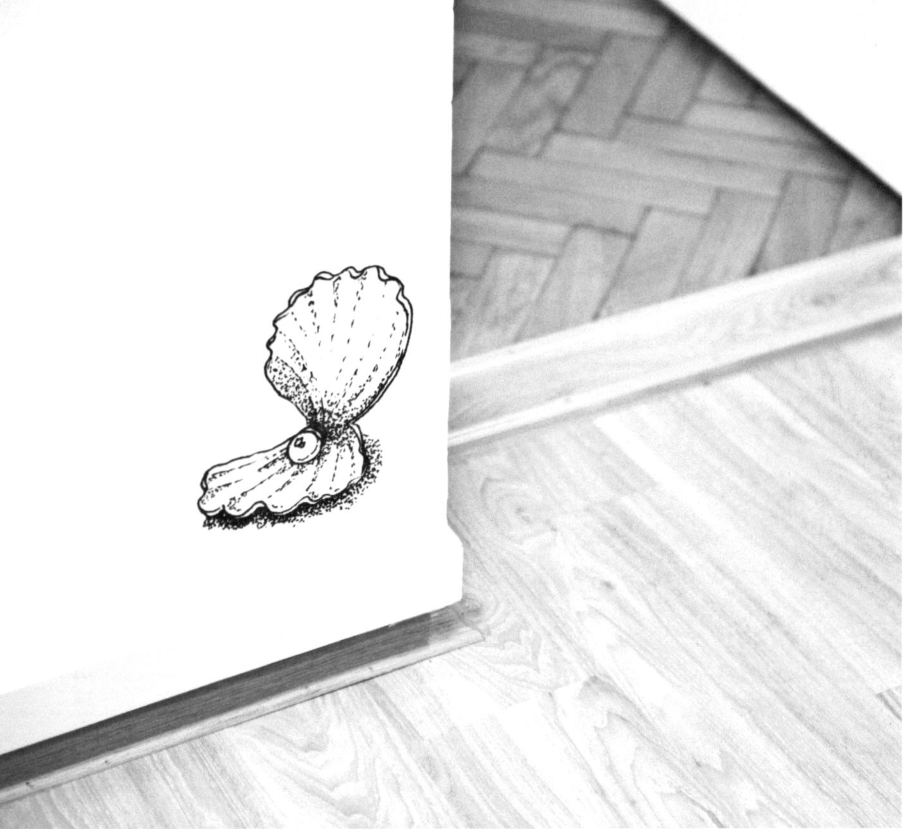

T4TURBAN

T4TURBAN
INFO@T4TURBAN.COM
MADINAH RD. THALIA ST. INTERSECTION
YANBU, SAUDI ARABIA - P.O. BOX 21452
T4TURBAN.COM

T4Turban

TURBAN TAILORS

Dammam, Saudi Arabia, *by Anagrama*

DESIGNER RAND ALBASSAM JAZZES UP THE HIJAB, AND TURNS THE TRADITIONAL TURBAN INTO A FASHION ITEM FAR BEYOND BELIEF.

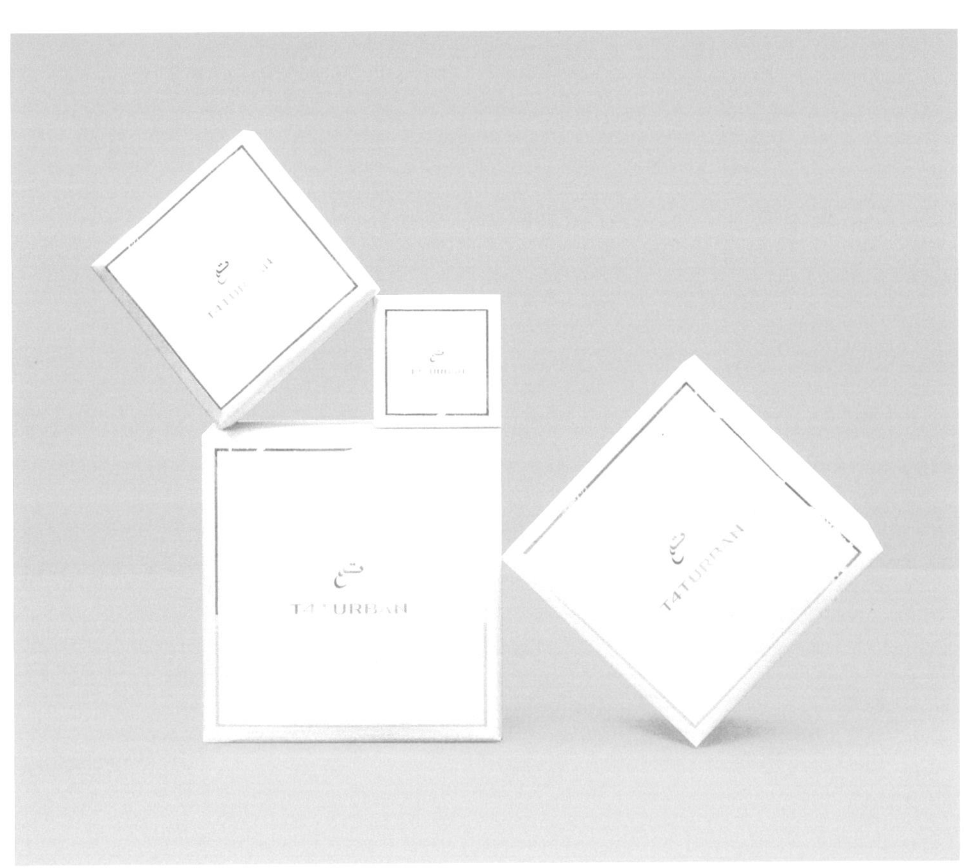

T4TURBAN tailors custom-made turbans for à la mode Muslim women. The company was established by Saudi entrepreneur Rand AlBassam, a trained fashion designer, trusting that Muslim tradition does not necessarily clash with today's trends. Working with patterns and colors that comply with Saudi Arabian culture without compromising on contemporary taste, she arrived at a comprehensive collection of tony turbans that revolutionize the Middle Eastern hijab, reviving a headpiece that has been neglected by the fashion industry for far too long. T4TURBAN products are mainly marketed by word-of-mouth and family members, but Anagrama assisted with graphics. Designed to befit Rand AlBassam's unconventional undertakings, their unobtrusive branding solution bridges between trends and tradition, too.

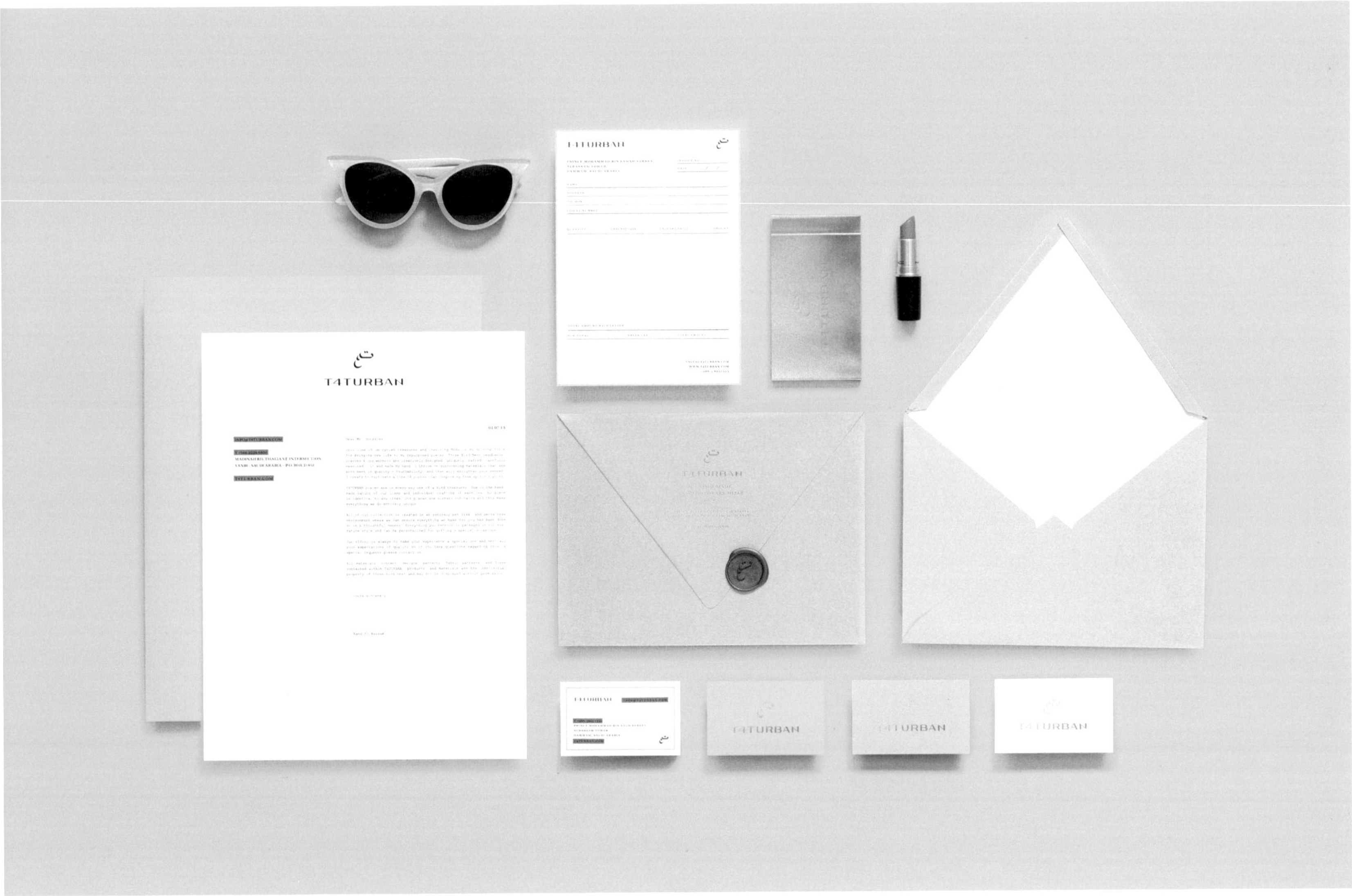

Maderista

CONCEPT CARPENTRY

Monterrey, Mexico, *by Anagrama*

MADERISTA'S MONIKER IS MADE-UP FROM THE WORD MADERA (SPANISH FOR WOOD), AND 'ISTA,' THE SUFFIX OF SPECIALISM.

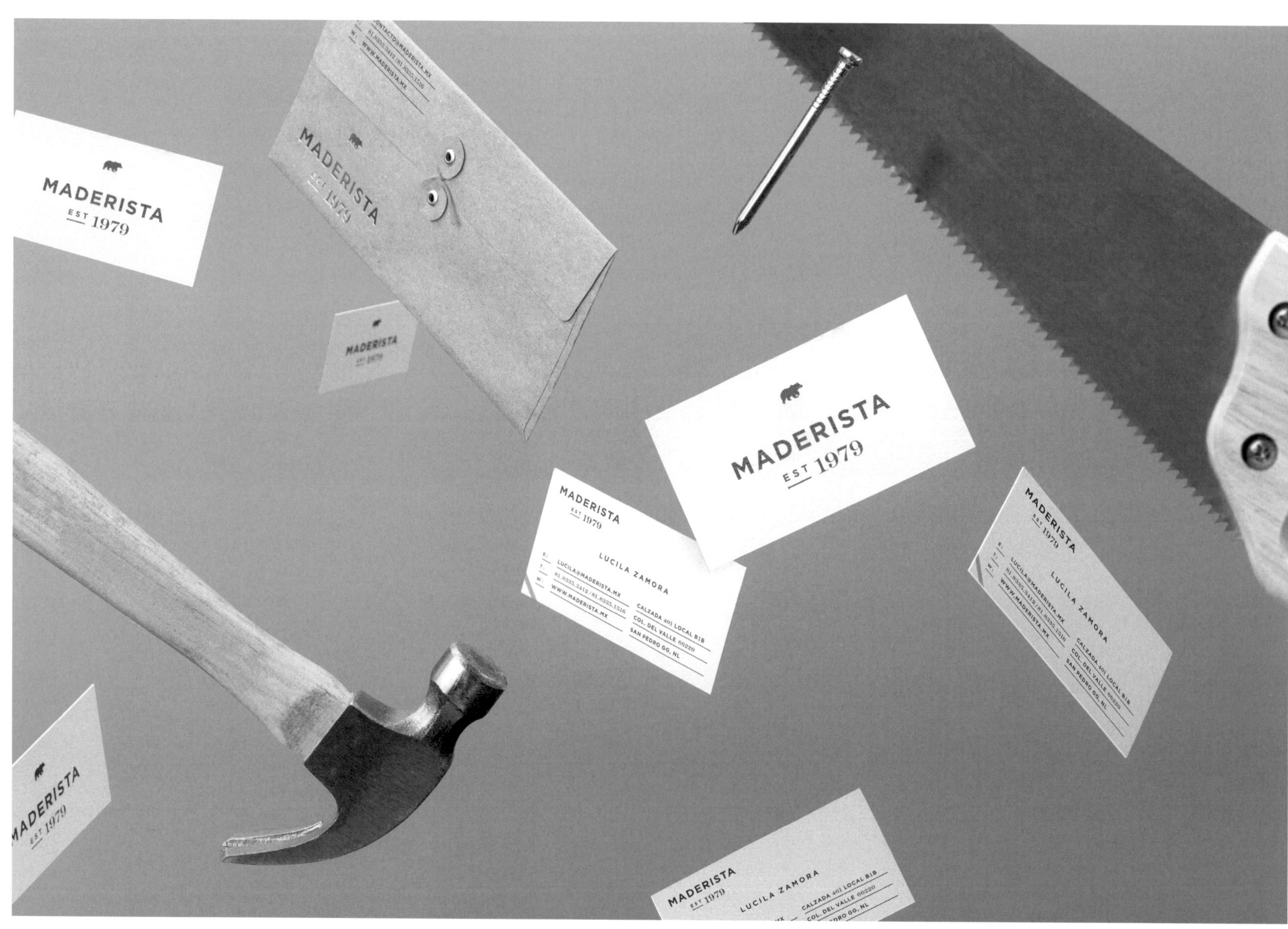

Maderista manufactures custom furniture from fine woods. Working with a team of diligent designers, they develop personalized proposals and products to be sold in the brand's own boutique. With more than 30 years of experience, Maderista approached Anagrama to consolidate its company with a rebrand that would express its expertise in a modern and all-encompassing way. The first measure was a new moniker, Maderista, a made-up compound consisting of madera (Spanish for wood) and the suffix 'ista,' a designation of profession, conviction, and character. The logo includes two icons: a bear, embodying the natural strength and robustness of wood, and a nail, symbolizing skilled craftsmanship—which the porous, off-white paper also conveys. Touches of hot-stamped gold comply with the classiness of the company's custom products, all of which are engraved with an orange line in the left-hand corner. A superb showroom setup portrays the plentitude of possibilities achieved through Maderista's personalized production.

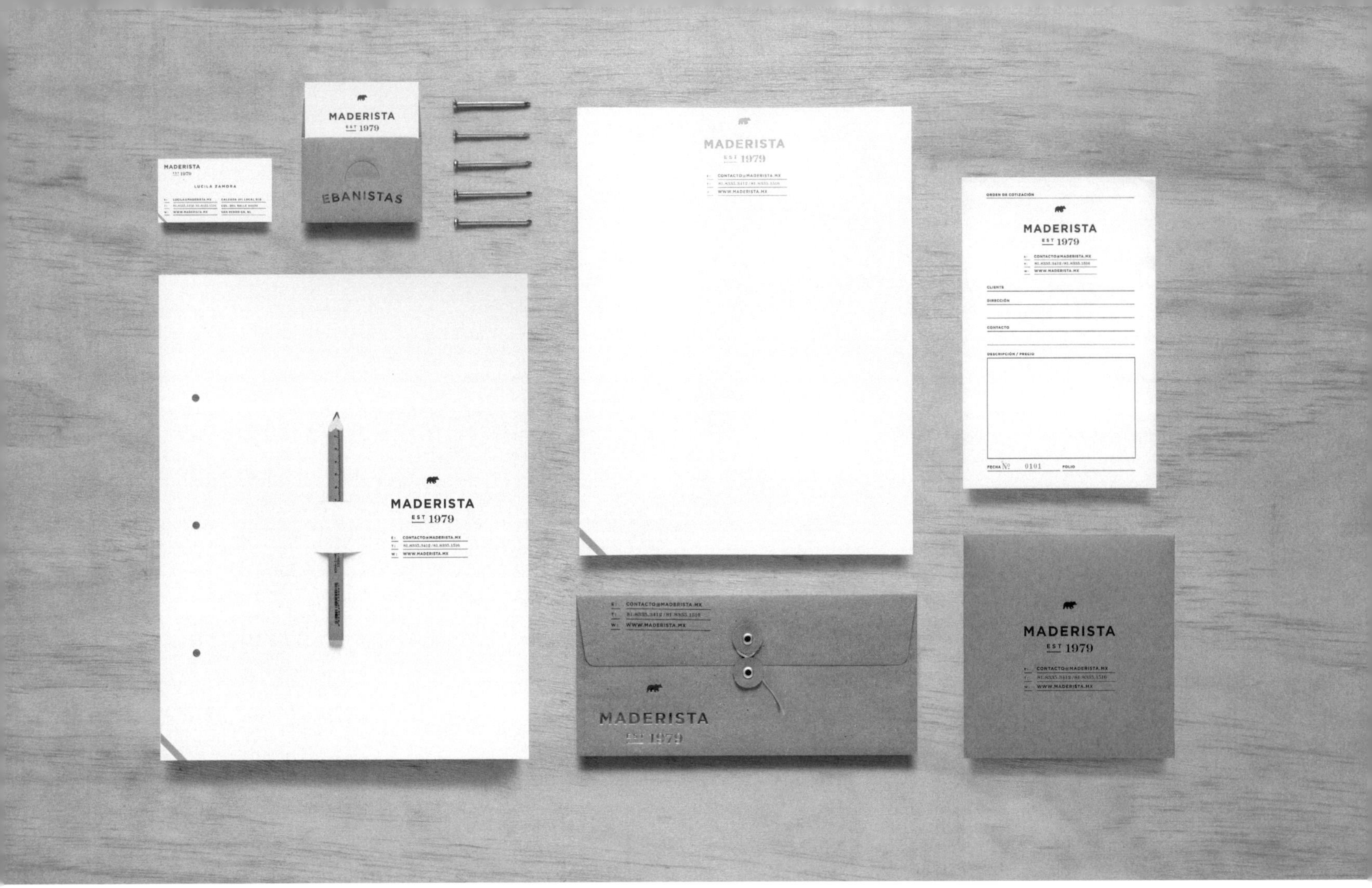

E: CONTACTO@MADERISTA.MX
T: 81.8335.3412/81.8335.1516
W: WWW.MADERISTA.MX
MADERISTA
EST 1979

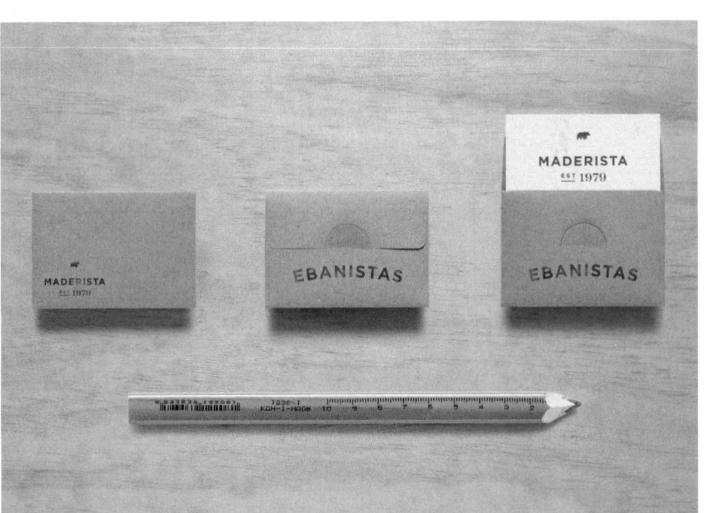
MADERISTA
EST 1979
EBANISTAS
MADERISTA
EST 1979
EBANISTAS

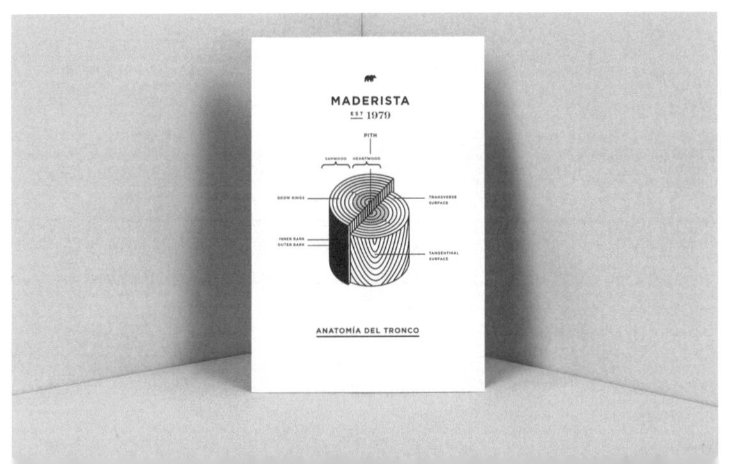
MADERISTA
EST 1979
PITH
ANATOMÍA DEL TRONCO

E: CONTACTO@MADERISTA.MX
T: 81.8335.3412/81.8335.1516
W: WWW.MADERISTA.MX
MADERISTA
EST 1979

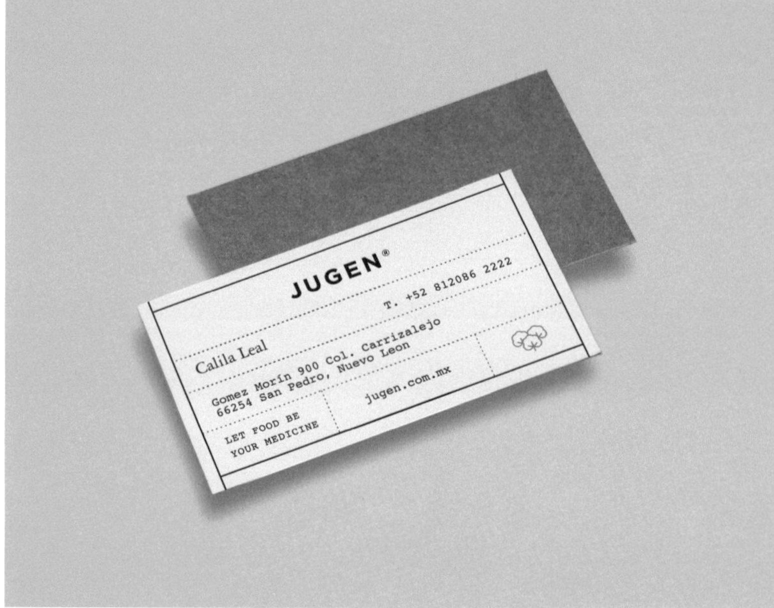

Jugen

FITNESS FOODS

Monterrey, Mexico, *by Anagrama*

JUICY JUGEN SETS NEW STANDARDS IN DETOX DRINKS AND SUPERFOODS FOR THE FIT. SPECIAL FEATURE: ITS SLIM 'N' SLEEK DESIGN SOLUTION.

Jugen specializes in salutary superfoods, like juices made from all-natural ingredients, composed to cleanse and detoxify the body. Anagrama's design approach draws on ancient apothecary bottles and incorporates soft hues inspired by herbal healing. Basing the brand on a clean and contemporary backdrop, they arrived at an aesthetic that connects healthcare with hipness. The interior is a modern mix between a bar and a suave chemist's concept store.

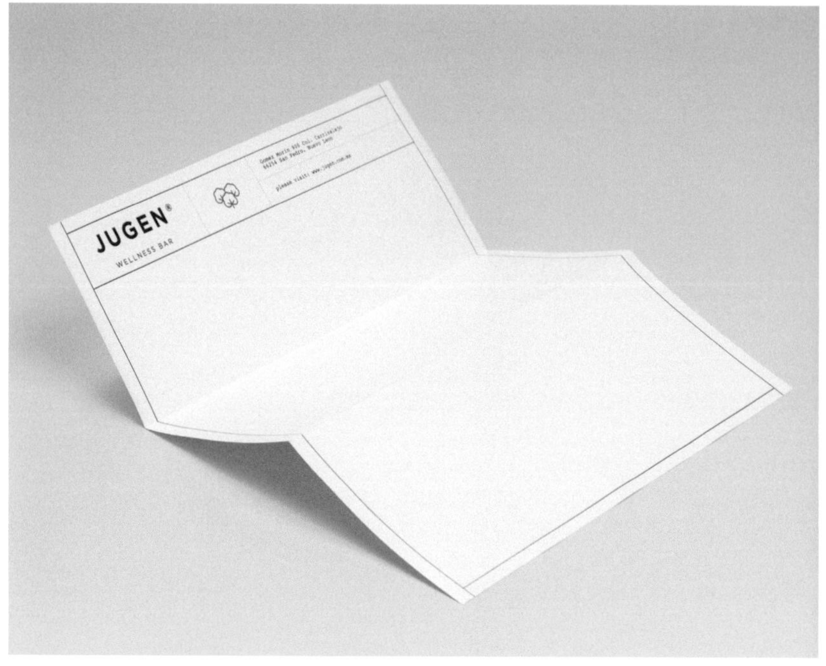

JUGEN®
WELLNESS BAR

HEALING ELIXIRS
GREEN SELECTION
ROOT SELECTION
FRUIT SELECTION
SUPERFOOD SMOOTHIES
TONICS
LET FOOD BE YOUR MEDICINE

Food Studio

CULINARY EVENTS

Oslo, Norway, *by Bielke + Yang*

FOOD STUDIO SERVES UP SAVORY STORIES,
LOCALLY SOURCED SPECIALTIES, AND A GOOD DEAL OF GREAT GRAPHICS.

Established by culinary consultant Cecilie Dawes, Food Studio does catering for foodie-fantasies such as kitchen themed table talks and creative cooking courses. Bielke+Yang have been part of the project from the very start, working closely with Dawes to develop a business strategy and set the tone for the brand. Together with a team of copywriters, film producers, and photographers, the designers helped create a holistic corporate identity inspired by Nordic nature and its rural narratives.

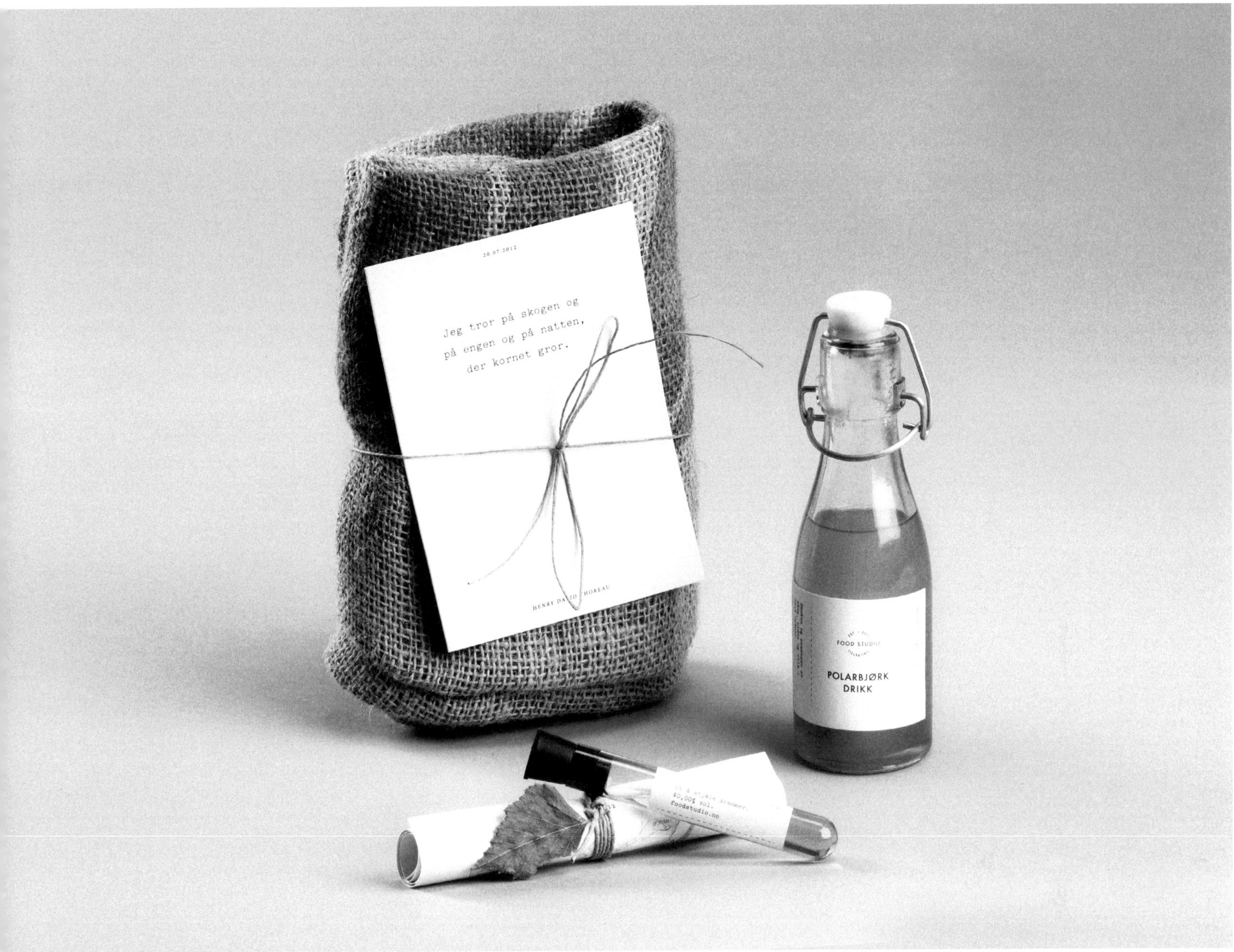

20.07.2012
Jeg tror på skogen og
på engen og på natten,
der kornet gror.
HENRY DAVID THOREAU
FOOD STUDIO
POLARBJØRK
DRIKK
foodstudio.no

20.07.12
VI HAR NÅ GLEDEN AV Å ØNSKE DEG VELKOMMEN
TIL SOMMERKVELDEN VÅR PÅ LILLEBORG.
VI VIL TA DEG MED TILBAKE TIL NATUREN,
TIL STILLHETEN, TIL KNITRINGEN OG LUKTEN AV
BÅL, TILBAKE TIL BARNDOMMENS FØRSTE SKOGSTUR
TIL LUKTENE, SMAKENE OG FARGENE.
MØT OPP I FOOD STUDIOS LOKALER VED
IVAN BJØRNDALSGT. 9 PÅ LILLEBORG
KL. 18:00 DEN 20.07.12. VEL MØTT!
IVAN BJØRNDALS GT. 9
KL 18:00
FOOD STUDIO
MED VENNLIG HILSEN
MAAEMO, TIM WENDELBOE
& FOOD STUDIO
20

FOOD STUDIO
LILLEBORG

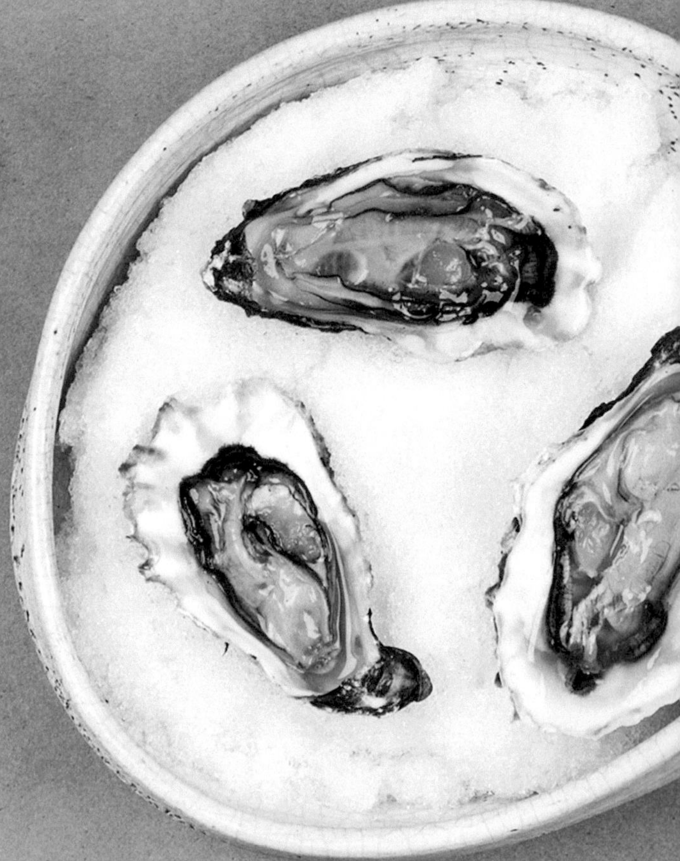

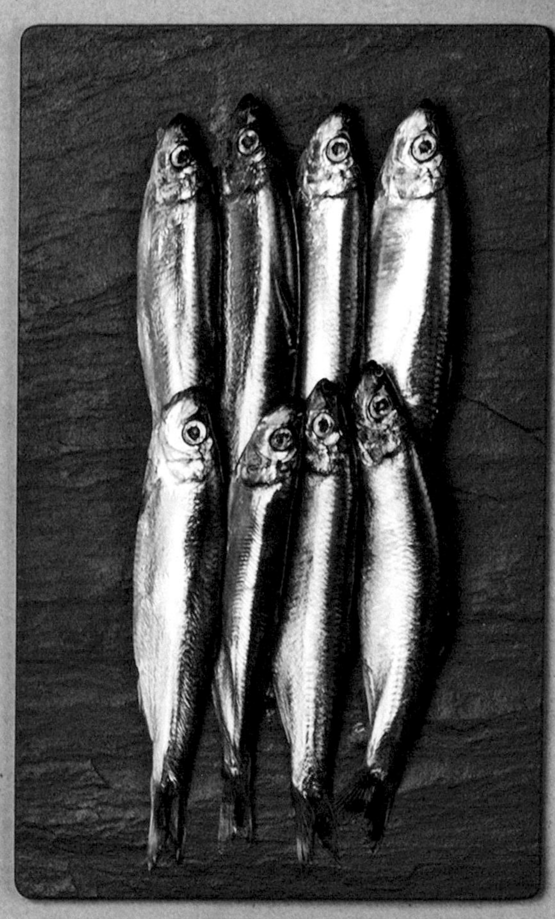

FOOD STUDIO
Food
Studio
№6
foodstudio.no

BØGEDAL No 218
Alkohol: 6,5 %
Brygget: 18/5 2010
Tappet: 8/6 2010
Food
Studio
No6

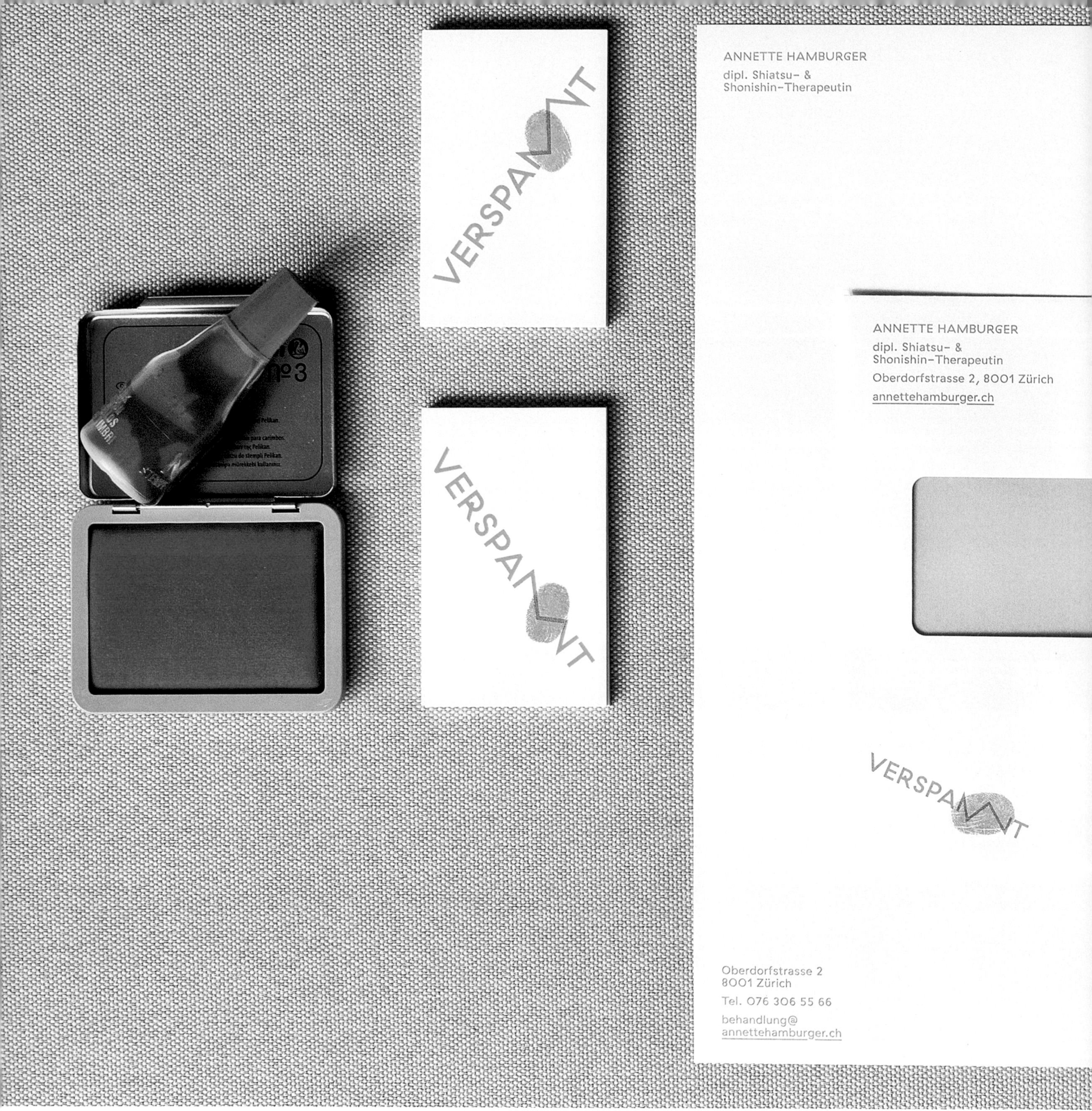

Annette Hamburger

PHYSICAL THERAPIST

Zurich, Switzerland
by David Büsser & Patrik Ferrarelli

AN IDENTITY AS INDIVIDUAL AS A FINGERPRINT: ANNETTE HAMBURGER'S SET OF SYMBOLS STANDS FOR THE PERSONAL PRESSURE TREATMENTS THE THERAPIST PRACTICES TO RELEASE HARDENED MUSCLES.

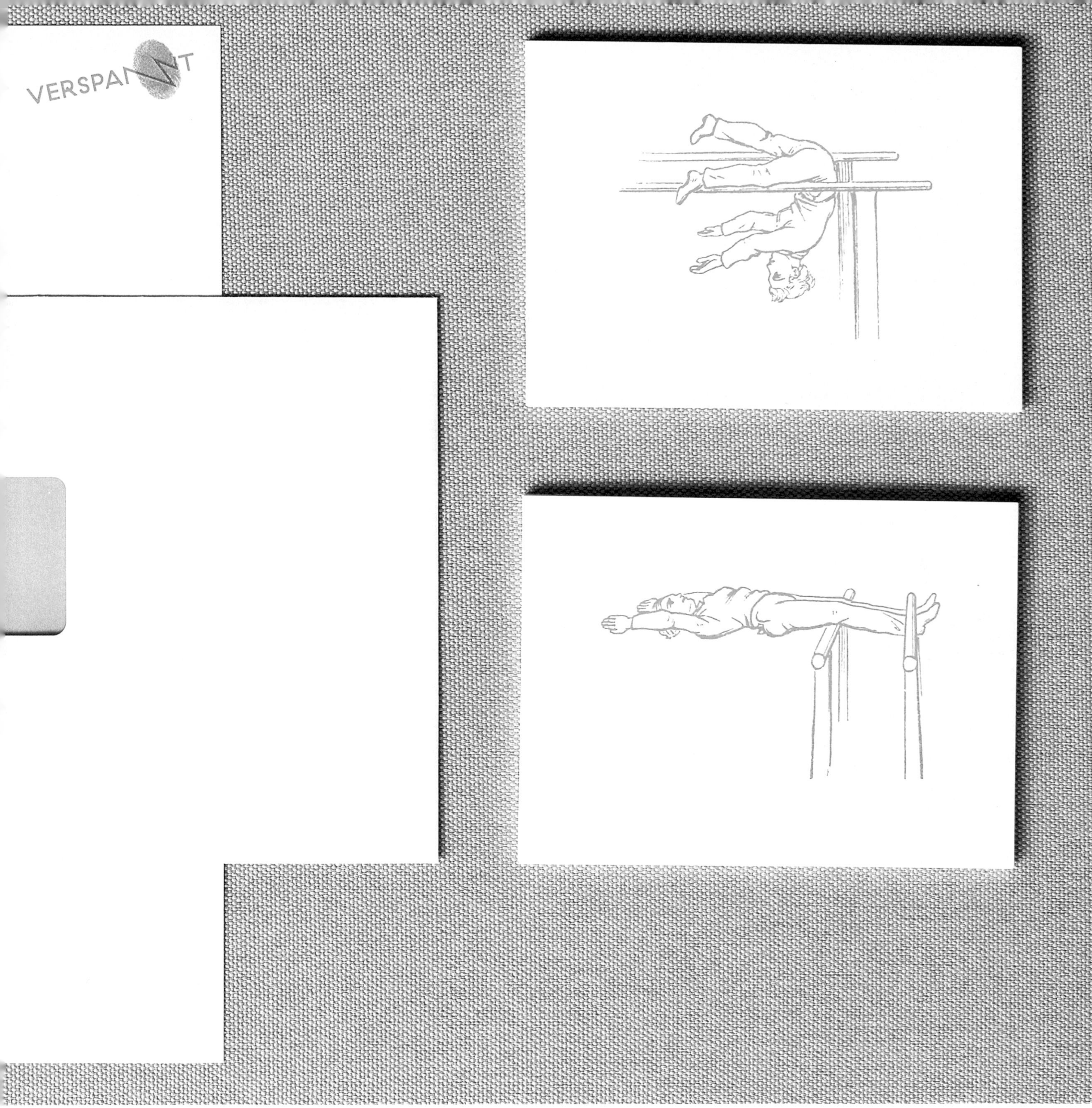

Annette Hamburger is a shiatsu and shonishin therapist providing treatment to unbend tense bodies. Having worked as a masseuse and manual lymphatic drainage specialist in Zurich's LABO Spa, she now practices independently in the premises of a local yoga studio. Designers David Büsser and Patrik Ferrarelli have helped Hamburger develop her own brand under the banner "verspannt," German for "tensed up." Their versatile visual identity draws on the therapist's expertise to treat tension by stimulating precise pressure spots. As these spots may vary for each of Hamburger's patients, Büsser and Ferrarelli based the brand on a series of symbols with differing details. The pink fingerprints are added manually by the therapist and alter with various applications.

Shave & Blade

BARBERSHOP & GROOMING GOODS

Riga, Latvia, *by Eskimo Design*

GET GROOMED, GENTLEMEN
SHAVE & BLADE REGALES WITH A
RAZOR-SHARP CORPORATE IMAGE

Shave & Blade is a barbershop and shaving brand catering to the wants of the well-to-do men of the world. To comply with the contemporary businessman's busy schedule, the shop is conceived as a lounge-like after-work salon inviting visitors to relax in comfortable chairs while being groomed. Eskimo Design developed brand marks and chose the hedgehog as a mascot with "masculine traits": independence, confidence, and obstinacy. Their product packaging for the company's grooming goods came out as sleek as the shop's smoothly shaved clients.

SHAVE & BLADE
GENTELMEN'S BARBER
POST SHAVE
BALM
300 ml / 10 fl oz
GIRTS VEJINS
Founder
CONTACTS
+371 292 86 773
girts@shaveandblade.com
www.shaveandblade.com

GENTELMEN'S
S&B
BARBER'S

SHAVE & BLADE

SHAVE & BLADE
SHAVE & BLADE
GENTLEMEN'S BARBER
SHAVE & BLADE
GENTLEMEN'S BARBER
SHAVE & BLADE
GENTLEMEN'S BARBER

SHAVE & BLADE
Founder
+371 292 86 775
girts@shaveandblade.com
www.shaveandblade.com
SHAVE & BLADE
GENTLEMEN'S BARBER
SHAVE & BLADE
GENTLEMEN'S BARBER
SHAVE & BLADE
GENTLEMEN'S BARBER

S&B S&B

S&B S B S&B &

S&B S&B S&B S&B

S&B

S&B

SHAVE & BLADE

SHAVE & BLADE S

SHAVE & BLADE

GENTELMEN'S BARBER

S&B and

S&B

and &

SHAVE & BLADE
GENTELMEN'S BARBER

SHAVE & BLADE
GENTELMEN'S BARBER

SHAVE & BLADE

S&B S&B

S&B

AND

S&B

GENTELMEN'S BARBER

·S&B·
SHAVE & BLADE
Gentlemen's barber

SSHAVE & BLADE

·SHAVE & BLADE·
GENTELMEN'S BARBER

Shave & Blade &B

Shave & Blade

SHAVE & BLADE
· GENTELMEN'S BARBER ·

S&B S&B S&B

·SHAVE & BLADE·
GENTELMEN'S BARBER

·S&B·

and

SHAVE & BLADE
Gentlemen's barber

and and

S&B S&B S&B

SHAVE & BLADE
GENTELMEN'S BARBER

SHAVE
&BLADE

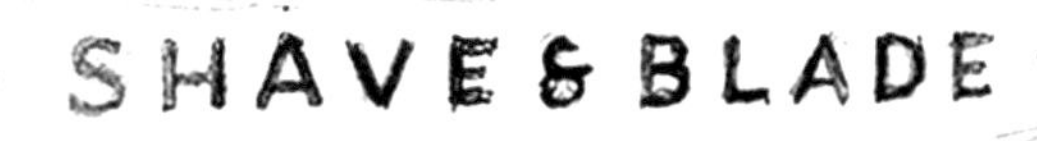

SHAVE & BLADE

SHAVE & BLADE S&B

SHAVE & BLADE S&B

Shave & Blade

Shave & Blade

SHAVE & BLADE

SHAVE & BLADE

SHAVE & BLADE

SHAVE & BLADE

SHAVE & BLADE

SHAVE & BLADE

S&B S&B

SHAVE & BLADE

SHAVE & BLADE

SHAVE & BLADE

SHAVE & BLADE

SHAVE & BLADE

SHAVE & BLADE

SHAVE & BLADE
Gentlemen's barber

SS SSHAVE & BLADE & &

S VE & BLADE

SHAVE & BLADE
Gentlemen's barber

S&B S&B

S

SHAVE & BLADE

SHAVE & BLADE

SHAVE & BLADE

SHAVE & BLADE

SHAVE & BLADE

SHAVE & BLADE
GENTELMEN'S BARBER

Shave & Blade

S&B
S&B
S&B
S&B

SHAVE
&BLADE

S&B

SHAVE
&BLADE

SHAVE
&BLADE
Gentlemen's barber

SHAVE & BLADE

SHAVE
&BLADE
Gentlemen's barber

SHAVE & BLADE
Gentlemen's barber

S&B

SHAVE & BLADE
Gentlemen's barber

SHAVE & BLADE
Gentlemen's barber

SHAVE & BLADE
Gentlemen's barber

SHAVE & BLADE
Gentlemen's barber

Shave & Blade
GENTELMEN'S BARBER

SHAVE
&BLADE
Gentlemen's barber

SHAVE & BLADE
Gentlemen's barber

Onni Flower Market

FLORIST

Jakarta, Indonesia, *by FullFill*

NO NEED FOR GAUDY GRAPHICS: FULLFILL'S BRANDING LETS ONNI FLOWER MARKET'S BEAUTIFUL BOUQUETS SPEAK FOR THEMSELVES.

A beautiful bouquet turns an ordinary day into a better day. Based on that idea, Onni Flower Market strategically opened its outlets in supermarkets and malls, selling flowers for any occasion and any day of the week. And as putting together a posy is a very personal procedure, the prospering start-up sets great store by customer care and a welcoming setting. FullFill's warm and welcoming corporate identity supports Onni's intimate approach and reinterprets the traditional flower shop concept with an enjoyably unobtrusive design featuring a lot of wood, white space, and only soft splashes of color.

ONNI FLOWER MARKET
EARTH LAUGHS IN FLOWERS
ONNI

ONNI

ONNI FLOWER MARKET
EARTH LAUGHS IN FLOWERS
ONNI

Skovin Gulv

OAK FLOOR SPECIALIST

Oslo, Norway, *by Heydays*

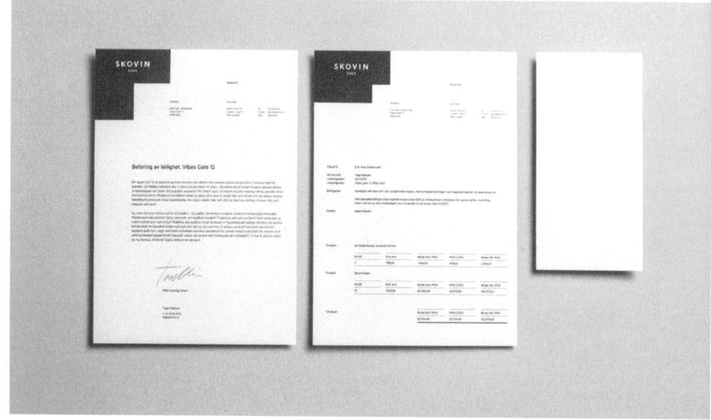

SKOVIN GULV SUPPLIES HIGH-STANDARD WOODEN FLOORING, AND STANDS ON FIRM GROUND ITSELF WITH BEAUTIFUL BRANDING BASED ON TIMBER AND TIMELESS TYPOGRAPHY.

Skovin Gulv specializes in oak flooring for the private market. The most fundamental of all interior furnishings, flooring also acts as the foundation of Heydays's corporate identity concept, where space is structured by parquet panels and floor plans. Although Skovin's superbly styled showroom is now located in Lysaker, on the outskirts of Oslo, the company name still refers to Skøyen, or Skǫðin, in old Norse, the Oslo neighborhood where the firm was founded.

SKOVIN
GULV

SKOVIN
GULV

SKOVIN

SKOVIN
GULV

SKOVIN
GULV

SKOVIN
GULV

Fatties

CONFECTIONERY

London, UK, *by Dot Dash*

FULL FAT AHEAD!
FATTIES COUNTERS ANY SLIMMING CRAZE
WITH A SET OF SUPER SWEET GRAPHICS.

Chloe Timms had been blogging about baked goods for a while when she decided to open her own bakery at the back of London's Broadway Market. As its name suggests, Fatties celebrates full flavor, proffering a product range that is lush instead of low-fat. The design direction Timms developed, together with Dot Dash, follows Fatties's flavorful bon-vivant vain. With bloated letters for the logo, a savory color scheme, and a marble pattern simulating the powder-covered surfaces of the confectioner's counters and bakery worktops, the designers hit the sweet spot.

FATT
IES

FATTIES

Försterei Reinbek

FORESTRY

Hamburg, Germany, *by Friendship Hamburg*

NATURALLY IN TOUCH WITH NATURE. REINBEK'S RANGER BARKS UP THE RIGHT TREE WITH THIS RESOURCEFUL REBRAND.

In 2012, Fritz Wolter, former forestry student, became one of Germany's youngest foresters when he assumed responsibility of around a thousand hectares of woodlands surrounding Reinbek, a city in the rural environs east of Hamburg. The change of command at the forestry coincided with a renovation of its old premises that included the opening of a new forest shop providing firewood and regional venison products. The extensive refurbishment was rounded off by a wide-ranging rebrand from the designers at Friendship Hamburg, who equipped the forestry with a set of hand-stamped stationery with natural charm.

Dachdeckermeister Garling

ROOFER

Hamburg, Germany, *by Friendship Hamburg*

FRIENDSHIP HAMBURG'S BUSINESS CARDS FOR THE CRAFTSPEOPLE AT GARLING RAISE THE ROOF—ERM, BAR—FOR SENSIBLE IDENTITY SOLUTIONS.

Master roofer Matthias Garling mounts and restores roofs that require renovation. Friendship Hamburg helped him boast about his business with a clever card. Translating Garling's services to a tiled design not only attracts a good deal of interest, but also demonstrates the different materials that the master roofer employs in his everyday work.

AUDIOVISUAL
ANDALUZ
AUDIOVISUAL

ANDALUZ
~ audiovisual ~

ANDALUZ
EST.
AUDIOVISUAL

ANDALUZ AUDIOVISUAL
ANDALUZ AUDIOVISUAL

ANDALUZ

ANDALUZ AUDIOVISUAL
ANDALUZ AUDIOVISUAL

ANDALUZ
~ audiovisual ~

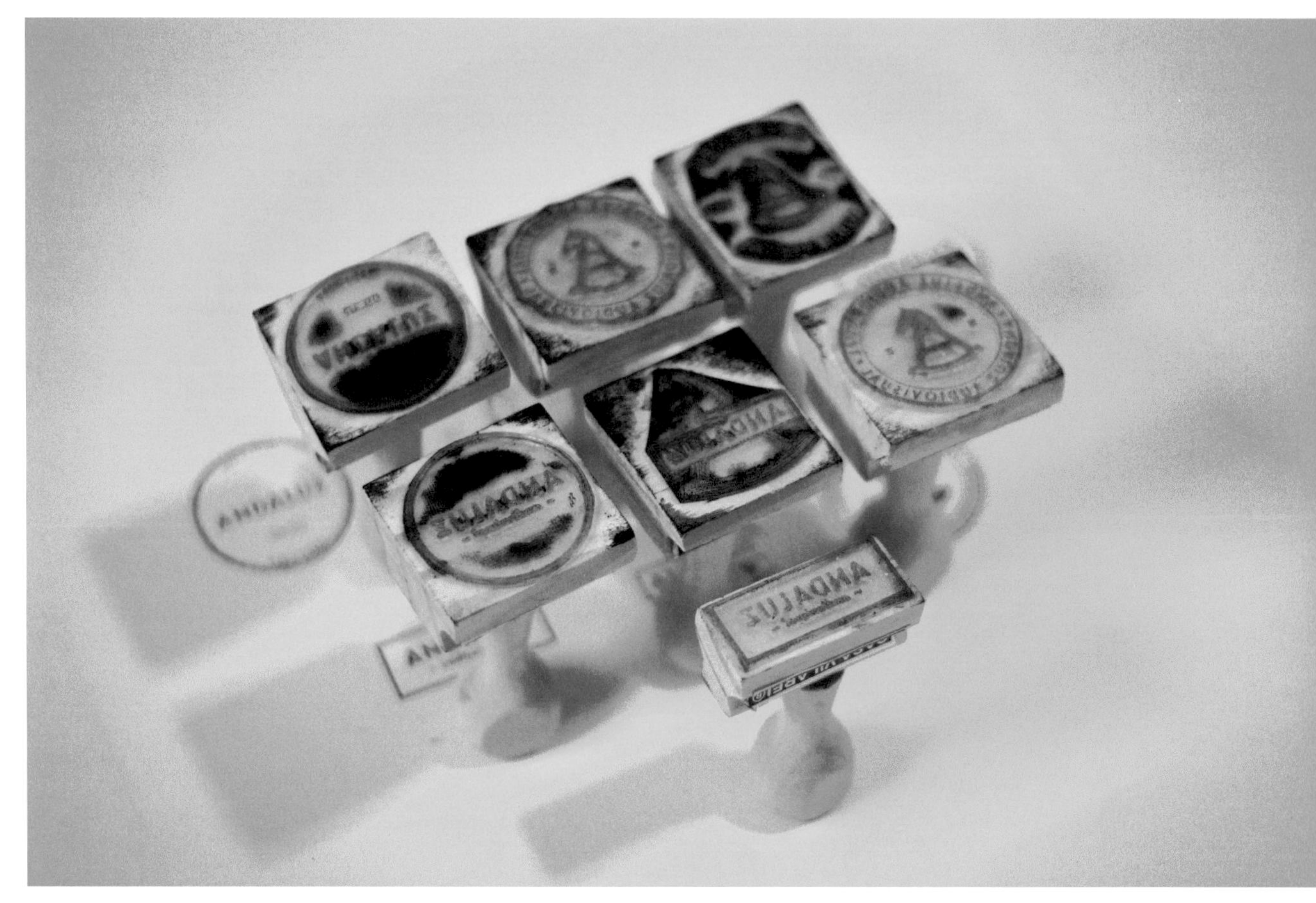

Andaluz Audiovisual

AUDIOVISUAL PRODUCTION

Rio de Janeiro, Brazil, *by Plau*

NOISY, NOT NEAT:
PLAU'S VISUAL IDENTITY
FOR ANDALUZ AUDIOVISUAL SETS
THE SCENE FOR THE SURREAL,
SLICK PRODUCTIONS.

Andaluz Audiovisual prepares, produces, and post-produces creative audio and ideo content. The company was established by a multicultural trio of filmmakers riven by the desire to experiment, combining technical with aesthetic qualities n order to perfect plots and productions. Setting high standards on (audio-)visual ommunications, the three brought the designers from Plau on board to develop a istinct brand image for their firm. The result references the short surrealist movie *In Perro Andaluz (An Andalusian Dog)* by Luis Buñuel with a monochrome clutter f dizzying distortions. The rocking horse logo was illustrated by Kako, an award-vinning Brazilian illustrator and founder of São Paulo-based design studio Kakofonia.

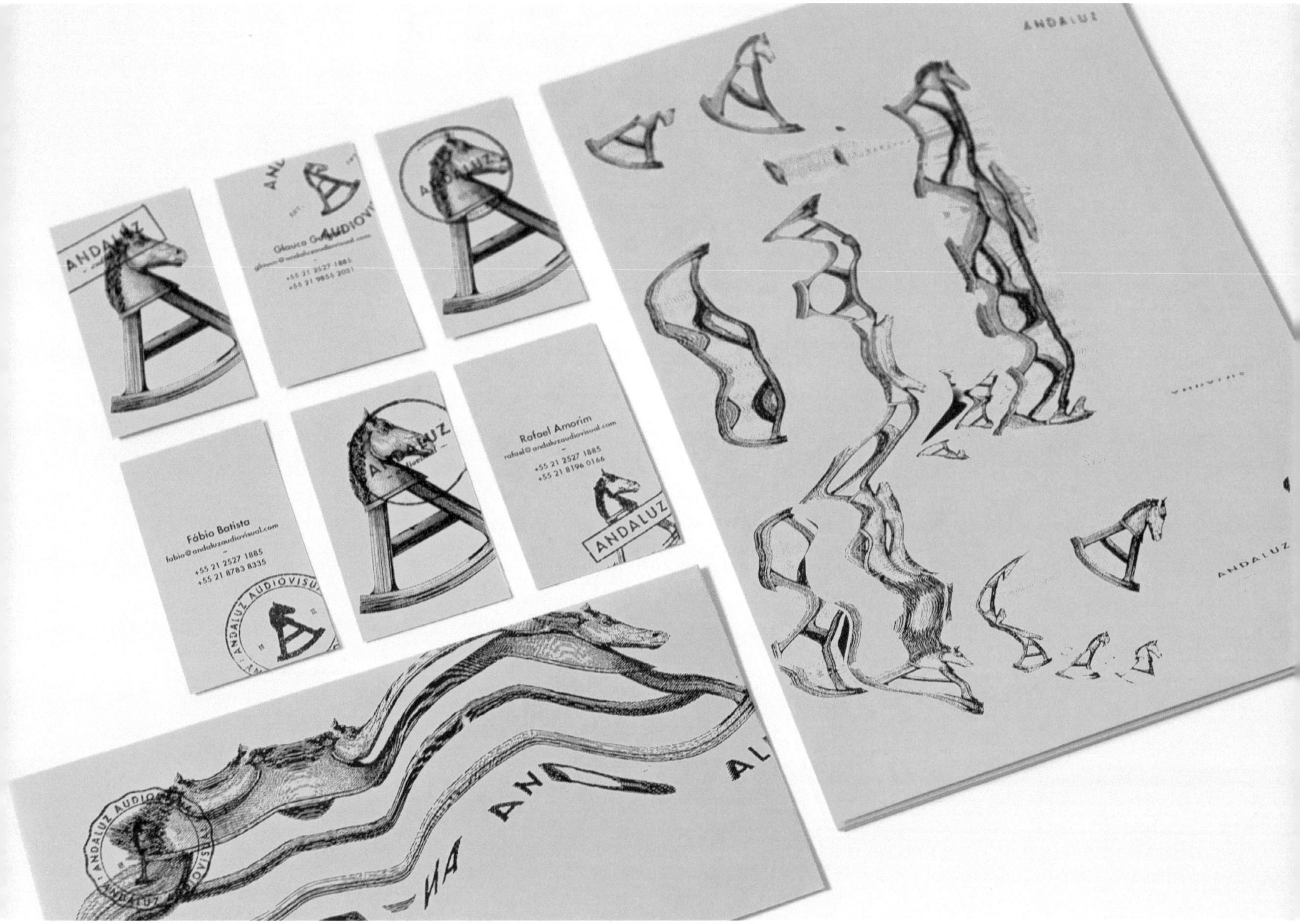

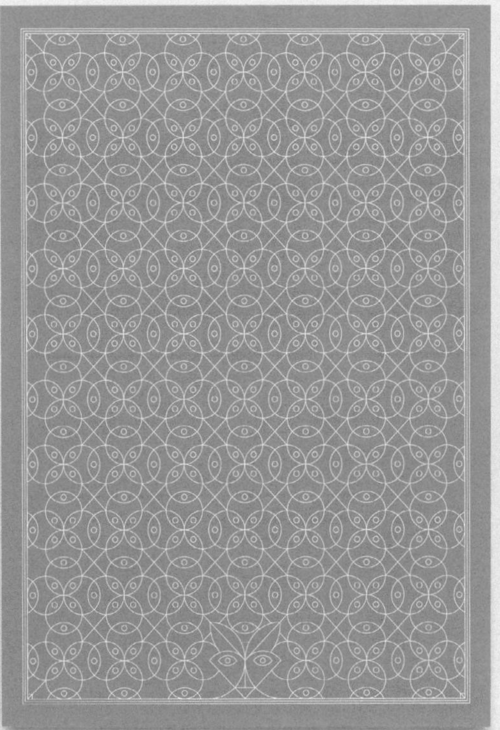

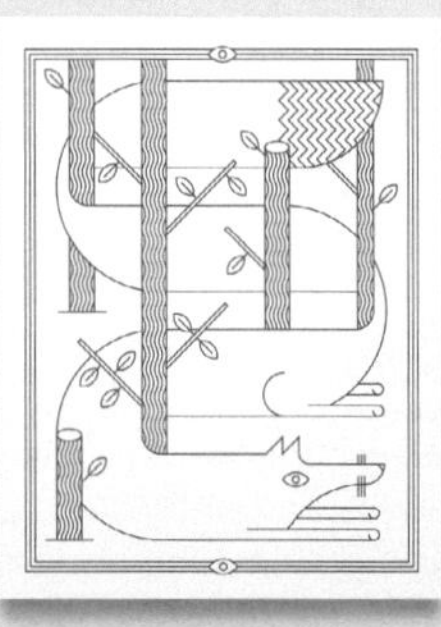

Frida von Fuchs

COMMUNICATIONS AGENCY

Berlin, Germany, *by Jonathan S. Garrett*

FOXY LADY! FRIDA VON FUCHS'S FABULOUS SET OF STATIONERY FEATURES A FUNNY CREATURE WHO IS HALF FRIDA, HALF FOX.

Frida von Fuchs is a communications and public relations agency founded by political scientist and experienced ad woman Femke Peter, and conceptor and copywriter Ben Bencivinni. The company coordinates campaigns and connects freelance creatives with commercial clients to collaborate on communication concepts. Its own beautifully illustrative branding concept was conceived by Jonathan S. Garrett, who drew a wondrous world around the company's cute mixed creature mascot.

FRIDA von FUCHS
Femke Peter
Geschäftsführerin
+49 160 96 87 31 89
femke-peter@fridavonfuchs.de
WWW.FRIDAVONFUCHS.DE
FRIDA von FUCHS
FRIDA von FUCHS

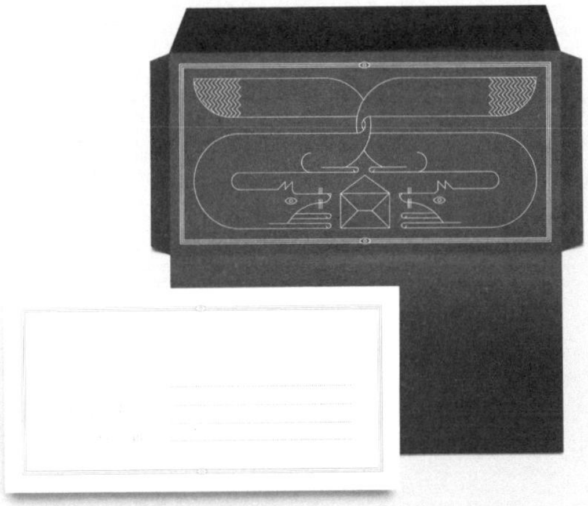

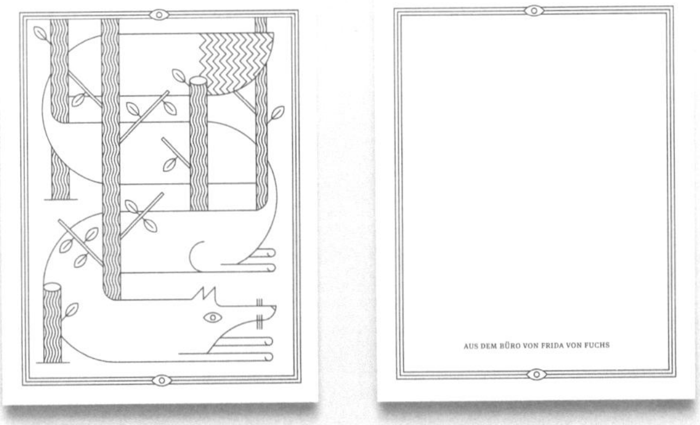
AUS DEM BÜRO VON FRIDA VON FUCHS

Nonusual's Gropes

BESPOKE BICYCLE PRODUCTS

London, UK, *by Ico Design Partners / Akira Chatani*

NIFTY AND NONUSUAL:
THE GREEN BRANDING SOLUTION FOR GROPES BICYCLE GRIPS.

A shared fancy for cycling sparked the creative collaboration between Akira Chatani and Ryo Yamada. The pair design, make, and sell bespoke bicycle accessories under the name Nonusual. Gropes are their leather handlebar grips, customizable coverings inspired by original leather-wraps, but restyled to be tied like shoelaces. Gropes are hand-made from high-quality leather with pre-punched holes, and come with extra-long laces. While the names Nonusual and Gropes were penned by strategic writers Regard, the visual product identity was conceived by Nonusual partner Akira Chatani and his designer colleagues at Ico Design Partners, who turned unwanted paper samples from the studio's previous projects into a tidy set of marketing materials. An ecologically, rather than economically driven decision led to labels, letterheads, packaging, and cards of varied colors and textures.

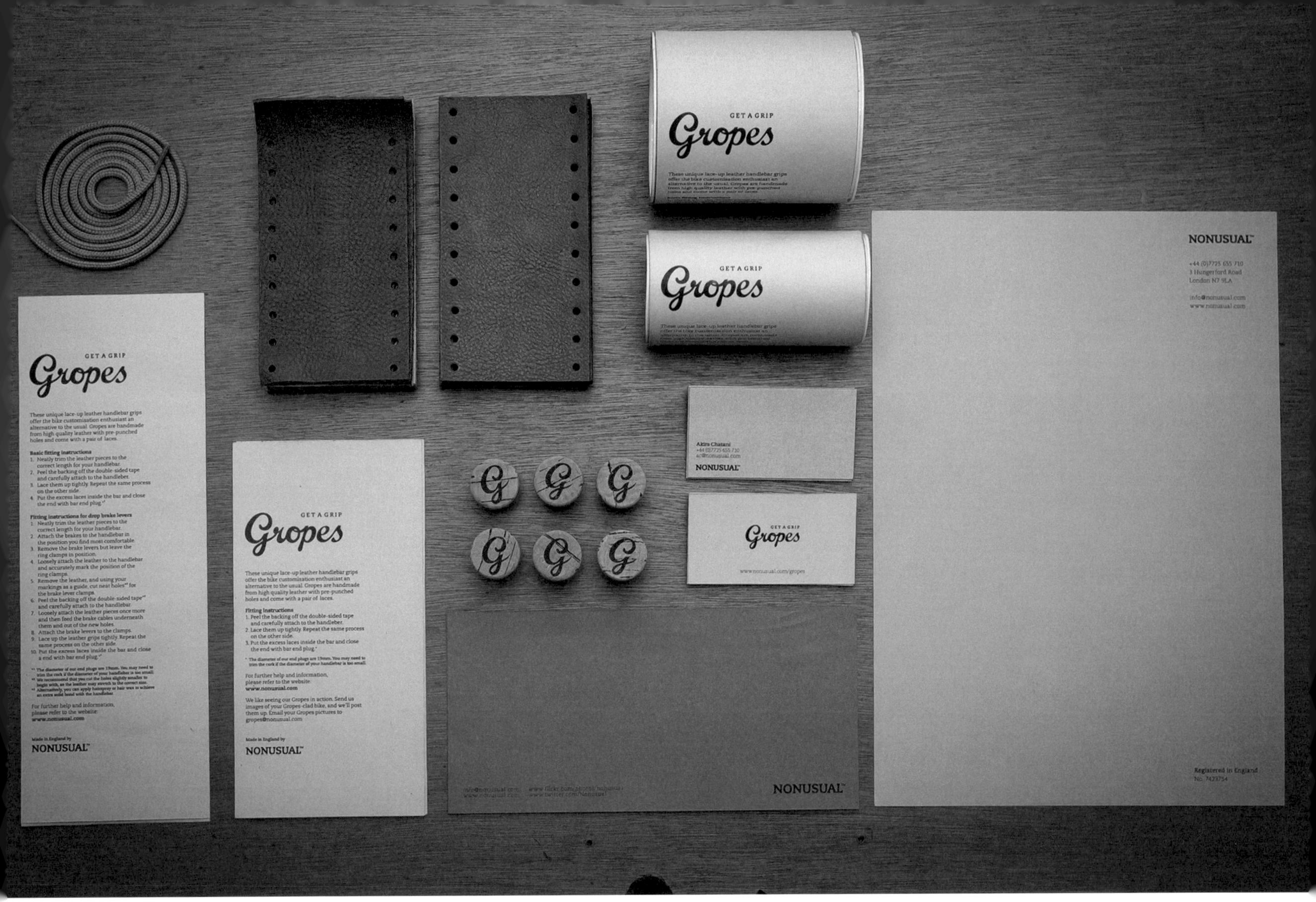

GET A GRIP
Gropes

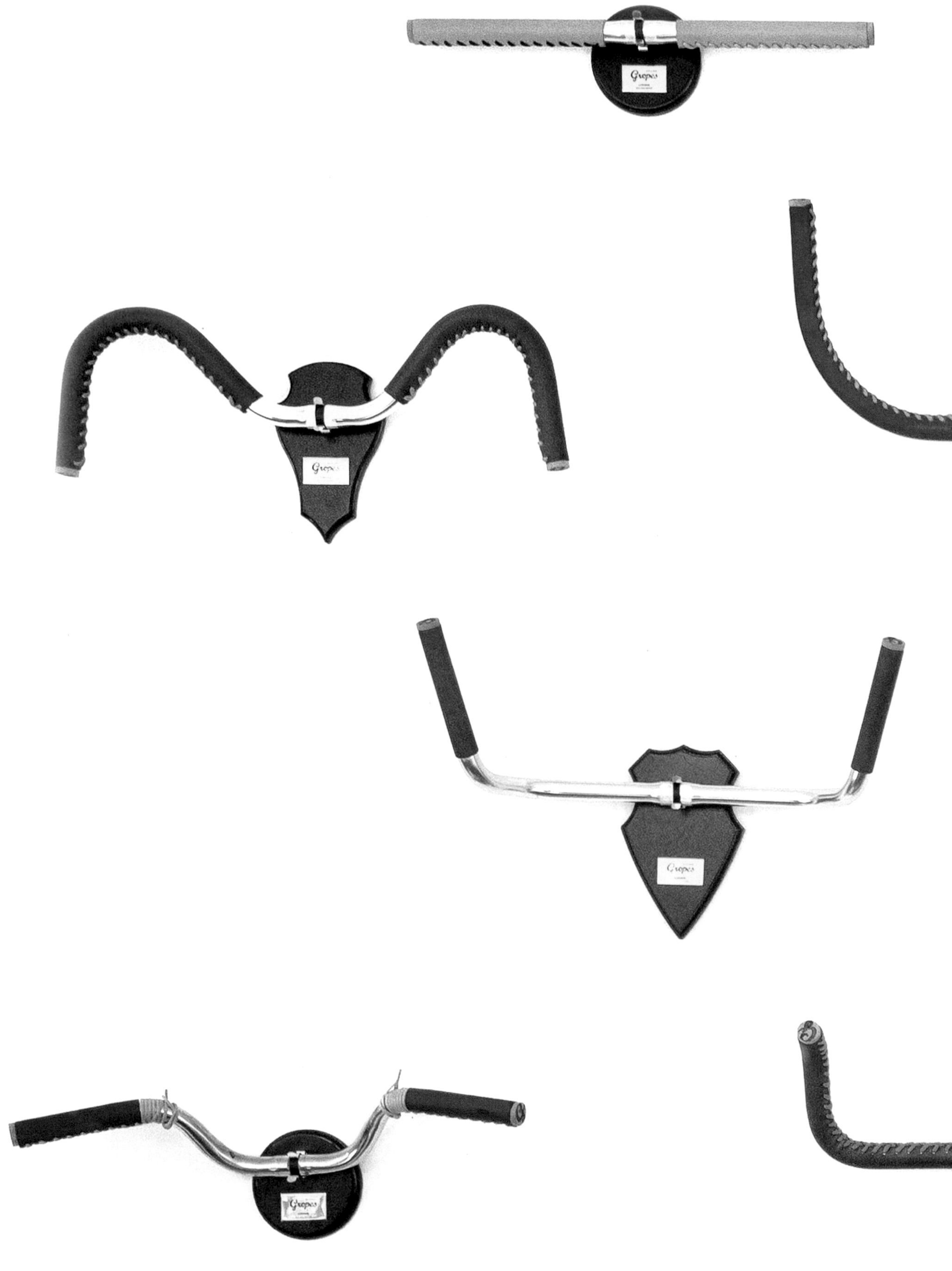

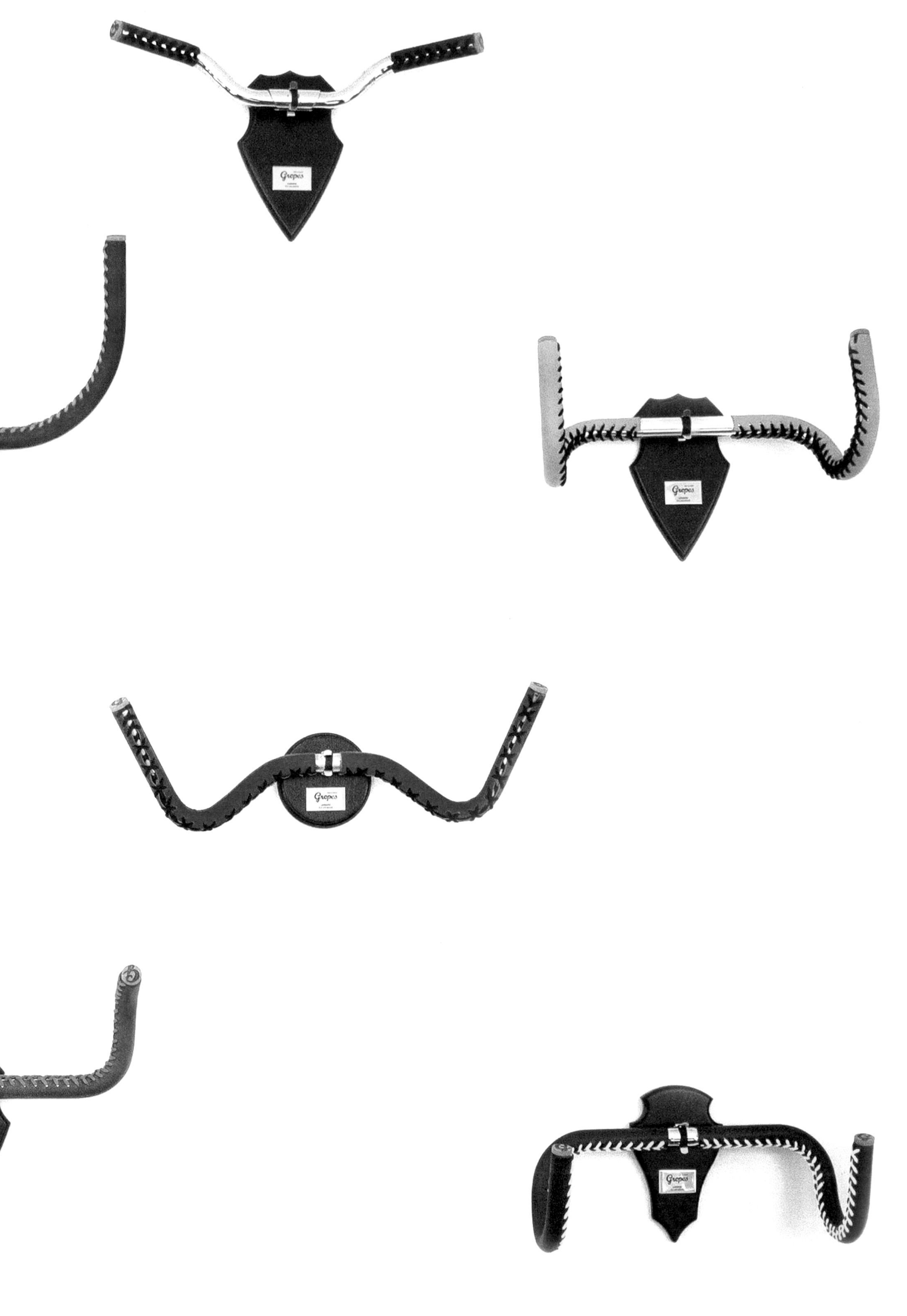

Ipsen & Co

BAKERY

Copenhagen, Denmark, *by Re-public*

CELEBRATING CENTURY-OLD COFFEE CULTURE IN CONTEMPORARY COPENHAGEN, THIS DANISH DELI SCORES WITH A COZY SETTING AND DELICATE DESIGNS.

IPSEN & SILJA

Charlotte Ipsen og Silja Mäkelä-Dichmann mødte hinanden — da de begge var i trygge jobs — godt nok med en broget fortid som selvstændige indenfor møbler, tøj, bed & breakfast etc. og med en stadig undren over, hvorfor så mange cafeer mister det personlige præg og livslysten efter et stykke tid.

Vi er ikke kokke, men kender nogen som er — de bedste endda! Ipsen & Co er lig med vores leverandører, krydret med personlighed og kærlighed og friske krydderurter. Det gode og simple og ligetil. Ipsen & Co bliver aldrig et koncept — vi er der og vi lever os ind i det og vi kan ikke lade være med at lave om hele tiden. Derfor vil man nok aldrig finde det samme på menuen længere tid ad gangen.

Når der skal bruges hjælp i cafeen, søger vi mere efter folk til et værested fremfor en café. Vi nægter at have mennesker ansat, som ser igennem kunderne eller ikke interesserer sig for det de laver eller andre mennesker. Så vi lægger ud med et barista kursus, så de ansatte kan lave verdens bedste kaffe og resten kommer med lysten og interessen.

IPSEN & BRØDET

Krummen & Kagen er et hjemmebageri, som selv bager alt deres brød og kager fra bunden efter egne opskrifter. Brødet langtidshæver på køl i minimum 12 timer, hvilket giver det fylde og smag. Kagerne laves med rigtig marcipan, ægte chokolade og andre gode råvarer. Fri for forblandinger og konserveringsmidler. Bageriet og deres egen butik på Østerbro er startet op af de to søskende Julie og Pernille i 2011. Sammen har de udviklet opskrifter, finpudset og fundet på nye hen ad vejen. Det vigtigste er, at tingene laves fra bunden. At der er smag og robusthed i brød og boller samt en fristelse og tilfredshed med hver en kage. Nøgleordet er kvalitet og mottoet er: Godt hjemmebag til folket.

IPSEN & OSTEN

Lomos er et lille 10 år gammelt firma, der har specialiseret sig i import af spanske-, franske- og italienske specialiteter. Firmaet er startet af 2 brødre Bill og Jimmi, som er opvokset i Spanien og med baggrund i restaurationsbranchen, ved hvor meget det betyder at få kvalitetsvarer hver gang. Derfor bestræber de sig på kun at importere de bedste varer til Danmark, mange af producenterne finder de selv under rejser til syden.

IPSEN & LAKSEN

Københavns Røgeri er hjertet i Lomos, og ambitionen er naturligvis at producere landets bedste røgede laks. Laksen indkøbes i Norge, hvor fisken farmes efter en særlig metode, som i grove træk går ud på at give fiskene mere plads i bassinerne, men vertikalt i stedet for horisontalt. Dette resulterer i nogle fisk, som er mindre, når de slagtes, og som med andre ord ligner vildlaks, og er næsten lige så glade! Lomos ryger kun pivfriske fisk. Laksene rammer København søndag aften efter at være blevet slagtet i Norge om lørdagen. Mandag morgen filleteres dyrene og tørsaltes herefter i 48 timer. Onsdag bliver de skyllet og passerer så et særligt tørreskab, der gør dem klar til røgovnen. Her tilbringer laksesiderne 36-48 timer hængende eller liggende over et såkaldt "fyr" af bøgesmuld, der langsomt brænder på gulvet af ovnen. Bortset fra nogle lejlighedsvise eksperimenter med at tilføje smuld fra æble- eller birketræ, er der hverken krydderier eller aroma i røgfyret, og laksene får således lov til at beholde mere af sin oprindelige smag i et friskt og ærligt udtryk.

IPSEN & SUPPEN

Kristian Bust er godt nok uddannet fotograf, men med en forkærlighed for god mad lægger han både navn til og står bag gryderne i køkkenet i sit nye spisested i Blågaardsgade.

Kristian Bust laver suppen til Ipsen & Co af årstidens grønsager og friske råvarer og den bliver laver helt fra bunden. Han følger samme motto som Ipsen & Co og tager det med mad og drikke alvorligt, men ikke højtideligt. Mad skal være til glæde og ikke kun til gavn, så fokus er på, at gøre få ting og gøre dem godt! Maven og ganen får altid det sidste ord. Så er hjertet også er med.

Ipsen & Co serves Copenhagen customers with superb coffee in cozy urroundings. Situated in the Danish capital's Frederiksberg district, the family-run offee shop and bistro benefits from a network of local suppliers and specialized mporters, who all share a common desire to put quality before anything else. n summer 2014, the space was taken over by two siblings, Lillebror and Line Rune—ne a trained gastronomer, the other a former pilot, and both passionate foodies. They ollow the previous owner's ambitious approach as well as the hospitable heritage of their parents and grandparents, all veteran caterers and coffee connoisseurs. Søren Severin of the studio Re-public has fitted Ipsen & Co with an identity inspired by functional vintage wine crates and classic coffee packaging that focuses on what's most essential: the quality of the product. Alongside savory illustrations, a set of tag lines was introduced to support the logo and translate the café's cozy atmosphere into welcoming words.

Trofana Alpin is a family-owned four-star lifestyle hotel located in the renowned winter sports resort Ischgl. With several ski lifts close by and a spa center with an indoor pool, hot tub, sauna, and steam room, it speaks to a sporty target-group with a sense for sociability, snugness, and rural rusticity. Traditionally Austrian and built to the taste of the Von der Thannen family who founded it, the hotel's communal areas and Tyrolean-style restaurant feature a lot of exposed timber for a warm and welcoming architectural ambience, while the interiors of its rooms and suites are rather contemporary, providing the perfect home for après-ski addicts and serious athletes. The Trofana Alpin brand, too, was redesigned by Bureau Rabensteiner to balance Tyrolea tradition with cosmopolitan clarity and convenience.

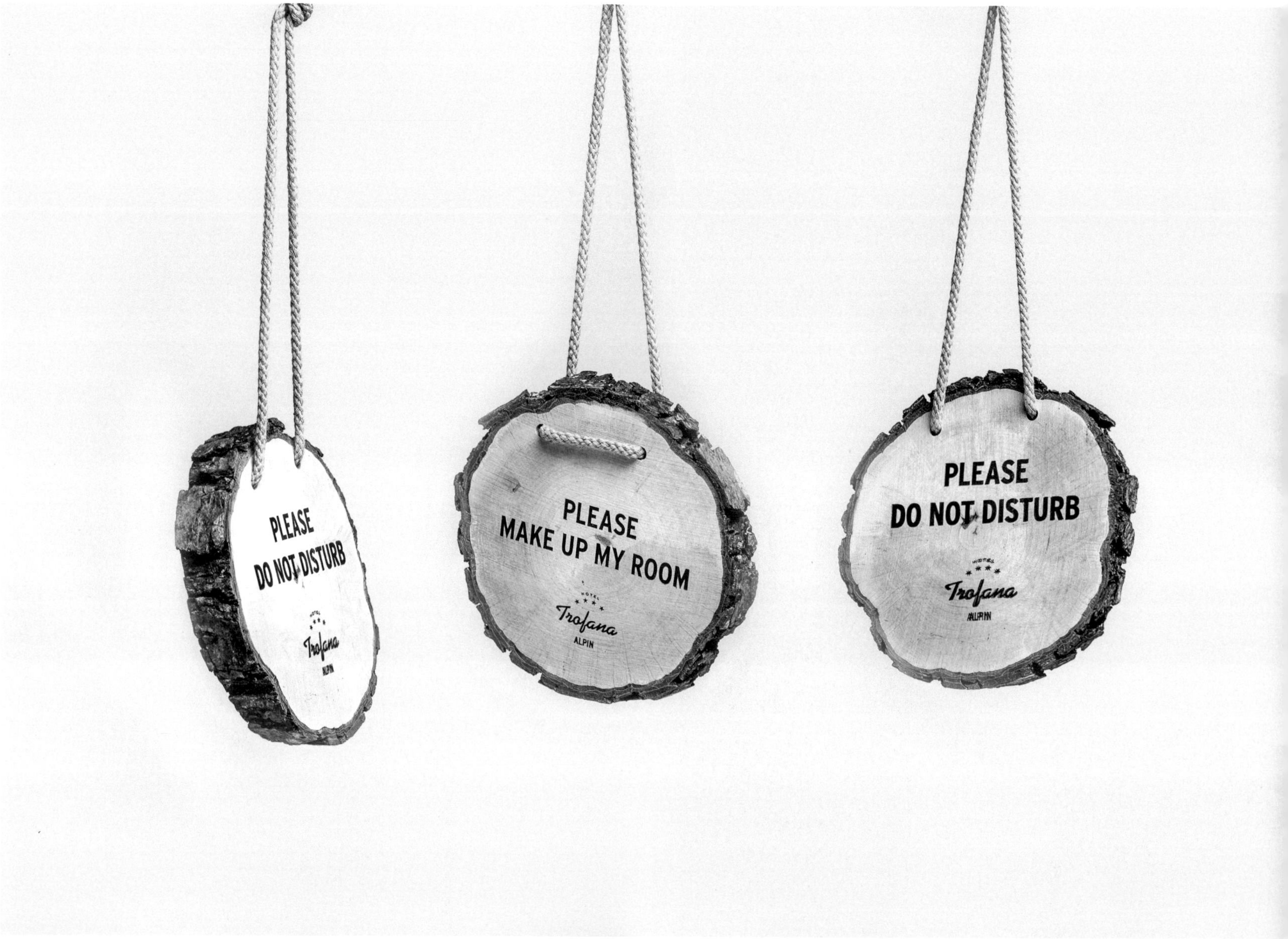

Trofana Alpin

HOTEL

Ischgl, Austria, *by Bureau Rabensteiner*

ISCHGL IS SMART-SET SKIING SURROUNDED BY A MAGNIFICENT MOUNTAINOUS IDYLL. SITUATED AT THE HEART OF THIS HOLIDAY HOTSPOT, TROFANA ALPIN WEDS AUSTRIAN HOSPITALITY WITH A SPORTY SPIRIT.

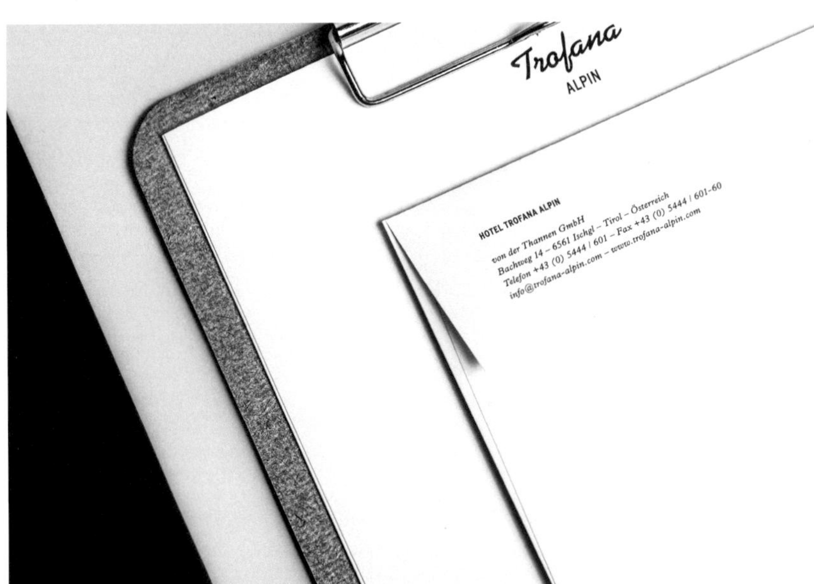
Trofana
ALPIN
HOTEL TROFANA ALPIN
von der Thannen GmbH
Bachweg 14 – 6561 Ischgl – Tirol – Österreich
Telefon +43 (0) 5444 / 601 – Fax +43 (0) 5444 / 601-60
info@trofana-alpin.com – www.trofana-alpin.com

HOTEL
Trofana
ALPIN

ALPIN
Zweigelt
ZWEIGELT · HEIDEBODEN · 2010 · BURGENLAND · GOLDENITS
Trofana
ALPIN
FAMILIE VON DER THANNEN

HOTEL
Trofana
ALPIN
von der Thannen GmbH – Bachweg 14 – 6561 Ischgl –Tirol – Österreich – Telefon +43 (0)
info@trofana-alpin.com – www.trofana-alpin.com
Bankverbindung: Volksbank Ischgl – IBAN AT16 4585 0005 2000 5066 – BIC
MADE IN TIROL
HOTEL
Trofana
ALPIN
FAMILIE VON DER THANNEN

PLEASE
KE UP MY ROOM
HOTEL
Trofana
ALPIN
tionen.

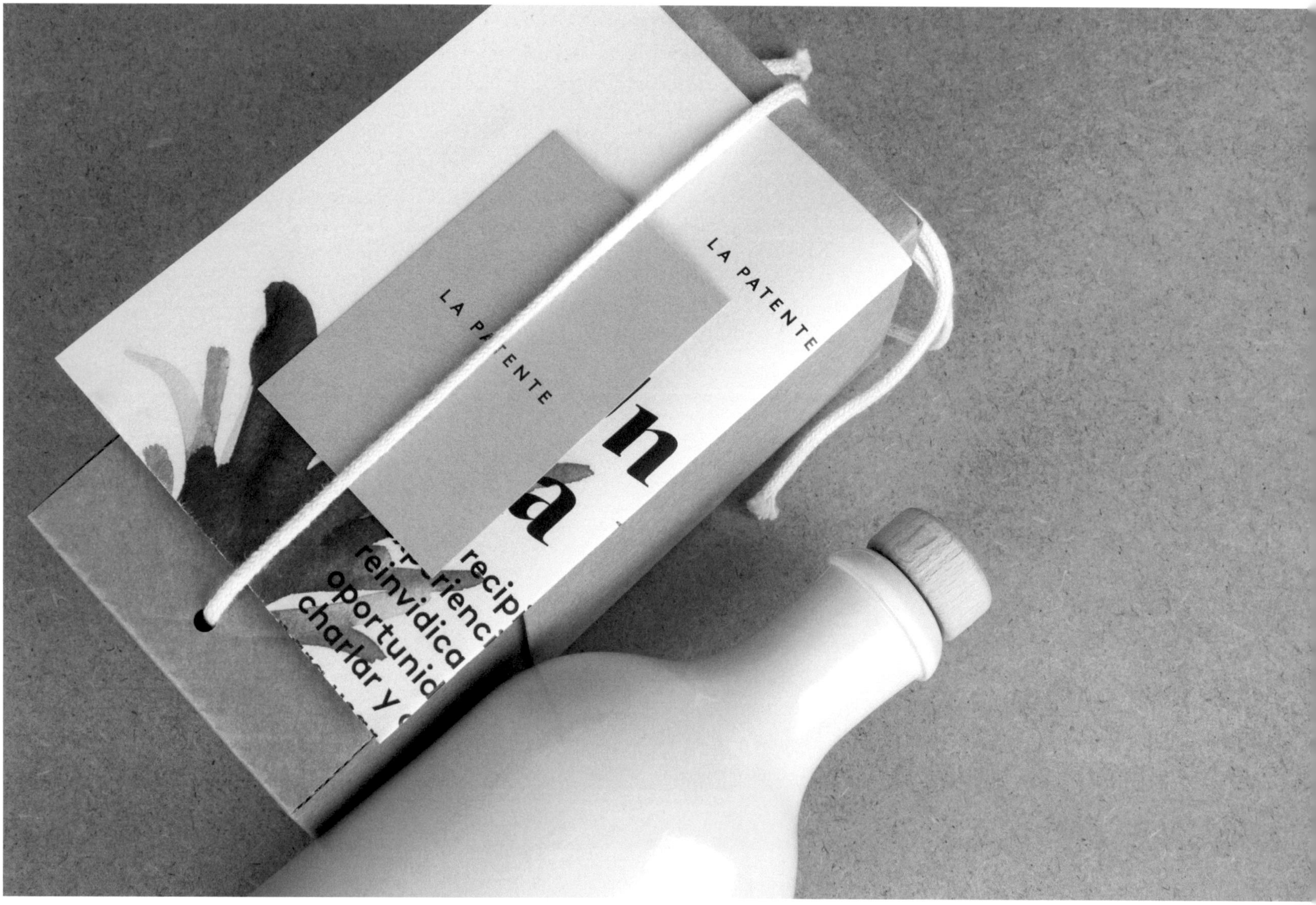

La Patente

CULINARY & CRAFT WORKSHOPS

Barcelona, Spain, *by P.A.R*

13 FEBRERO

Cocina ligera

Descubre técnicas y recetas para preparar platos más ligeros y sencillos ¡sin aburrirte mientras comas!

LA PATENTE

15 FEBRERO

Iniciación a la cocina japonesa

En este taller descubriremos que hay gastronomía más allá del sushi

LA PATENTE

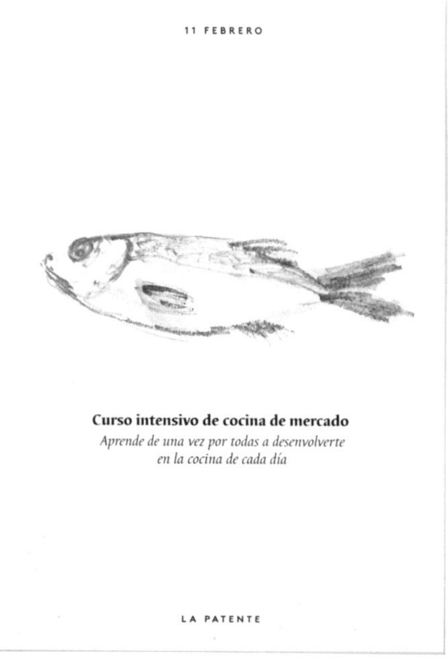

11 FEBRERO

Curso intensivo de cocina de mercado

Aprende de una vez por todas a desenvolverte en la cocina de cada día

LA PATENTE

26 FEBRERO

Pasta fresca artesanal

Aprende a elaborar tu propia pasta fresca artesanal con la que elaborar sabrosos platos

LA PATENTE

NO PATENT MEDICINE, BUT LESSONS FOR LIFE: LA PATENTE HAS MADE IT ITS MISSION TO MAKE MORE OF THE MUNDANE.

La Patente is a workshop venue that specializes in survival training for the ressed, contemporary soul. Addressing its services at ambitious amateurs with n interest in cooking, gardening, and crafts, it teaches them to treasure tradition nd to consciously slow down. Craftsmanship and traditional techniques are core to La Patente's curriculum, and all activities are characterized by a certain collaborative spirit and hands-on participation. P.A.R's corporate identity reflects the school's principles with a nod to naturalness, with handmade watercolor illustrations contributed by Pol Montserrat.

Queremos reinterpretar lo cotidiano con un estilo urbano, original y con sentido del humor, que da valor a *lo hecho a mano* o *lo de toda la vida*. Nuestra intención es que cualquiera pueda sentir que está en su cocina o en su salón preparando algo con los amigos.

Anvil Property Smith

PROPERTY MANAGEMENT

Johannesburg, South Africa, *by Nicholas Christowitz*

THE HOUSING INDUSTRY IS HARDER THAN METAL.
ANVIL PROPERTY SMITH ASTOUNDS WITH AN IMPACT-PROOF IDENTITY TRUE TO ITS TAGLINE.

Anvil specializes in the leasing and sale of commercial and industrial property, commercial and industrial property management, and property advisory services. The firm's founder and managing director Matthew Marvin seeks to promote "commercial property intelligence" and puts transparency at the forefront of his practice. Striving for a straightforward branding solution that would communicate his clear-cut company concept, he briefed Nicholas Christowitz and got what he wanted: a bold alternative in order to stand out among the bright and garish property businesses that dominate the Johannesburg market.

PROPERTY SMITH

Matthew Marvin

-----

mattm@anvilproperty.co.za
+27 82 569 0402

Upper Grayston Office Park,
150 Linden Street, Sandton, 2196
tel: +27 87 700 3120
fax: +27 11 326 6456

-----

www.anvilproperty.co.za

Speicher7

HOTEL

Mannheim, Germany, *by Deutsche & Japaner*

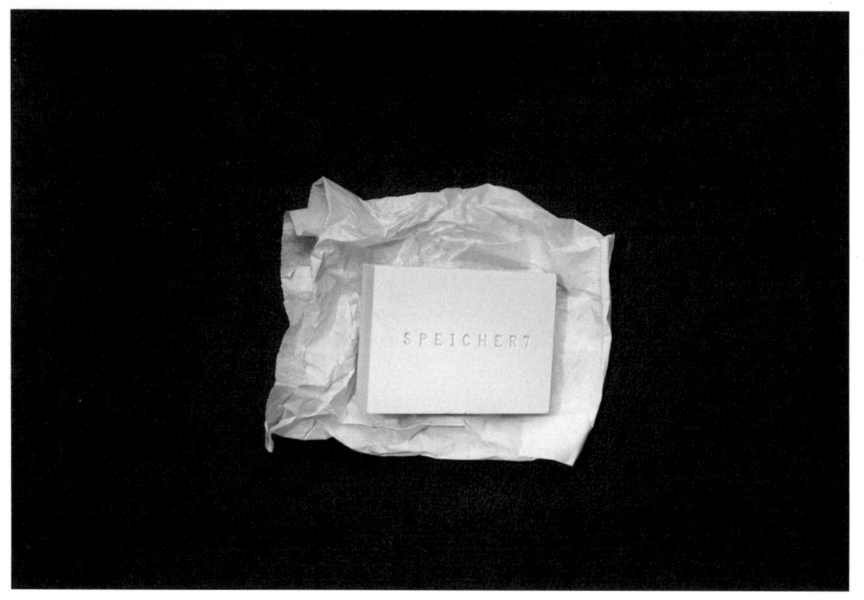

FINALLY ASHORE. HARBOR HOTEL SPEICHER7 INVITES SOJOURNERS TO FLOAT OFF INTO SEVENTH STYLE HEAVEN.

Speicher7 is the latest venture of two versatile entrepreneurs and coffee shop owners—florist M. Jürgen Tekath and Thorsten Kraft, formerly the director of a retirement home. Based in an abandoned warehouse building in the wharf area of Mannheim, directly on the bank of the River Rhine, the harbor hotel houses 20 rooms, a bar, and "Flow," the yoga and meditation room with a sauna that is considered the house's great soul. Tekath and Kraft raise the bar when it comes to combining well-being and style. Sleep is meditation, they say, and it is ensured with their COCO-MAT mattresses made from 100 percent natural materials. Every little detail is selected carefully, they declare, and they grant their guests the benefits of AESOP cosmetics. The hotel's intriguing interior has been implemented with the help of Schmucker & Partner's architectural practice; and its splendid corporate communications were developed by the designers Deutsche & Japaner, who delivered a comprehensive set of stationery, bar menus, note pads, pencils, soaps, laundry bags, shirts, and blankets based on a classy custom-lettered logo.

nvitation

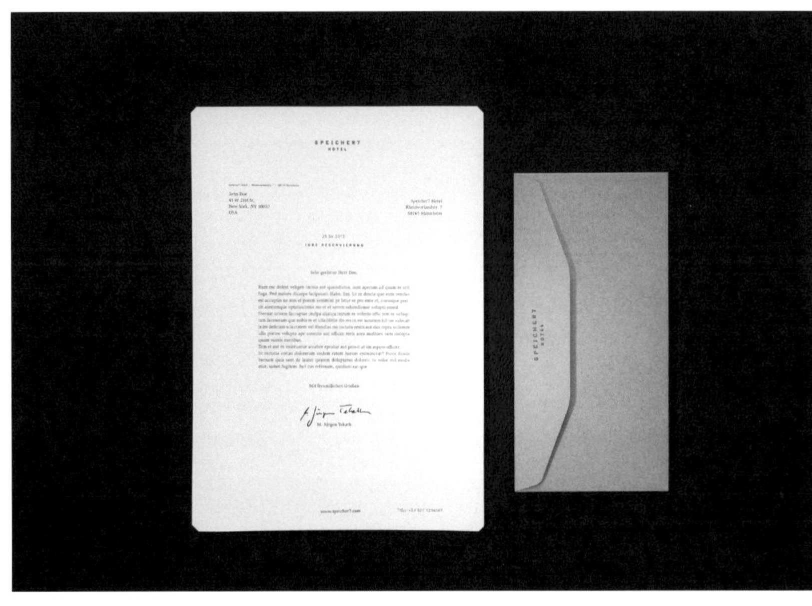

Door Tag

Notepad

Postcards

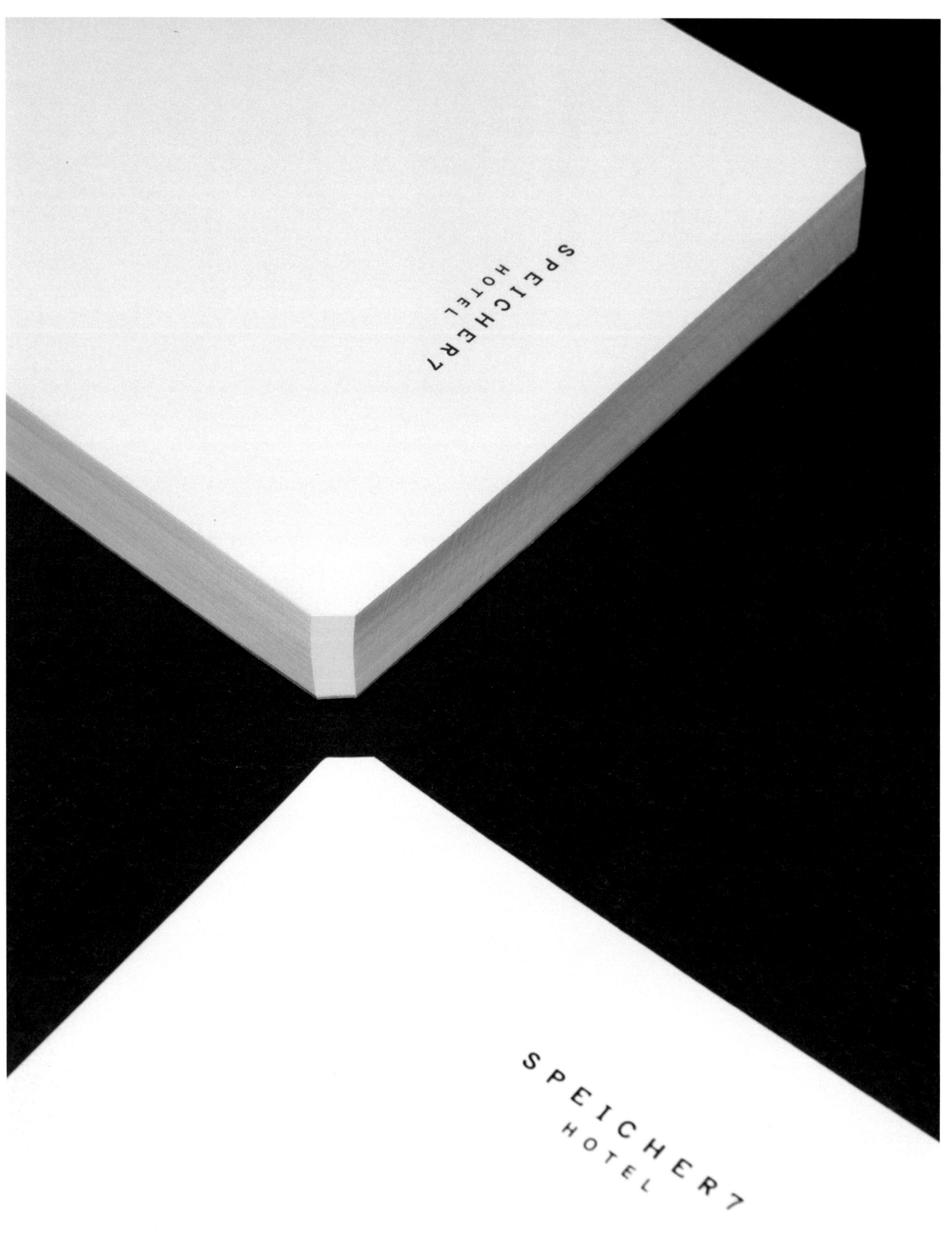
SPEICHER7
HOTEL
SPEICHER7
HOTEL

Postcards

WALT
WALK DON'T RUN
Hat Maker EST. 1981
With Compliments
walt-hats.de
bespoke@walt-hats.de
WALT

WALT

WALT HATS
WALK DON'T RUN
Hat Maker EST. 1981

Date ~

Invoice No. ~

WALT

Sold To ~

Address ~

Item(s) ~	No. ~	Cost ~

WALK DON'T RUN
Hat Maker EST. 1981

WALT ~ Account Holder: Daniel Thies ~ Account No. 30542626 ~ Sort code. 60-10-39
Cheques to be made to 'Mr Daniel Thies' and sent to Große Bergstr. 252, 22767 Hamburg, Germany
IBAN: GB74NWBK60103930542626 ~ BIC: NWBKGB2L ~ VAT No. DB 120 1980 52
bespoke@walt-hats.de ~ walt-hats.de

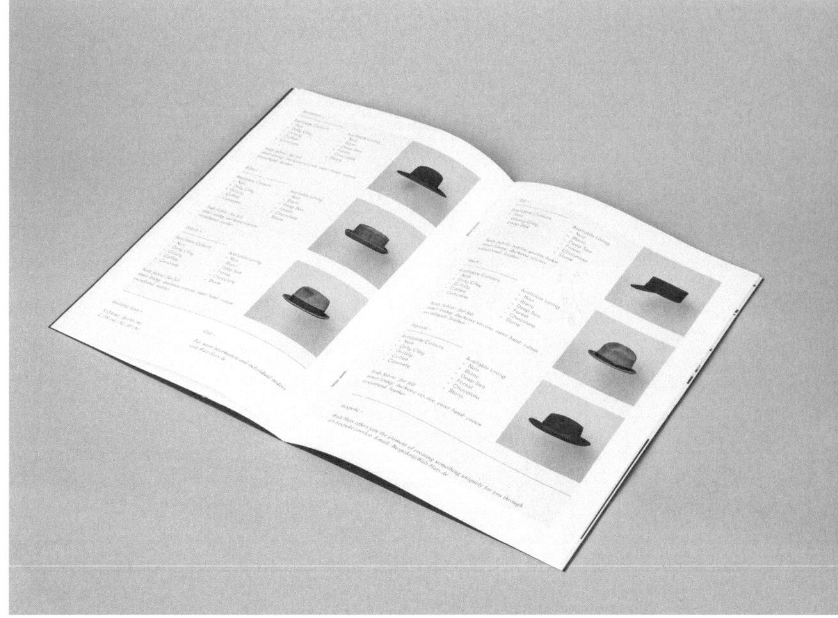

Walt Hats

HAT MAKER

Hamburg, Germany, *by YUKIKO*

WALK DON'T RUN!
WALT HATS COUNTERS TODAY'S HASTE WITH TRADITIONALLY CRAFTED HIP HEADWEAR.

Housed in a historic commercial complex in Germany's hanseatic heart, Walt's workshop creates custom hats for the gentleman of today. The brainchild of Bird's Nest Collective, an advertising agency with interdisciplinary interests, the company was conceived to bridge the gap between contemporary hastiness and classic craftsmanship. All their hats are handmade, from the first mold over the stitched logo down to the lining, and can be customized to the customer's wish. When it came to communications, YUKIKO was commissioned, and came up with a fabulous promotional film, photo stills of floating hats, and a sleek silhouette-style symbol.

Rain Or Shine

ICE CREAM PARLOR

Vancouver, Canada
by Glasfurd & Walker

THE NEED FOR DELICATE ICE CREAM DOES NOT DEPEND ON WEATHER CONDITIONS; NEITHER DOES OUR WISH FOR DELIGHTFUL CORPORATE IDENTITIES. THIS SUSTAINABLE SCOOP SHOP, RAIN OR SHINE, SERVES SWEETNESS AND STYLE IN ALL SEASONS.

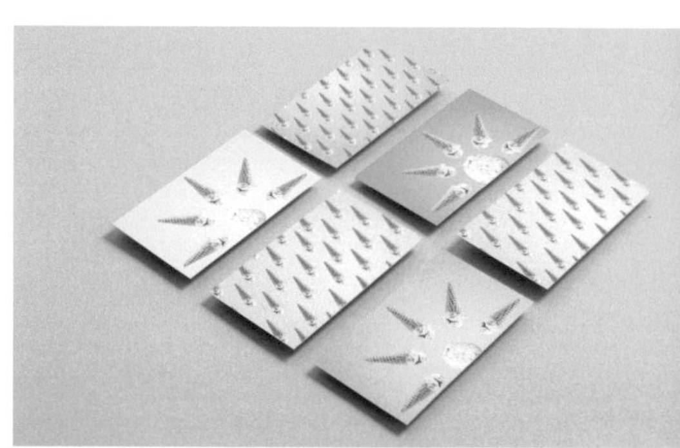

Josie Fenton and her husband Blair Casey worked in education and finance before they co-founded their craft ice cream company, Rain Or Shine, promising to give Vancouver the scoop. Driven by their devotion to delicious dessert, they make everything from scratch and carefully select all ingredients—most are sourced locally, seasonally, and organically. The masterful menu tells of Taco Tuesdays and manifold milkshakes. Apart from some seasonal toppings, everything is available year-round. And as the couple considered a cool corporate image as important as an all-seasons ice cream supply, they commissioned Glasfurd & Walker with the creation of a sweet set of graphics. The result is raining ice cream and cones!

Rain OR
ICE CREAM

Rain OR Shine
ICE CREAM
RAINORSHINEICECREAM.COM

At Les

FASHION LABEL

Tokyo, Japan, *by Michael Thorsby*

ASPIRING LABEL AT LES COMBINES CELINESQUE CLARITY WITH ADVENTUROUS ACCENTS À LA ACNE, AND PRESENTS ITSELF AS MONOCHROME AND MINIMALIST, ALBEIT WITH THE MANDATORY MARBLE PATTERN.

At Les is a ladies' fashion label freshly founded by Furusawa-san, a Tokyo-based designer whose collections combine Celinesque clean and classy cuts with experimental elements and adventurous accents à la Acne. Michael Thorsby's minimal corporate design approach stems from the clarity of lines found in customary Japanese clothing, like the traditional Wataboshi wedding hat, whose straight shape is picked up upon by some of At Les's pieces, but interpreted with an innovative twist.

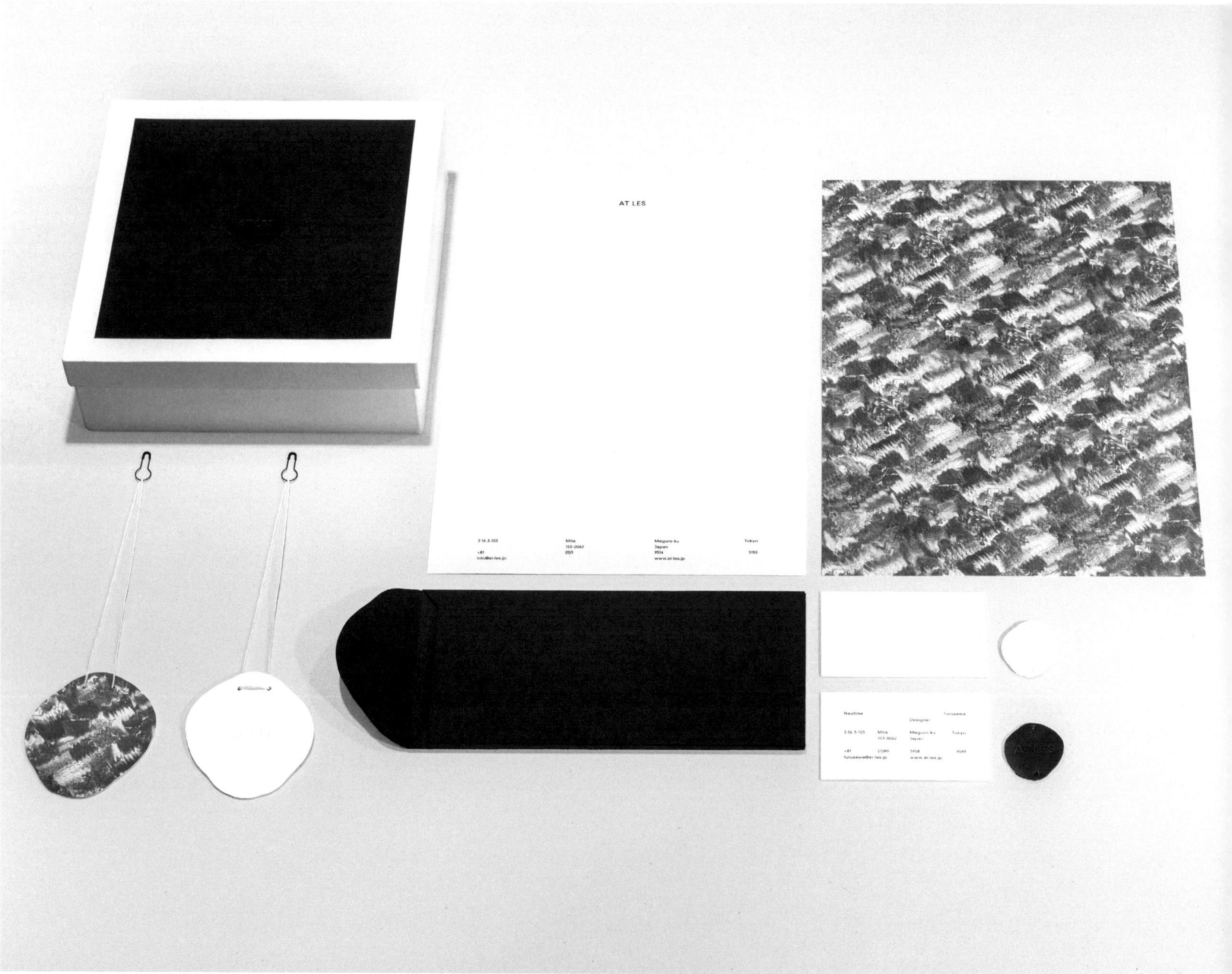

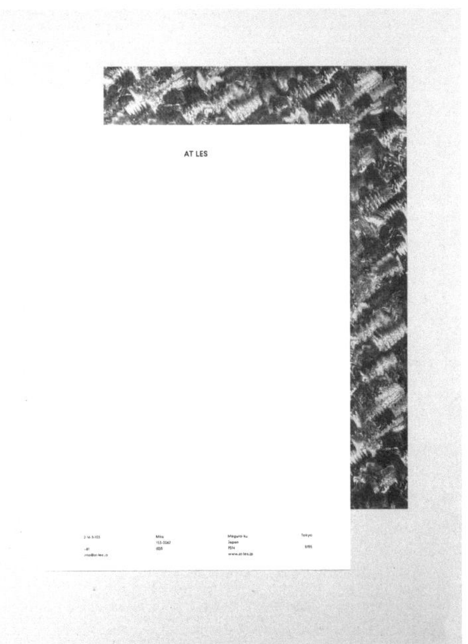
AT LES

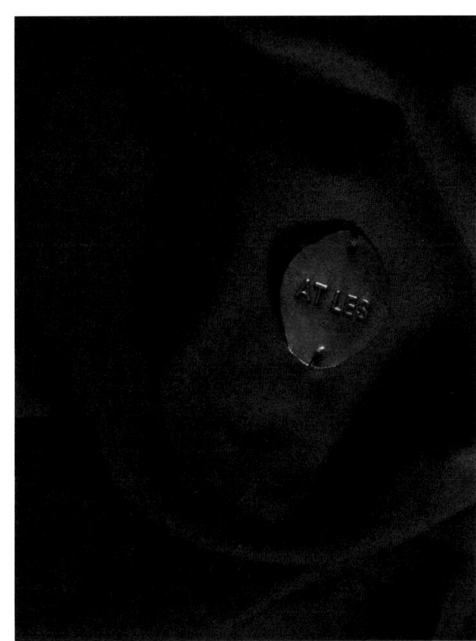
AT LES

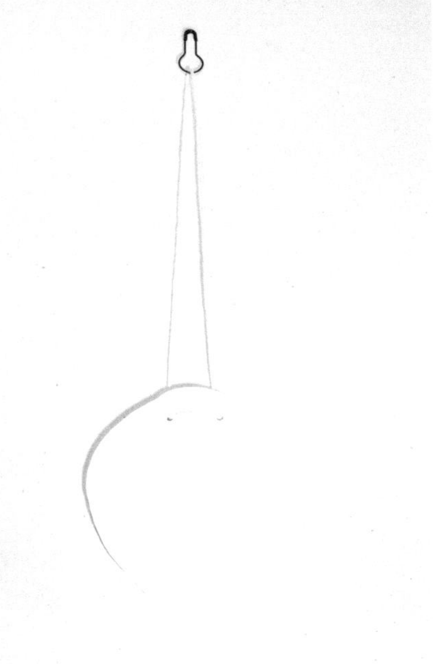

Hay Market

RESTAURANT

Hong Kong, *by Foreign Policy Design Group*

CAVALIER AND CONTEMPORARY:
HONG KONG RESTAURANT HAY MARKET'S
STYLE SEEMS AHEAD BY A NOSE.

Hay Market is a high-class restaurant sitting on the sprawling grounds of the Sha Tin Racecourse. Home to Hong Kong's Jockey Club, this is a world-class cadre founded by British colonists. Called in to develop a design direction for the brand new gastronomy business, Foreign Policy Design Group drew on the racecourse's colonial pedigree and played with the lofty visual language of its supercilious stables. The result is a vivid mix of vintage British typography and Victorian advertising illustrations, set against simple geometrically structured grounds and a candy-colored palette inspired by shimmery jockey silks.

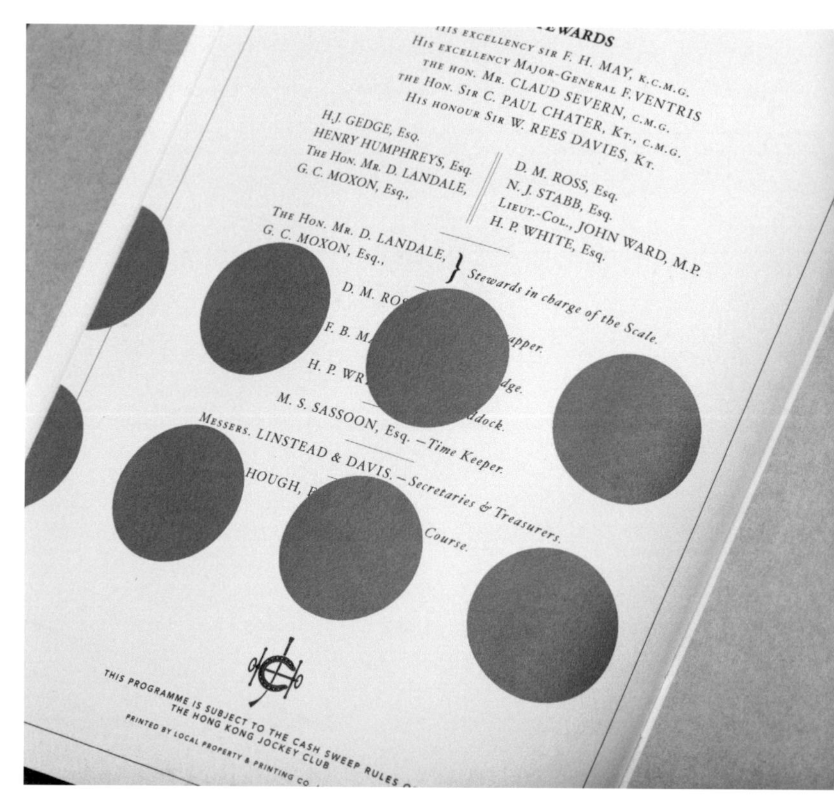

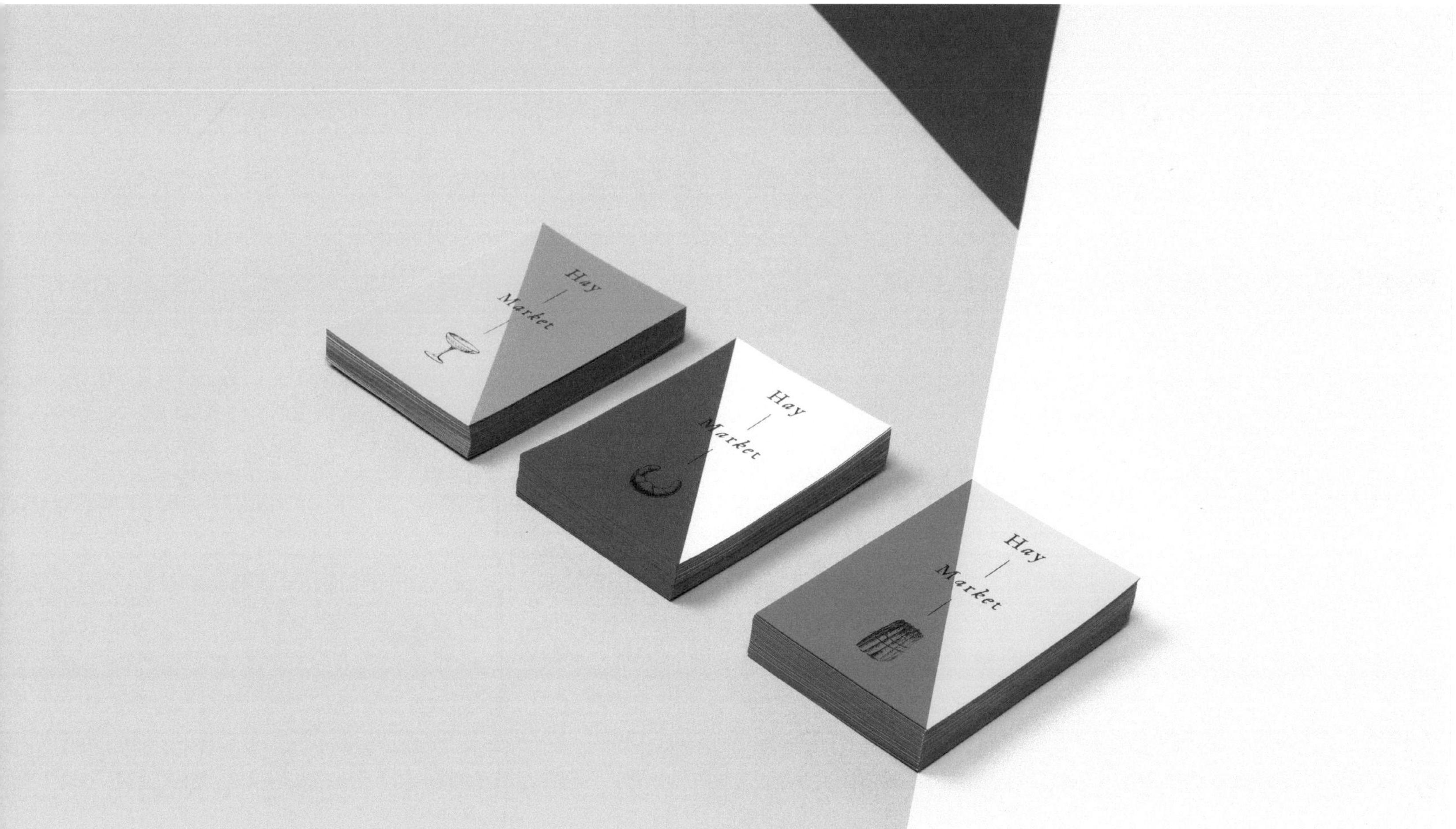

MAIN COURSE SELECTIONS
ON CARROT POTATO PANCAKE
6 OZ M4 WAGYU STRIPLOIN
FRENCH FRIES AND TRUFFLE MAYONNAISE
FRESHLY BAKED QUICHE LORRAINE
GRATINATED PANCAKE WITH GREEN ASPARAGUS,
FONTINA CHEESE AND SMOKED NORWEGIAN SALMON
BATCH
1846 March 7
THE STOCK DEPARTMENT
PLUS 10% SERVICE CHARGE. NO SERVICE CHARGE APPLICABLE ON CHARGES
DEBITED TO HONG KONG JOCKEY CLUB MEMBER'S ACCOUNT

Hay
Market
Hay
Market
Hay
Market
Hay Market
喜馬當先
2/f Grandstand II
Sha Tin Racecourse
Hong Kong
entertainment.hkjc.com
+852 3690 3690
Hay — Market
TABLE
No 36
Hay — Market
TABLE
No 18

The Pressery

MILK MAKER

London, UK, *by Natali Stajcic, Chi-San Wan, and Tim Jarvis*

THE PRESSERY SETS STRAIGHTFORWARD SIMPLICITY AGAINST THE SUSPICIOUSLY OVERDESIGNED SUPERFOODS ONE SEES STACKED ACROSS SUPERMARKET SHELVES.

Disillusioned with the general grocery grub, false eco-seals, and supposedly healthy supermarket foods, Natali Stajcic and Chi-San Wan set out to develop authentic almond milk as an alternative to the boastfully bottled drinks that dominate the market. The result was well-received by family and friends, and The Pressery was first presented to the public at London's Lower Marsh weekly weekend market. Sourced from raw Spanish almonds that are activated overnight, then cold-pressed with filtered water in their East London kitchen, the milk comes with no preservatives, additives, or artificial sweeteners. The company's corporate identity is as sincere and simple, designed by the duo with help from professional designer Tim Jarvis from Profission studio. In line with The Pressery's genuine guiding principle, its stripped-down style clearly shows that less can indeed be more.

THE
PRESSERY
ALMOND MILK
ORIGINAL
ORGANIC RAW ACTIVATED

THE
PRESSERY

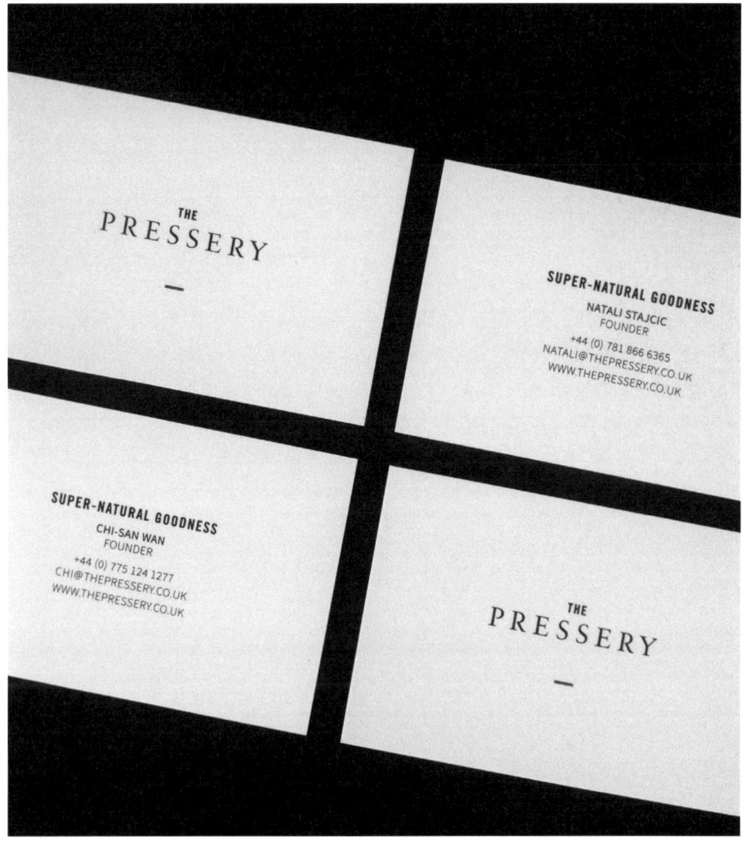
THE
PRESSERY
SUPER-NATURAL GOODNESS
NATALI STAJCIC
FOUNDER
+44 (0) 781 866 6365
NATALI@THEPRESSERY.CO.UK
WWW.THEPRESSERY.CO.UK
SUPER-NATURAL GOODNESS
CHI-SAN WAN
FOUNDER
+44 (0) 775 124 1277
CHI@THEPRESSERY.CO.UK
WWW.THEPRESSERY.CO.UK
THE
PRESSERY

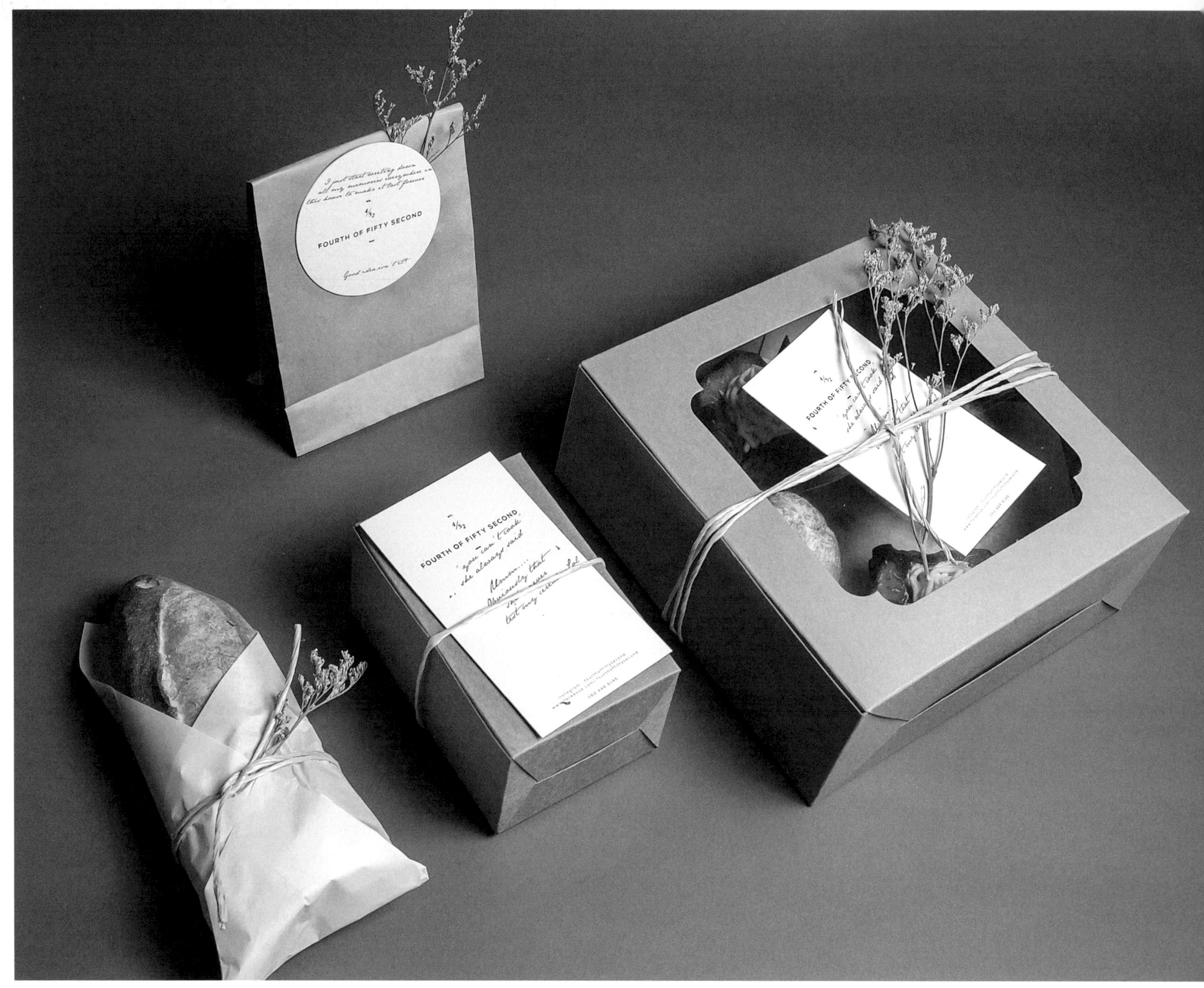

4/52

COFFEE SHOP

Bangkok, Thailand, *by Wide and Narrow*

COFFEE IS THE MOTHER OF INVENTION. AND LOTS OF IT MAKES FOR FAR-FETCHED IDEAS. WIDE AND NARROW'S IDENTITY FOR THIS BANGKOK-BASED CAFÉ DIGS DEEP INTO NARRATIVES OF NUTTY NEIGHBORS.

4/52, or Fourth of Fifty Second, is a coffee shop and café housed in a three-story building in Bangkok. Its name is derived from its doorplate number, while the rest of Wide and Narrow's branding is based on some weird work of fiction: the designers made up a story of a man living on the floor above the café, desperately fighting his Alzheimer's disease, scribbling a multitude of memos and instructions to himself all over his home. Drawing on their curious character, Wide and Narrow designed corporate communications covered with notes, and put a plethora of pencils across the coffee shop for guests to jot down some thoughts themselves.

FOURTH OF FIFTY SECOND
FOURTH OF FIFTY SECOND
FOURTH OF FIFTY SECOND

HERE

Rzany & Hund

DERMATOLOGIST

Berlin, Germany,
by Weiss-Heiten

MODEL, AGENT, OR ACNE PATIENT—WE ALL APPRECIATE PLEASANT DESIGN. DERMATOLOGISTS RZANY & HUND SURPRISE WITH SOME SUPERB STATIONERY-STYLE SET-CARDS.

Berlin-based dermatologists Prof. Dr. med. Berthold Rzany Sc.M. and Dr. med. Martina Hund met at Charité, the city's most renowned hospital and medical school, where both worked as senior physicians. In 2012, they opened their own practice on Ku'damm, the broad boulevard commonly considered to be Berlin's Champs-Elysées, to treat and advise private patients with skin problems and corresponding concerns. In spite of their slogan "Ease. Relax. Trust. Eyes closed.", patients in their practice are welcome to keep an eye out for decent design. For unlike most doctors, dermatologists Rzany & Hund seem to set great store by their graphics. Their wise decision to work with Weiss-Heiten was rewarded with a clear and consistent corporate identity, carried throughout from the print collateral to the practice's interior.

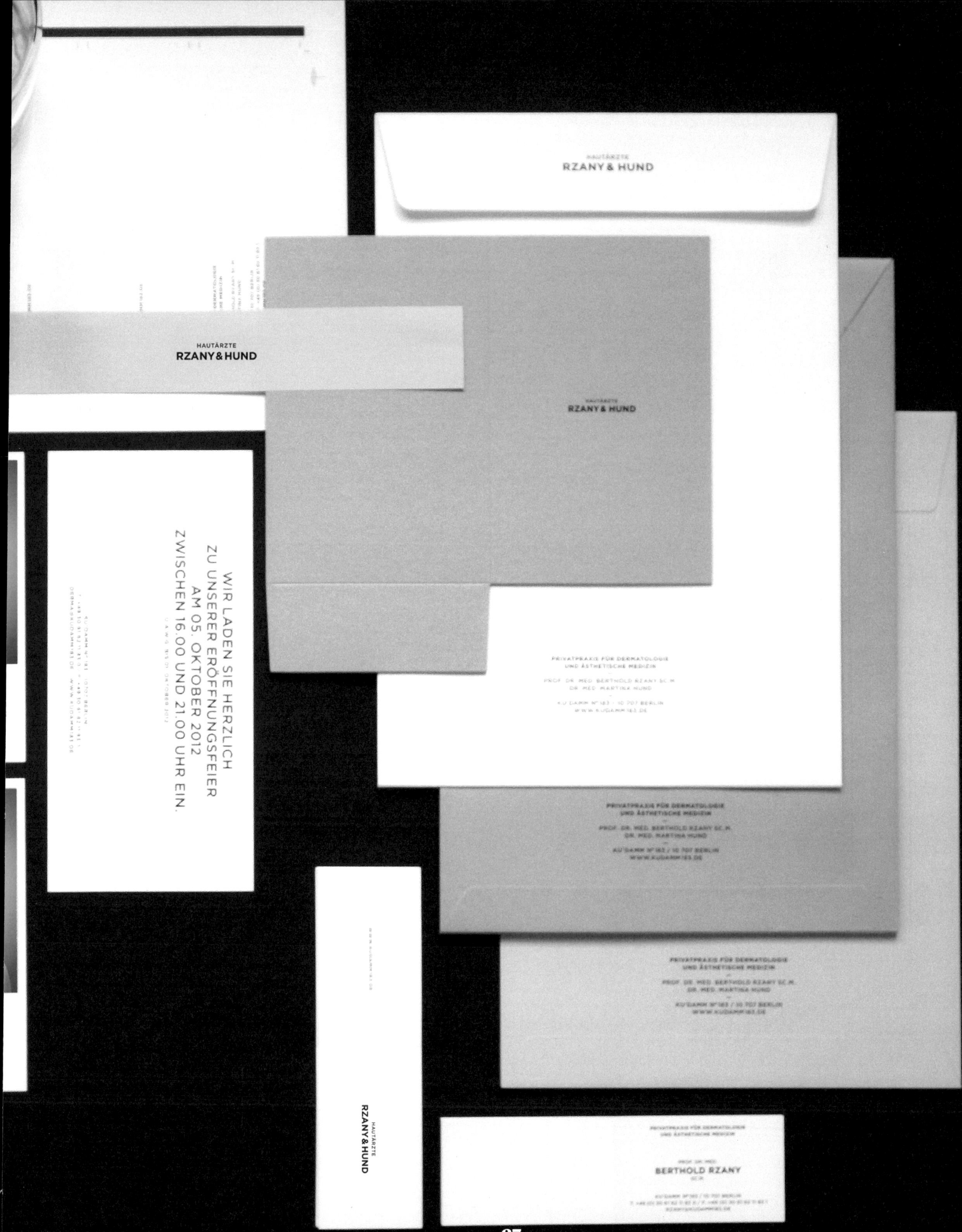

HAUTÄRZTE
RZANY & HUND

HAUTÄRZTE
RZANY & HUND

HAUTÄRZTE
RZANY & HUND

WIR LADEN SIE HERZLICH
ZU UNSERER ERÖFFNUNGSFEIER
AM 05. OKTOBER 2012
ZWISCHEN 16.00 UND 21.00 UHR EIN.

PRIVATPRAXIS FÜR DERMATOLOGIE
UND ÄSTHETISCHE MEDIZIN

PROF. DR. MED. BERTHOLD RZANY SC.M.
DR. MED. MARTINA HUND

KU'DAMM N°183 / 10 707 BERLIN
WWW.KUDAMM183.DE

PRIVATPRAXIS FÜR DERMATOLOGIE
UND ÄSTHETISCHE MEDIZIN

PROF. DR. MED. BERTHOLD RZANY SC.M.
DR. MED. MARTINA HUND

KU'DAMM N°183 / 10 707 BERLIN
WWW.KUDAMM183.DE

HAUTÄRZTE
RZANY & HUND

PRIVATPRAXIS FÜR DERMATOLOGIE
UND ÄSTHETISCHE MEDIZIN

PROF. DR. MED.
BERTHOLD RZANY
SC.M.

KU'DAMM N°183 / 10 707 BERLIN

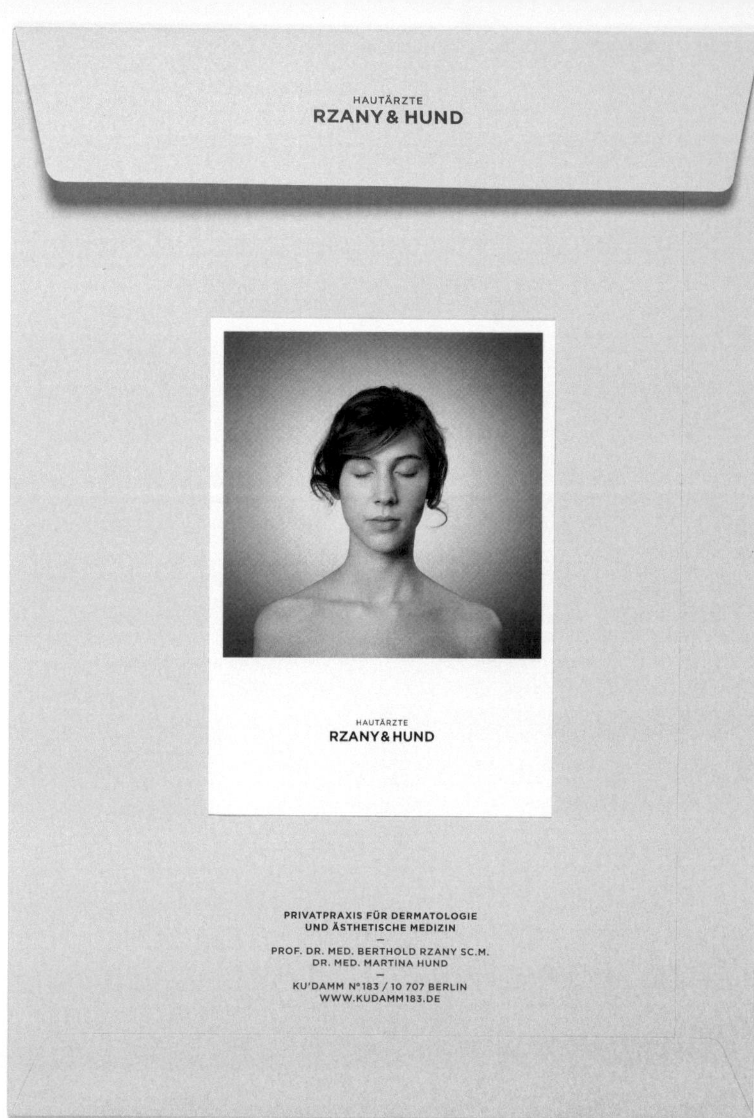

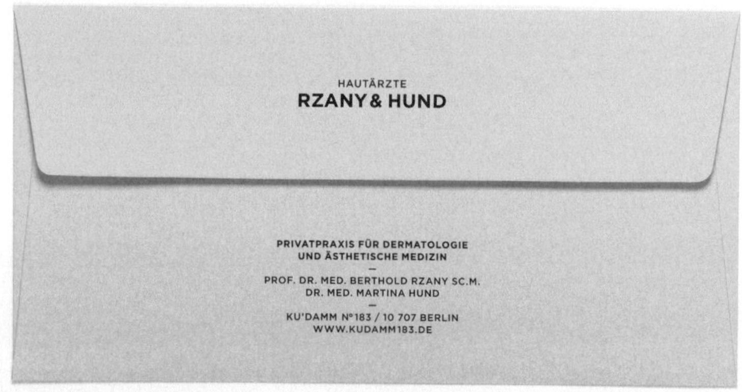

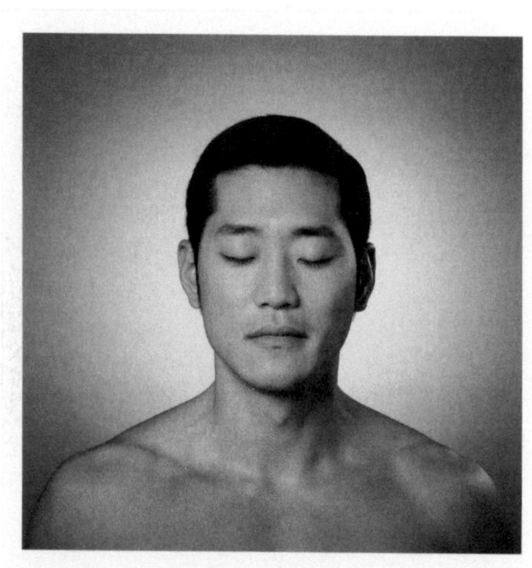

HAUTÄRZTE
RZANY & HUND

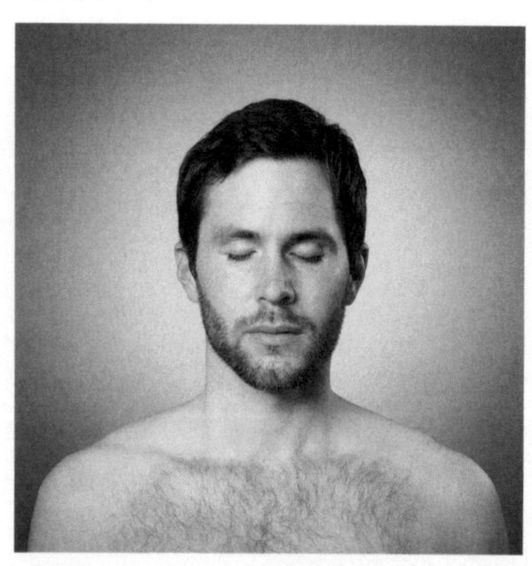

HAUTÄRZTE
RZANY & HUND

HAUTÄRZTE
RZANY & HUND

WWW.KUDAMM183.DE

HAUTÄRZTE
RZANY & HUND

PRIVATPRAXIS FÜR DERMATOLOGIE
UND ÄSTHETISCHE MEDIZIN

PROF. DR. MED.
BERTHOLD RZANY
SC.M.

KU'DAMM N°183 / 10 707 BERLIN
T. +49 (0) 30 61 62 11 83 0 / F. +49 (0) 30 61 62 11 83 1
RZANY@KUDAMM183.DE

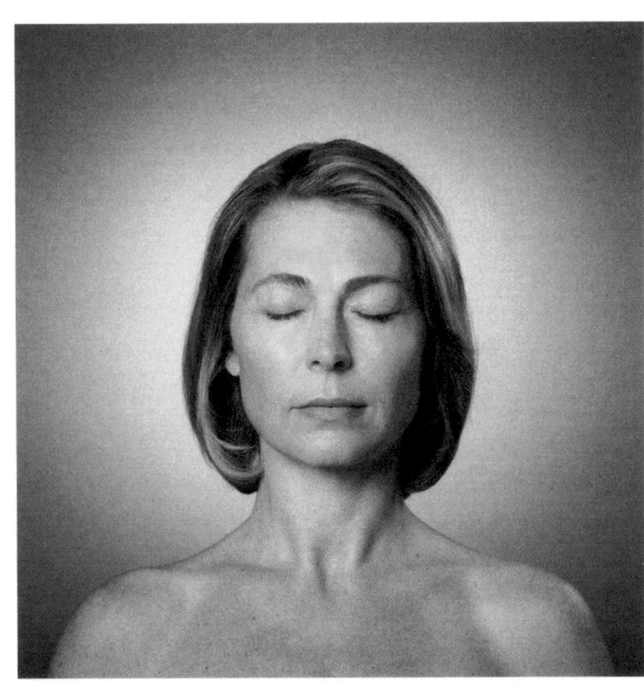

HAUTÄRZTE
RZANY & HUND

DAN!
DAN ARISA DALMAU
MUSIC / ORG. D'ESPECTACLES
GRÀCIA, BCN
637 729 849 / 932 841 049
INFO@DANARISA.COM
WWW.DANARISA.COM
DAN!
BOM!
BOM!
KAA!
PIM!

DAN!
BOM!
BOM!
BOM!
TAA!
TOO!
TAA!
DAN!
KAA!
BOM!
TAA!
TAA!
TOO!
KAA!
KAA!
DAN!
BOM!
BOM!
KAA!
PUM!
PAM!
PUM!
PAM!
TAA!
TAA!
TAA!

DAN!

PERCUSSIONIST

Barcelona, Spain, by Alex Dalmau

ALEX DALMAU DRUMS UP PERCUSSIONIST DAN ARISA'S SOLO PERFORMANCES WITH SOME RESOUNDING RUBBER STAMP STATIONERY.

Dan Arisa is a Catalan musician and member of the jazz-fusion band Pegasus, formed by Josep Mas "Kitflus", Max Sunyer, Rafael Escoté, and Santi Arisa. Seeking to present himself as a solo percussionist with a powerful set of stationery and promotional pieces, Arisa approached Alex Dalmau, who did not beat around the bush, and brought on a personal brand based on the percussionist's professional toolkit. Several rubber stamps have been produced to print all promotional material manually, transforming the process of branding into a drum technique.

Casa Virginia

RESTAURANT

Mexico City, Mexico, *by Savvy Studio*

HOME IS WHERE THE ART IS. WELL-RECEIVED BY ROMA'S BOHEMIAN RESIDENTS, RESTAURANT CASA VIRGINIA HOSTS HOMELY HAUTE CUISINE DINNERS IN AN AESTHETICALLY DESIGNED AMBIANCE.

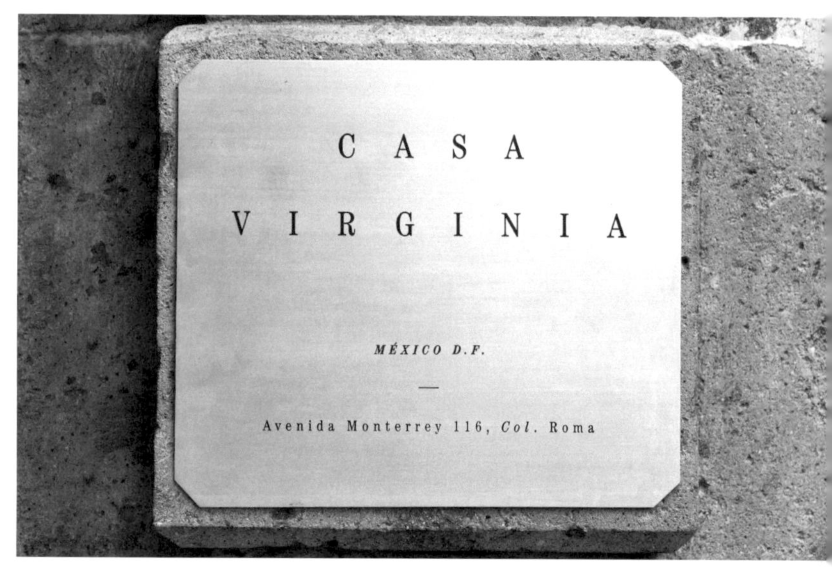

Casa Virginia is a culinary project by celebrated Mexican chef Mónica Patiño. Located in Mexico City's artsy and residential Roma area, the restaurant combines the coziness of nonchalant neighborhood eateries with high-end creative cuisine. Seeking to translate that two-tracked atmosphere to Casa Virginia's corporate identity and its visual applications, Savvy Studio combined graphic simplicity with special finishes, such as gold foiling, that mirror Patiño's meticulous cooking processes and the costly ingredients she uses. Savvy's designers call the result a contemporary reinterpretation of the graphic grandeur that dominated Mexico during the golden 20s. Interior decorators and architects Habitación 116 have added appropriate fine furnishings.

CABERNET MERLOT
MUJER
CASA
VIRGINIA
MÓNICA PATIÑO
CASA
VIRGINIA
MÉXICO D.F.

SELECT STORE SLASH GARMENT GALLERY PAR LA ROY FRAMES FASHION AS ART. LIKE PORTRAITS, ITS PRODUCTS ARE PRESENTED AGAINST GRAPHIC GROUNDS OF ARTISTIC PALLOR.

Par La Roy

GARMENT GALLERY

Monterrey, Mexico, *by Savvy Studio*

Fashion parlor Par La Roy promotes fresh brands by select creatives; due to its curatorial retail concept, it could be described as a gallery boutique. Conceived by Savvy Studio in close collaboration with creative colleague Emilio Álvarez, the space is indeed designed as a white cube, with white walls, white ceilings, and clean white chattels, and defined by a simple layout to let fashion collections and products come to the fore. Interspersed with only a few soft pastel-colored letters on the walls, the white interior provides a perfectly desaturated backdrop for the boutique's displays and ever-changing collections. The custom type that Savvy Studio's designers drew for Par La Roy is based on the combination of the material properties of metallic tubes, and sets a sense of structure and relief, creating volume and variability.

G . F Smith

PAPER MAKER & MERCHANT

London, UK, *by Made Thought*

THE STORY OF G . F SMITH IS ONE OF PULP, PAPER AND PROSPERITY. BASED ON THEIR BROAD PRODUCTION KNOW-HOW, BRITAIN'S PREMIER PAPER MERCHANTS-TURNED-MAKERS PROVIDE AN EVER-GROWING PAPER COLLECTION THAT HAS PROVEN PARTICULARLY POPULAR AMONGST AMBITIOUS CREATIVES. CREATIVELY AMBITIOUS THEMSELVES, THE COMPANY COMMISSIONED MADE THOUGHT FOR A VISUAL MAKEOVER THAT MIRRORS THE FIRM'S LEGACY WHILST LEAVING ENOUGH LEEWAY FOR FUTURE AMBITIONS.

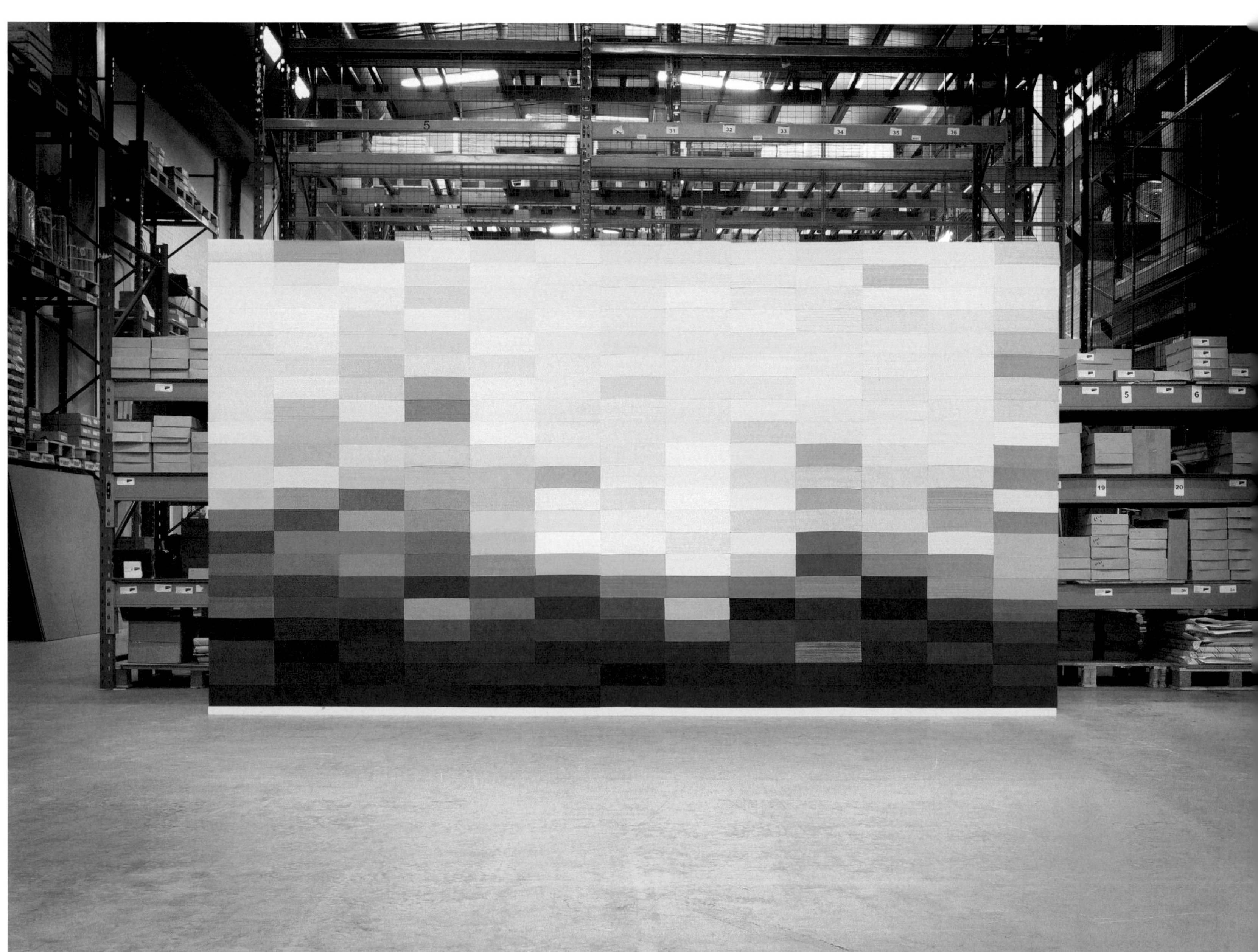

G . F Smith has been producing paper since 1885, when George Frederick Smith founded the firm following his fascination with the material and the creative makers who used it.
It was Smith's passion for paper and its possibilities that paved the way for the firm's future: famous not only for its expansive range of papers, but also for its immense expertise regarding production processes, G . F Smith has become the primary paper supplier for the British printing and publishing industry, and an international crowd of challenging creatives. Since the sixties, when the first graphic design courses were set up across the country's art colleges, the company has assisted ambitious designers in assuming closer control of print and paper specifications—and set great store on their own graphic representations. In 1965, the firm appointed its first design consultant to develop a strong company identity spanning stationery, sample books, and promotional collateral. Regular revisions followed, keeping the company's corporate communications topical and top of the line. Most recently, a comprehensive rebrand by Made Thought included a custom typeface and two marks, one of custodianship and one that acknowledges G . F Smith's current role as curator of its remarkable paper collection. The new identity intends to reflect the company's legacy and the craft that lies behind its services and current status.

Megan Simpkins
G . F SMITH
Beth-Louise Powell
G . F SMITH
Colin Smith
G . F SMITH
Lee Said
G . F SMITH
Gail Mellors
G . F SMITH
Tim Berry
Commercial Manager
Mobile 0774 775 6276
tdberry@gfsmith.com
G.F Smith
Lockwood Street
Hull HU2 OHL

G . F
SMITH
1885 ONWARDS

G . F
SMITH
G . F
SMITH
G . F
SMITH

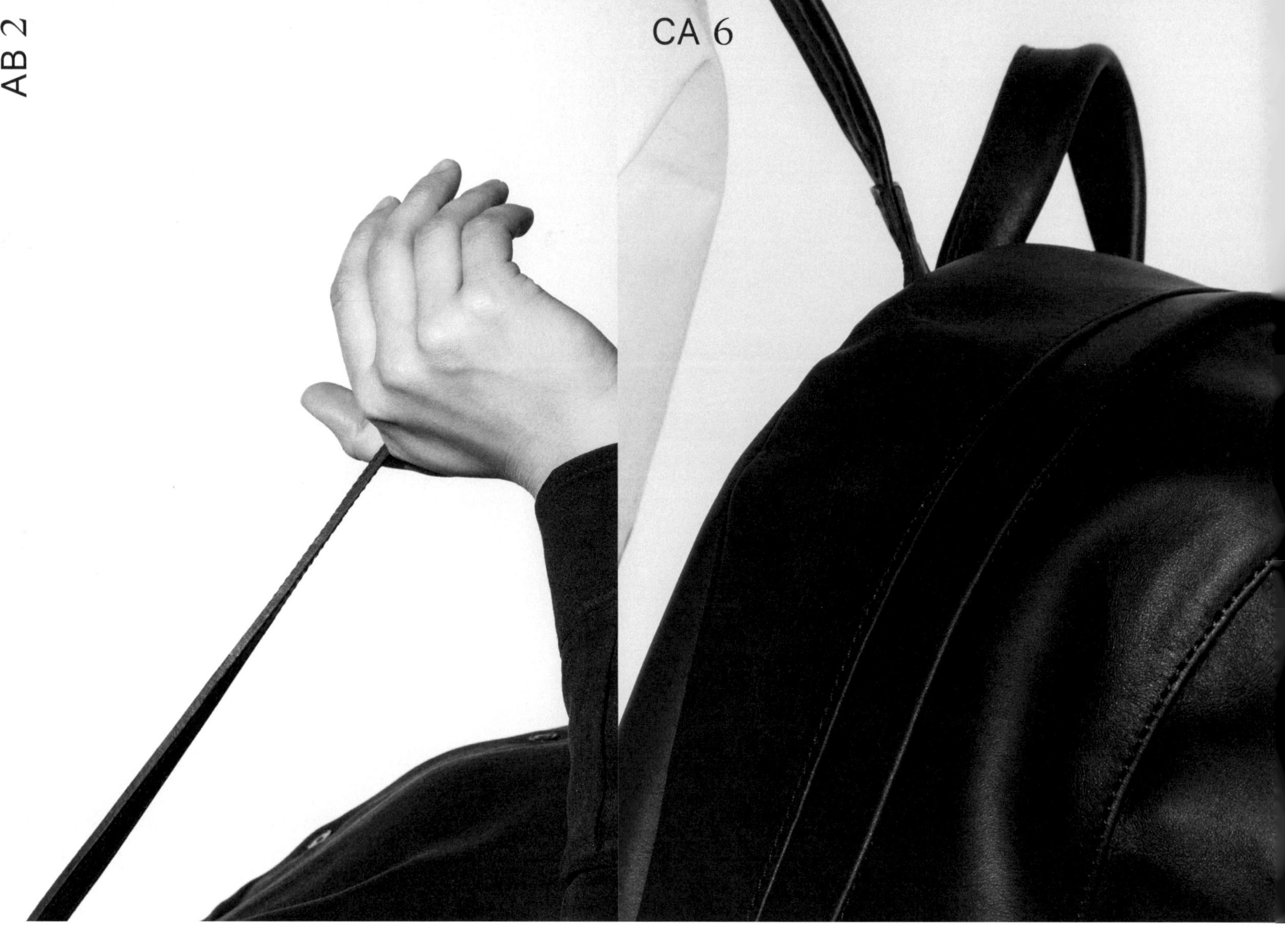

PB 0110

LEATHER BAGS

Hannover, Germany, *by Haw-lin Services*

THE BREE FAMILY HAS BEEN BURNING FOR BAGS SINCE THE SEVENTIES. PB 0110 IS ONE OF THEIR SON'S AMBITIOUS SOLO PROJECTS, A BRILLIANTLY BRANDED LINE OF LEATHER BAGS.

Born into a family of diligent bag producers, Philipp Bree left the business his parents Wolf Peter and Renate Brigitte Bree had founded in the seventies—supposedly with less than 10,000 German marks in their pockets—to launch his own brand called PB 0110 in 2012. Having headed the successful family firm with his brother for over 10 years, Bree substantially shaped the brand's development while staying true to the original ideas of his father. His first solo collections, too, build on the traditional Bree tendency towards simple shapes and pure materials. Philipp Bree merges the artisan approach of his parents with his own taste and a personal penchant for essential everyday products that assume personality over time. His accessory line combines contemporary style with the aura of cult classics. Haw-lin Services contributed a corresponding brand identity, bridging the gap between the timely and the timeless with a tactful typographic solution.

PB
0 1 1 0

(   )

PB 0110 e.K.
Birkenweg 50, 30657 Hannover
Germany
T +49 (0)511 806028-61
F +49 (0)511 806028-64
contact@pb0110.com
www.pb0110.com

Philipp Bree, Owner
PB 0110 e.K.
Birkenweg 50, 30657 Hannover
Germany
T +49 (0)511 806028-61
F +49 (0)511 806028-64
M +49 (0)172 4133250
p.bree@pb0110.com
www.pb0110.com

Christian Metzner, Design
PB 0110 e.K.
Birkenweg 50, 30657 Hannover
Germany
T +49 (0)511 806028-61
F +49 (0)511 806028-64
M +49 (0)176 96507693
c.metzner@pb0110.com
www.pb0110.com

PB
0 1 1 0

(   )

PITTI UOMO
17. – 20. June 2014
Florence

SEEK
08. – 10. July 2014
Berlin

CIFF
03. – 06. August 2014
Copenhagen

TRANOÏ FEMME
26. – 29. September 2014
Paris

PB 0110 SHOWROOM PARIS
27. JUNE – 01. JULY
Temple / galerie et éditions
20, rue de la Corderie
75003 Paris

I would like to invite you to visit me at one of the upcoming trade shows in Florence, Berlin, Copenhagen or Paris.

Sincerely yours,

Philipp Bree

PB
0110

( )

Please join me for some drinks and music
at the presentation of my first leather
and linen accessories collection.

rsvp@pb0110.com

Sincerely,

Philipp Bree

SHOWROOM
Potsdamer Straße 81, 10785 Berlin
15. – 19. January 2013
1 PM – 7 PM

SEEK
15. – 17. January 2013
Berlin

TRANOÎ
19. – 21. January 2013
Paris

PB
0110

( )

How-lin Services
z.Hd. Nathan Cowen
Friesenstraße 22
10965 Berlin
Germany

Betreff: Becoming soon
10. September 2012

Seite 1/1

Lieber Herr Nathan Cowen,

Zwei Merkmale charakterisieren die BREE Kollektion seit jeher: Innovationsfreude und Langlebigkeit. Für ein Produkt, das so sehr im Fokus der Mode steht wie Taschen, ist dieser Ansatz in den frühen 1970er-Jahren keineswegs selbstverständlich. Die Suche nach dem neuesten Trend und gleichzeitig der Respekt vor tradierten Werten gleichen vielmehr einem Spagat. Doch diese Übung macht den Meister – und sie prägt die Marke.

Schon 1972, also erst zwei Jahre nach der Gründung des Unternehmens, erhalten Produkte von BREE die ersten Designpreise. Es ist die konsequente Suche nach der kongenialen Synthese aus Funktion und Form, die den frühen Erfolg der Marke ausmacht. Das Streben nach gestalterischer Perfektion findet auch weiterhin hohe Anerkennung und wird heute vom BREE Designteam konsequent weiterentwickelt. Kein anderer Taschenhersteller weltweit ist so oft ausgezeichnet worden. Doch das Wichtigste daran: Immer mehr Kunden wissen eine solche Designqualität zu schätzen. 1993 hat BREE nicht nur Handelspartner in der Schweiz und Luxemburg, sondern auch in Hongkong und Japan, USA und Kanada. In diesem Jahr bezieht das Unternehmen die neue Zentrale in Isernhagen bei Hannover. Doch das Wichtigste daran: Immer mehr Kunden wissen eine solche Designqualität zu schätzen.

Mit freundlichen Grüßen,

Philipp Bree

PB 0110 e.K.
Birkenweg 50, 30657 Hannover, Germany
T +49 (0)511 806028-61, F +49 (0)511 806028-64
contact@pb0110.com, www.pb0110.com

Volksbank Hannover
Kto. 660 947 300, BLZ 251 900 01
IBAN DE33 2519 0001 0660 9473 00, BIC VOHADE2HXXX

Philipp Bree, Owner
USt-IdNr. DE815389936, St-Nr. 25/106/06292
HRA 202552

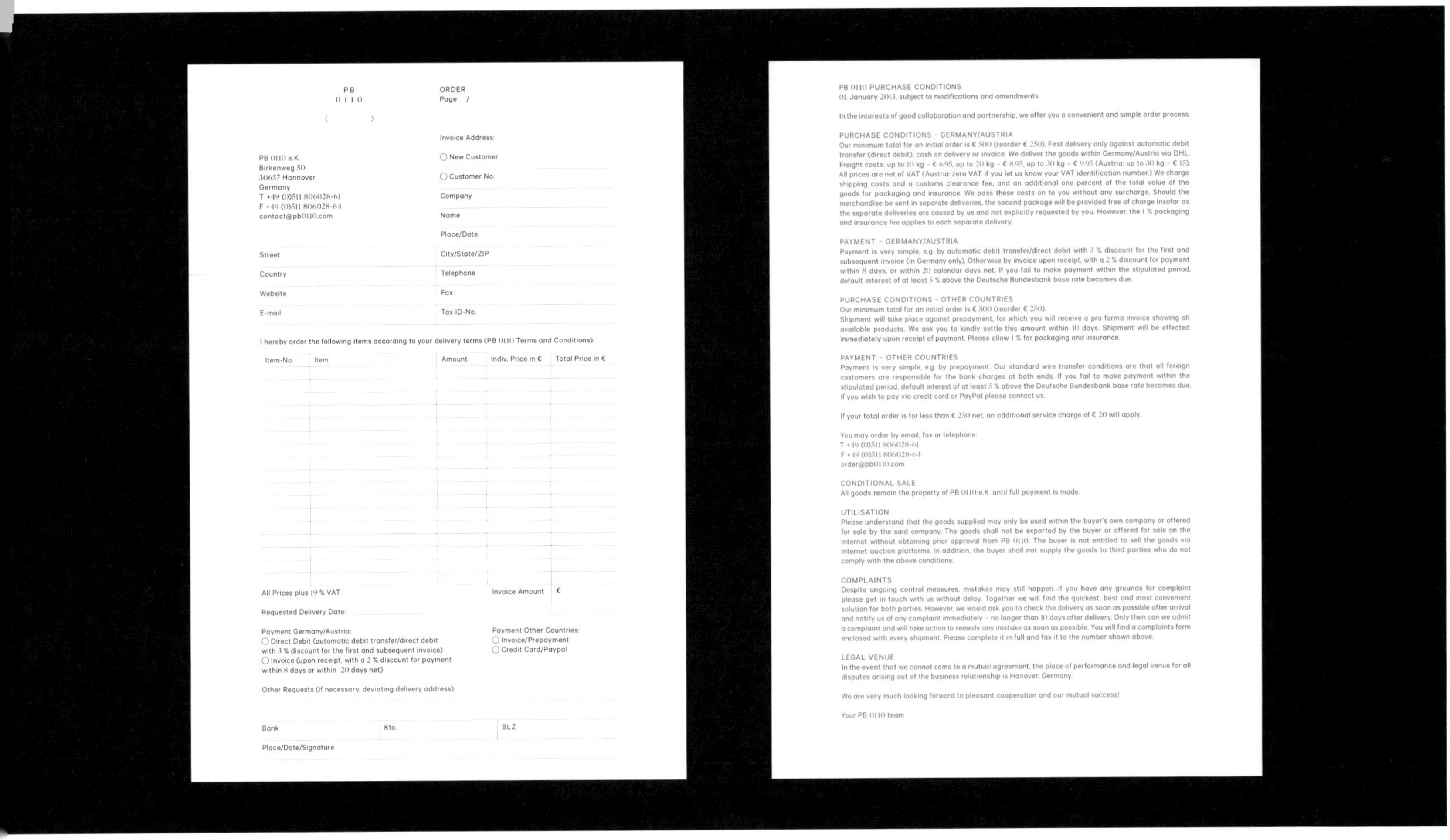

PB
0110

( )

ORDER
Page /

Invoice Address:

PB 0110 e.K.
Birkenweg 50
30657 Hannover
Germany
T +49 (0)511 806028-61
F +49 (0)511 806028-64
contact@pb0110.com

○ New Customer

○ Customer No.

Company

Name

Place/Date

Street	City/State/ZIP
Country	Telephone
Website	Fax
E-mail	Tax ID-No.

I hereby order the following items according to your delivery terms (PB 0110 Terms and Conditions):

Item-No.	Item	Amount	Indiv. Price in €	Total Price in €

All Prices plus 19 % VAT

Invoice Amount €

Requested Delivery Date:

Payment Germany/Austria:
○ Direct Debit (automatic debit transfer/direct debit with 3 % discount for the first and subsequent invoice)
○ Invoice (upon receipt, with a 2 % discount for payment within 8 days or within 20 days net)

Payment Other Countries:
○ Invoice/Prepayment
○ Credit Card/Paypal

Other Requests (if necessary, deviating delivery address):

Bank	Kto.	BLZ

Place/Date/Signature

PB 0110 PURCHASE CONDITIONS
01. January 2013, subject to modifications and amendments

In the interests of good collaboration and partnership, we offer you a convenient and simple order process.

PURCHASE CONDITIONS – GERMANY/AUSTRIA
Our minimum total for an initial order is € 500 (reorder € 250). First delivery only against automatic debit transfer (direct debit), cash on delivery or invoice. We deliver the goods within Germany/Austria via DHL. Freight costs: up to 10 kg – € 6.95, up to 20 kg – € 8.95, up to 30 kg – € 9.95 (Austria: up to 30 kg – € 15). All prices are net of VAT (Austria: zero VAT if you let us know your VAT identification number.) We charge shipping costs and a customs clearance fee, and an additional one percent of the total value of the goods for packaging and insurance. We pass these costs on to you without any surcharge. Should the merchandise be sent in separate deliveries, the second package will be provided free of charge insofar as the separate deliveries are caused by us and not explicitly requested by you. However, the 1 % packaging and insurance fee applies to each separate delivery.

PAYMENT – GERMANY/AUSTRIA
Payment is very simple, e.g. by automatic debit transfer/direct debit with 3 % discount for the first and subsequent invoice (in Germany only). Otherwise by invoice upon receipt, with a 2 % discount for payment within 8 days, or within 20 calendar days net. If you fail to make payment within the stipulated period, default interest of at least 5 % above the Deutsche Bundesbank base rate becomes due.

PURCHASE CONDITIONS – OTHER COUNTRIES
Our minimum total for an initial order is € 500 (reorder € 250).
Shipment will take place against prepayment, for which you will receive a pro forma invoice showing all available products. We ask you to kindly settle this amount within 10 days. Shipment will be effected immediately upon receipt of payment. Please allow 1 % for packaging and insurance.

PAYMENT – OTHER COUNTRIES
Payment is very simple, e.g. by prepayment. Our standard wire transfer conditions are that all foreign customers are responsible for the bank charges at both ends. If you fail to make payment within the stipulated period, default interest of at least 5 % above the Deutsche Bundesbank base rate becomes due. If you wish to pay via credit card or PayPal please contact us.

If your total order is for less than € 250 net, an additional service charge of € 20 will apply.

You may order by email, fax or telephone:
T +49 (0)511 806028-61
F +49 (0)511 806028-64
order@pb0110.com

CONDITIONAL SALE
All goods remain the property of PB 0110 e.K. until full payment is made.

UTILISATION
Please understand that the goods supplied may only be used within the buyer's own company or offered for sale by the said company. The goods shall not be exported by the buyer or offered for sale on the Internet without obtaining prior approval from PB 0110. The buyer is not entitled to sell the goods via Internet auction platforms. In addition, the buyer shall not supply the goods to third parties who do not comply with the above conditions.

COMPLAINTS
Despite ongoing control measures, mistakes may still happen. If you have any grounds for complaint please get in touch with us without delay. Together we will find the quickest, best and most convenient solution for both parties. However, we would ask you to check the delivery as soon as possible after arrival and notify us of any complaint immediately – no longer than 10 days after delivery. Only then can we admit a complaint and will take action to remedy any mistake as soon as possible. You will find a complaints form enclosed with every shipment. Please complete it in full and fax it to the number shown above.

LEGAL VENUE
In the event that we cannot come to a mutual agreement, the place of performance and legal venue for all disputes arising out of the business relationship is Hanover, Germany.

We are very much looking forward to pleasant cooperation and our mutual success!

Your PB 0110 team

PB
0110

( )

3

3

Kostas Murkudis Bleibtreustraße 26 10707 Berlin Germany

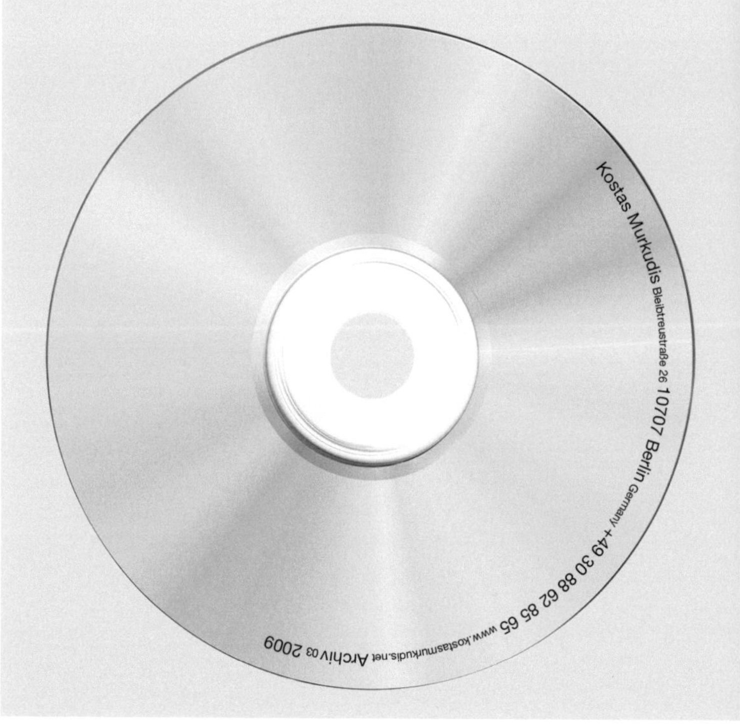
Kostas Murkudis Bleibtreustraße 26 10707 Berlin Germany +49 30 88 62 85 65 www.kostasmurkudis.net Archiv 03 2009

Kostas Murkudis

FASHION LABEL

Berlin, Germany, *by Haw-lin Services*

KOSTAS MURKUDIS CREATES VISIONARY WARDROBES FOR VENTURESOME WEARERS. HAW-LIN SERVICES CLOTHED HIS COMPANY WITH A COLLECTION OF CORPORATE COMMUNICATIONS THAT TRANSLATES THE LABEL'S VOLATILE VISUAL LANGUAGE INTO TYPOGRAPHIC TERMS.

Although Kostas Murkudis has assisted classy couturiers Wolfgang Joop and Helmut Lang, advised Nicolas Ghesquière at Balenciaga, and designed for the likes of big brands like Closed, his own label has remained a laboratory since its foundation in 1994. Producing many of his pieces in very limited editions, Murkudis frees himself from fashion's curse of blindly following buyers' and customers' expectations by instead continuing to create collections as adventurous and architectural as the ones that brought him a big fan base back in the nineties. Rebranding the renowned designer, Haw-lin Services came up with a corporate look and feel no less autonomous than Murkudis's fashion collections. The minimal concept is based on a simple type-size change that supports the hierarchy of information. The brand mark has been punched into all stationery materials using a manual pattern notcher.

Kostas Murkudis Bleibtreustraße 26 10707 Berlin Germany +49 30 88 62 85 65

Valerie von Kittlitz Assistant to Kostas Murkudis Bleibtreustraße 26 10707 Berlin Germany +49 177 86 21 896

Kostas Murkudis Bleibtreustraße 26 10707 Berlin Germany +49 30 88 62 85 65

Valerie von Kittlitz Assistant to Kostas Murkudis Bleibtreustraße 26 10707 Berlin Germany +49 177 86 21 896

Kostas Murkudis Bleibtreustraße 26 10707 Berlin Germany +49 30 88 62 85 65 www.kostasmurkudis.net Subject Communication Date 06.02.2014 Page 1/1

Haw-lin Services
Nathan Cowen
Mehringdamm 61, 2. Hof, 3. OG
10961 Berlin

Sehr geehrter Herr Cowen,

Tio qui occus quae earum rerferatur, ium harumquos ditisqu aspidel igendeniae ipsandam quo ipsum doluptae si a cones essitibus et ex eum fugitature exerchictur, cus.

Exped untiberi comnis doluptas soluptibeati quiatum qui ut lautati onsequae nonse ent, sinverciis et accum fugiaerit reperum et aut archit aut moluptat.

Ma ipis volor solorpor rat ea nihit que di di imolorent minum quiberspitam voluptata nem. Rae cuptatur mosam re ium restior iasperum voloreiunt re qui solupta tionse pa cus dolore proreperunt velitibus ne sitaquiduci dolupis aut ex ea veribusamus niendel icimagnatus esequossit hilibus aut dolor sitat.
Uptas dignim quia sediore possiniat aspid quas res dis ressitistium ratiis ut versped que et dolupta que sinctus molor mo cuptae modicte vendaeprent lam iuntis re dolupturi recto ipsapisit, occusa quiaspiet et pra natiis esequid quuntius maximos apitibus et provid quia dis et am id mos demodisti ditiae es quatiant et, non nimusantoris id quistia nectae. Ro cor as estios re volorrovitem iditatecti omnis apiscium facid magnimp orpore sequi dolor audis illuptatiis rest, et labo. Oluptat rest, ipsunture rem voluptatio. Libeaquate odi ut volupisquos moluptatquia voluptatur andae nonsequas quodit exero consequ iatiorestias alis magnimolupta volestrum autectia quid ut etur aperuntiunt.

Quunt acculpa dolorunt aut res ad molorat iatemodi blam aut ex et ea volut porerci musamet quiasit re poris aut il ipsae pos ipsa qui beat.

Kostas Murkudis

4D

Lumbürr Co.

OUTDOOR GOODS

Toronto, Canada, *by Ben Johnston x Mark Simmons*

LUMBÜRR CO. BRINGS US EVERYTHING WE NEED FOR A JOLLY JAUNT, AND MAKES LAUNCHING A LIFESTYLE BRAND LOOK AS EASY AS A WALK IN THE PARK.

Lumbürr Co. provides beautifully branded products built around a perfect day in the park. From blankets and bicycles to garden game gadgets, its collection is carefully handcrafted in the company's Toronto wood workshop. The brand is the brainchild of industrial designer Mark Simmons, who founded it upon his return from a two-year trip to Sweden, where he received his master's degree in sustainable design. Luckily, his studies left him enough time for picnics and playing Kubb, so that he returned from the northern lowlands packed with inspiration to invest in his new venture. Combining a Scandinavian sense for sustainability with Canadian craftsmanship, Mark Simmons made it Lumbürr Co.'s mission to make products that promote well-being throughout their life-cycle, from the initial choice of their materials down to their final disposal. The careful consideration present in Lumbürr Co.'s collection culminates in the brand's corporate design that Simmons developed with befriended graphic designer Ben Johnston

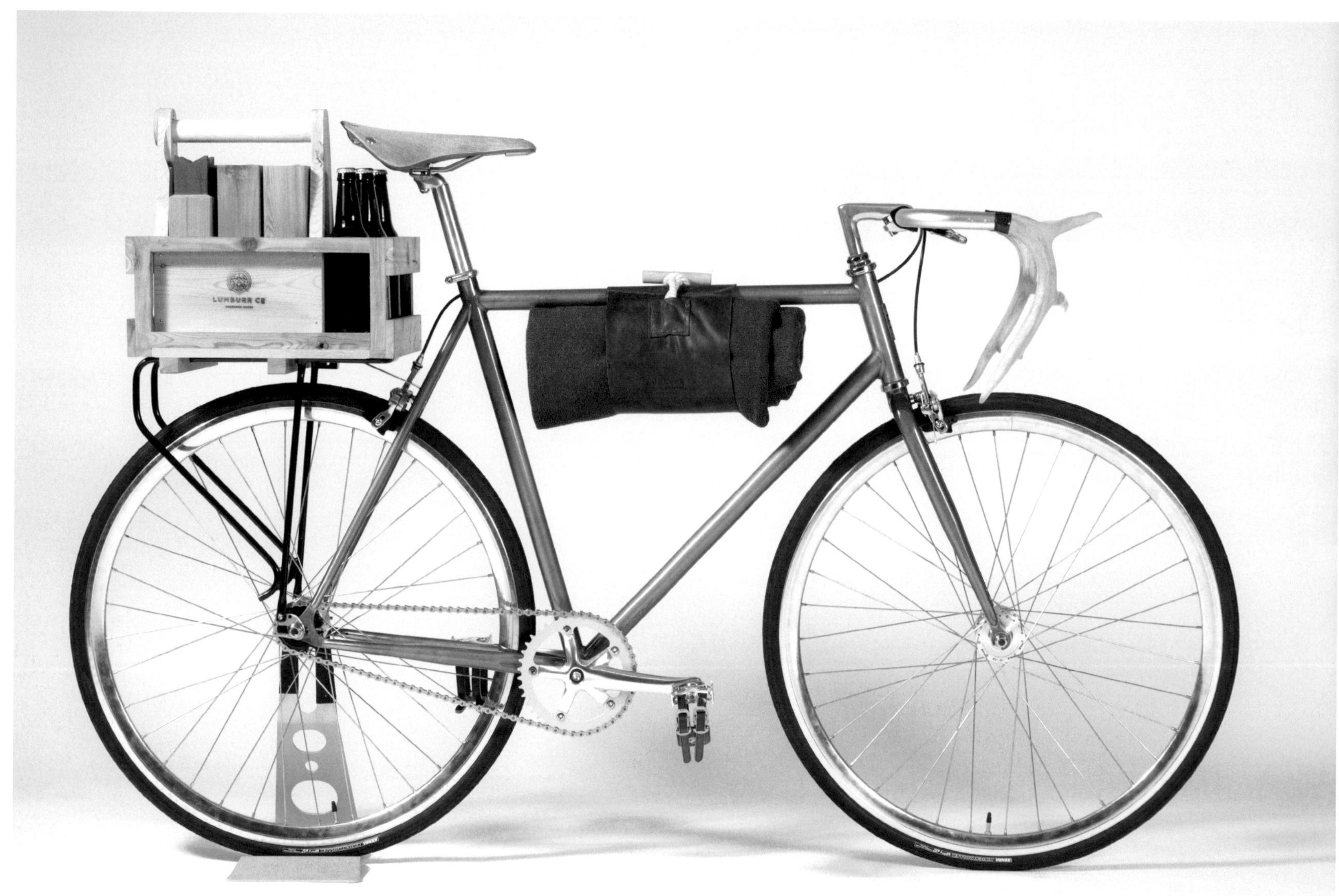

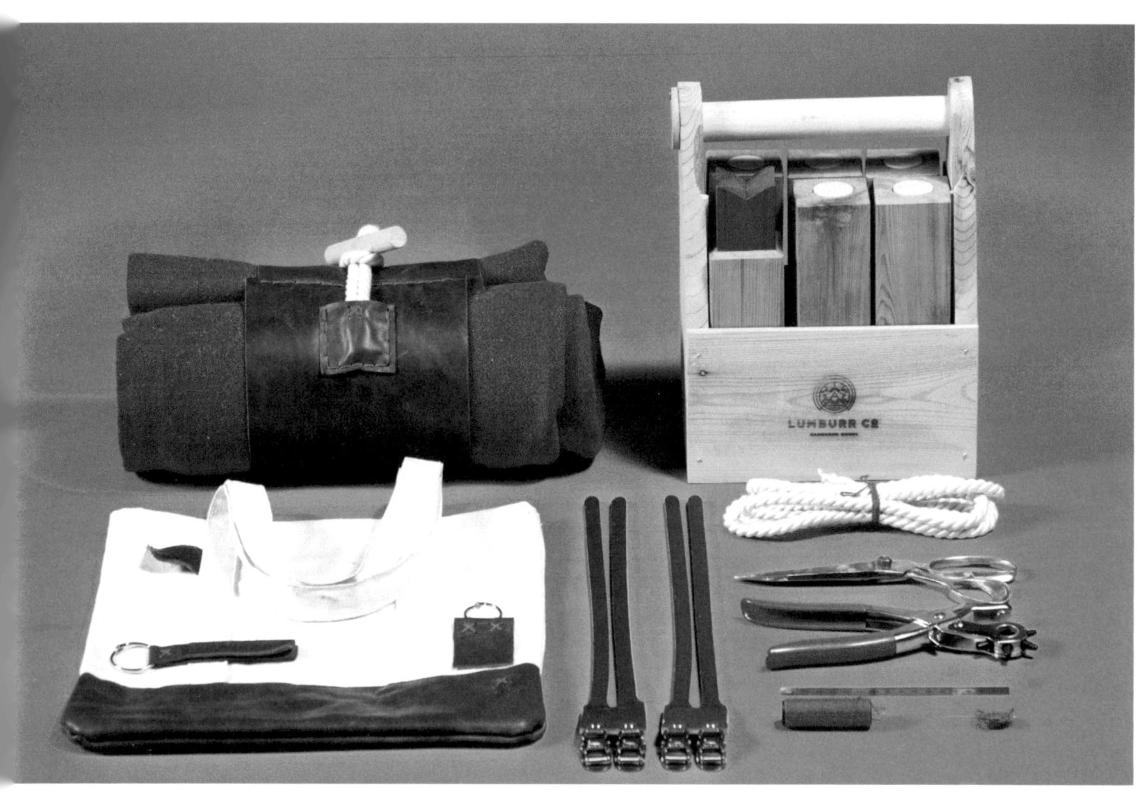
LUMBURR Cº

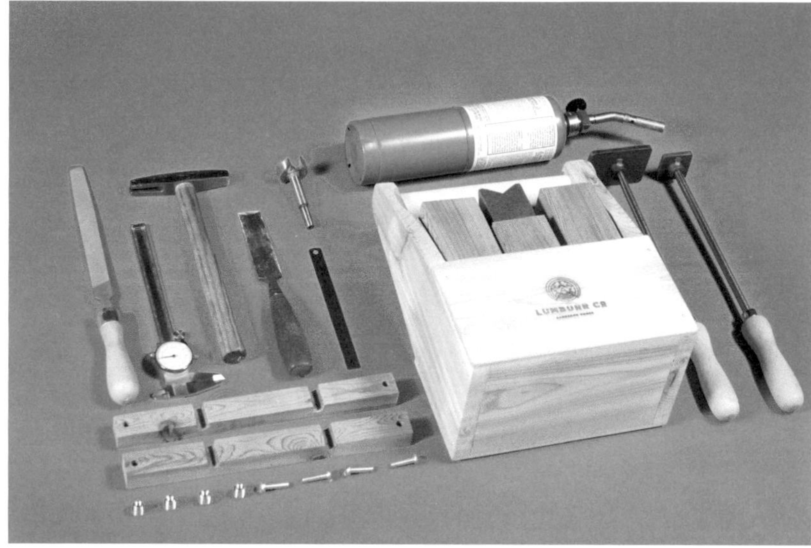
LUMBURR Cº

LUMBÜRR Cº
LUMBÜRR Cº

LUMBÜRR Co
HANDSOME GOODS

LUMBÜRR Co

DAMN FINE LIFESTYLE

LUMBÜRR Co

Le Baigneur

GENTLEMEN'S GROOMING

Paris, France, *by Atelier Müesli*

THE MODERN MAN AND THE SEA:
LE BAIGNEUR BRINGS A NEW WAVE OF BEAUTY BALMS
AND SUPPORTS THE SEASHORE WITH SUSTAINABLE STYLE.

Paris-based beauty boutique Le Baigneur bestows upon menfolk a hand-made high-standard skin care system. Besides supplying bespoke balms to soothe stressed skin after shaving and stiff breezes, it supports the care of continental coastlines, donating a part of its profits to the Surfrider Foundation Europe. Atelier Müsli's branding for Le Baigneur is based on the company's crafty approach, and communicates its core values (sustainability and simplicity), as well as savoir-vivre. They developed geometric groundwork, taking cues from the classic mosaic-tiled flooring of ancient spas that they then mixed with earnest seals inspired by the collateral of good old craft guilds. Guided by the aim to support an authentic gentlemanly spirit, they waived preppy corporate polish in favor of simple design work, and conceived of a bright but budget-friendly two-tone palette, printing on unpretentious, uncoated paper stock.

SOINS DU VISAGE
SOINS DU CORPS
ACCESSOIRES
WWW.LEBAIGNEUR.FR
LE
BAIGNEUR
SOINS DE QUALITÉ
POUR HOMME
PARIS
EXIGEANT
Une gamme de soins pour le visage et le corps, 100% naturel, certifiée bio et spécialement conçue pour l'épiderme masculin.
RESPECTUEUX
Un choix d'emballages sans plastique, 100% recyclables et fabriqués en France.
ENGAGÉ
Le stockage et l'expédition de nos produits est confiée à une Entreprise Adaptée gérée par l'Association des Paralysés de France. 1 % du chiffre d'affaire annuel est reversé à l'association environnementale Surfrider Foundation Europe.

ARGILE VERTE · EXTRAIT DE
CALENDULA BIO
HUILE
DE CHANVRE BIO
PULPE D'ALOE VERA BIO
HUILE ESSENTIELLE
DE VETIVER BIO
GREEN CLAY
ORGANIC
CALENDULA EXTRACT
ORGANIC
HEMP OIL
ORGANIC ALOE VERA PULP
ORGANIC VETIVER
ESSENTIAL OIL
PEAU
SÈCHE
APAISANT
ET
NOURRISSANT
DRY
SKIN
SOOTHS
AND
NOURISHES

1
SAVON À BARBE N°1 +
BOL EN PORCELAINE
SHAVING SOAP N°1 +
PORCELAIN BOWL
LE BAIGNEUR
BOL À BARBE
SAVON À BARBE
1
SHAVING SOAP
SHAVING BOWL
N°1
150 GR

SAVON
TONIFIANT
TONIFYING
SOAP

LE BAIGNEUR

LE
BAIGNEUR
SOINS DE QUALITÉ
POUR HOMME
PARIS
FABIEN MEAUDRE
Gérant · Fondateur
35 rue des Trois Bornes
75011 Paris
Mobile 06 58 17 99 21
Mail contact@lebaigneur.fr
Site www.lebaigneur.fr

SAVONS
NATURELLEMENT
SAVON
RELAXANT
100 GR

SOINS DE QUALITÉ POUR HOMME
LE BAIGNEUR
SOAP
100 GR
SAVON
RELAXANT
RELAXING
SAVON
RELAXANT
SAVON NATURELLEMENT
HYDRATANT ET DOUX
LE BAIGNEUR VOUS CERTIFIE
LA FABRICATION ARTISANALE
DE CE SAVON SELON LA MÉTHODE
TRADITIONNELLE DE
SAPONIFICATION À FROID.

SOINS DE QUALITÉ POUR HOMME
LE BAIGNEUR
SOAP
100 GR
SAVON
TONIFIANT
TONIFYING
SAVON
TONIFIANT
SAVON NATURELLEMENT HYDRATANT ET DOUX
LE BAIGNEUR VOUS CERTIFIE LA FABRICATION ARTISANALE DE CE SAVON SELON LA MÉTHODE TRADITIONNELLE DE SAPONIFICATION À FROID.
Fabriqué par la Savonnerie de Beaulieu
NATURE & PROGRÈS

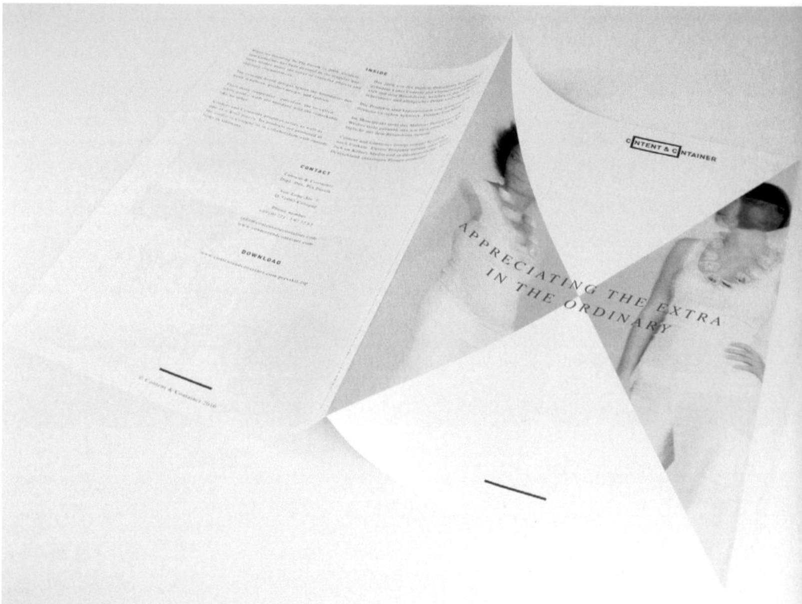

Content & Container

CERAMICS & ACCESSORIES STUDIO

Cologne, Germany, *by Bureau Bleen*

CONTENT & CONTAINER CELEBRATES THE CRAFTY CRUDITY THAT CONTEMPORARY CREATIONS TEND TO BLANKET BENEATH SLEEK SURFACES. BUREAU BLEEN'S BRANDING FOR THE FIRM FINDS BEAUTY IN IMPERFECTION, TOO.

Pia Pasalk produces one-of-a-kind-pieces of pottery and small series of accessories inspired by the "wabi-sabi philosophy of Japan." With experimental designs that turn flaws into the focus and errors into elements of style, her company Content & Container celebrates the charm of the imperfect and the inconspicuous. Bureau Bleen's branding for the business picks up on the somewhat crude occurrence of Content & Container's perfectly flawed product, putting a certain intended imperfection at the center of all communications. The quirky typographic logo connects Content & Container quite literally, merging the two terms into a vivid visual moniker.

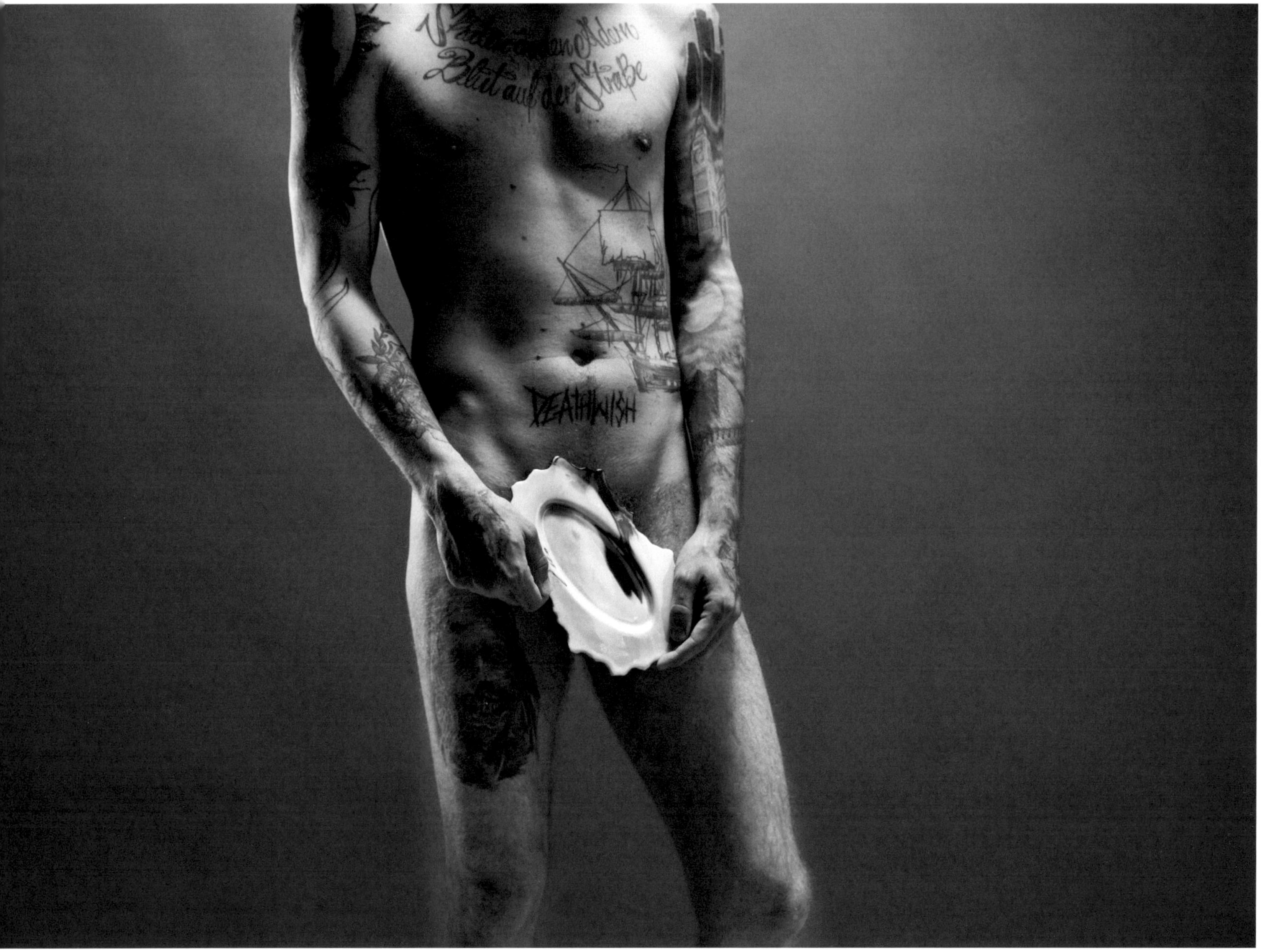

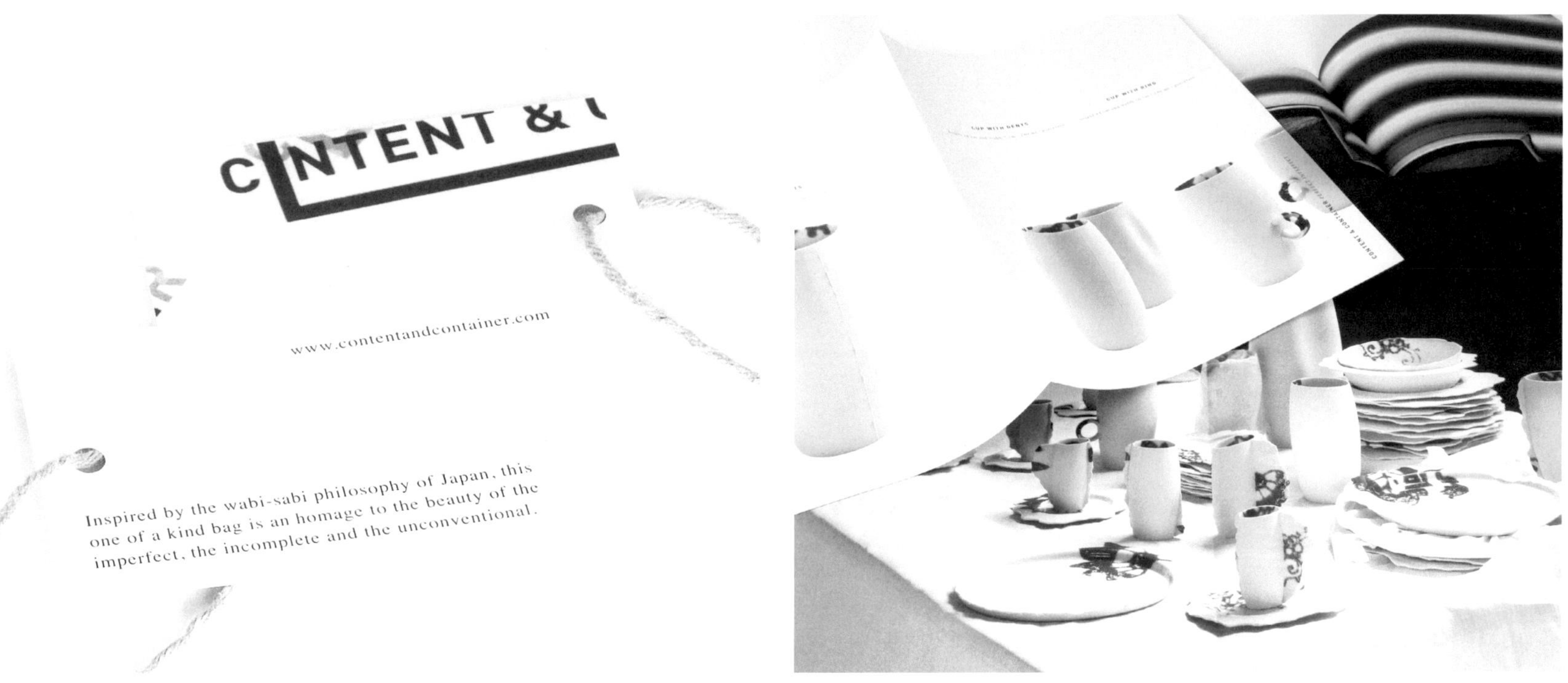
CONTENT & C
www.contentandcontainer.com
Inspired by the wabi-sabi philosophy of Japan, this one of a kind bag is an homage to the beauty of the imperfect, the incomplete and the unconventional.

Outpost

GENERAL STORE

Wayne, IL, USA, *by Knoed Creative*

WELCOME TO WAYNE, WHERE TWO SELF-MADE MERCHANTS STOPPED THE MARCH OF TIME, GIVING THE LOCAL GENERAL STORE A NEW LEASE ON LIFE.

Joe Vajarsky and his wife Caroline Scheeler from Wayne, Illinois have watched a small store on their sleepy town's main road go in and out of business for almost 20 years. Seemingly trapped in a time long gone, the shop sat vacant for several years before the couple struck a deal with the owner to buy the building and open Outpost, their modern take on an old-fashioned general store. Serving up fresh, local food, flowers, and spirits alongside selected vintage wares, they sought a visual concept to speak to Wayne's customers, who sometimes come shopping on horseback.

Knoed Creative's corporate identity honors the heritage of the town and concept of the store with a monogram inspired by vintage letterforms, a utilitarian logo stamp, manila paper, and hand-painted signage.

OUTPOST
GENERAL STORE
FRESH · LOCAL
FOOD TO GO
COFFEE · SNACKS
BEER · SPIRITS · WINE
VINTAGE AND ANTIQUE WARES
FLOWERS
DRY GOODS · SUNDRIES

OUTPOST
GENERAL STORE

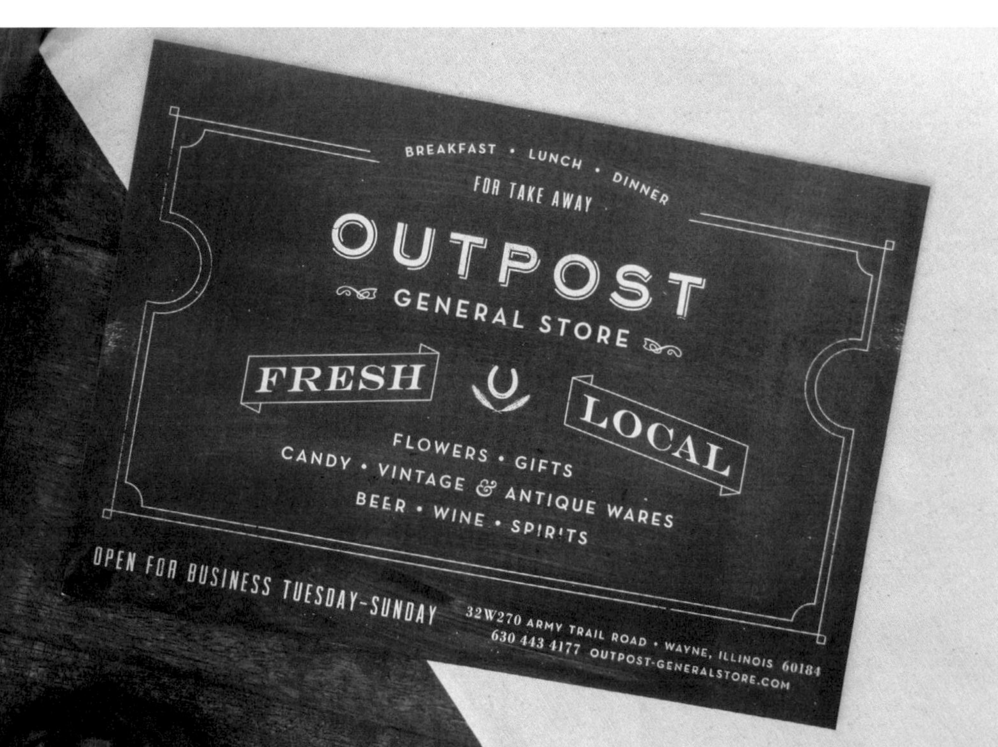
BREAKFAST · LUNCH · DINNER
FOR TAKE AWAY
OUTPOST
GENERAL STORE
FRESH
LOCAL
FLOWERS · GIFTS
CANDY · VINTAGE & ANTIQUE WARES
BEER · WINE · SPIRITS
OPEN FOR BUSINESS TUESDAY-SUNDAY
32W270 ARMY TRAIL ROAD · WAYNE, ILLINOIS 60184
630 443 4177 OUTPOST-GENERALSTORE.COM

OUTPOST
GENERAL STORE

OUTPOST
GENERAL
STORE

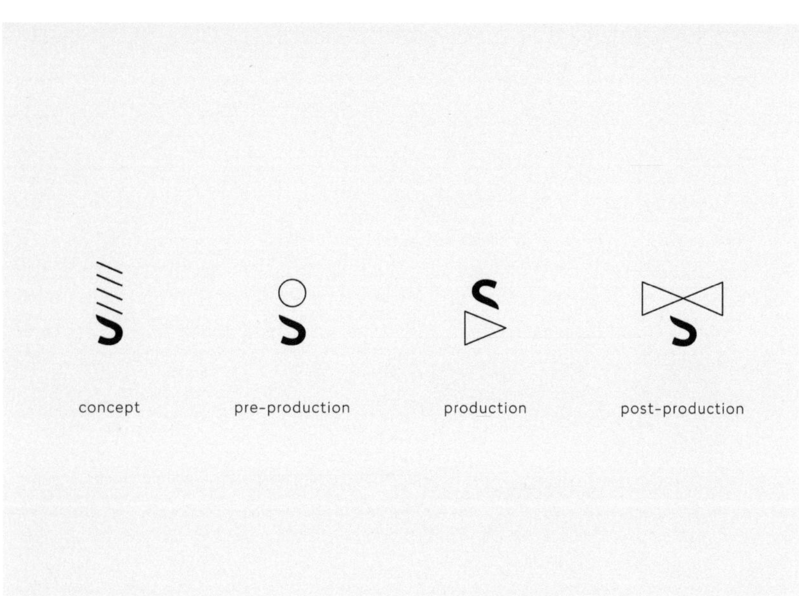

Supersaga

AUDIOVISUAL PRODUCTION

Ghent, Belgium, *by Elvire Delanote*

FLEMISH FILMMAKING MEETS SWEDISH MANAGEMENT SKILLS: LUCAS BOLS AND JULIE LINDH SAY THEY TURN ANY SAGA INTO A "SUPERSAGA." DESIGNER ELVIRE DELANOTE BESTOWED THEIR BRAND WITH A BEFITTING SUPER IMAGE.

Supersaga is the product of Belgian producer Lucas Bols and Swedish problem-solver Julie Lindh's shared passion for pictures and stories. The two came together to specialize in what they call supernatural storytelling: professional audiovisual production powered by emotion and endless energy. Certain to turn each and every saga into a "supersaga," they hired Elvire Delanote to contribute some super good graphics. The designer delivered a sliced 'S' symbol suggestive of Supersaga's strong sense for motion and mission to maintain a story's momentum. The company thrives on complementation, carefully coordinating and collaborating with its committed clients. The stationery has been letterpressed to leave a strong impression, and the compositions are centered around Supersaga's productions, which are always conceived to progress from the story's core.

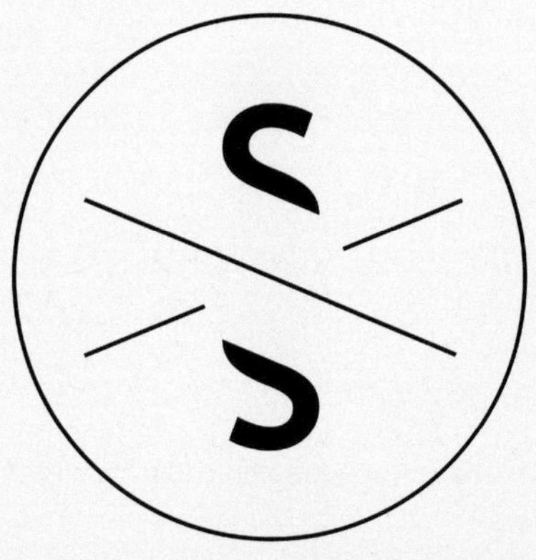

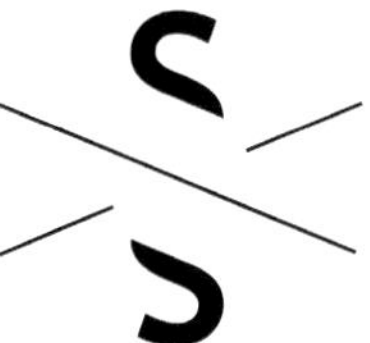

Supersaga is a creative audiovisual studio based in Ghent that tells the stories of exceptional people and products. With endless passion and drive, they bring high-end creative vision and production know-how to every video. Supersaga creates unique and refreshing stories that leave a strong and memorable impression, great videos that move and emove people. They turn every saga into a supersaga.

Põhjala

BREWERY

Tallinn, Estonia, *by Marke Saaremets*

"California inspired: sharks—San Diego—premier stainless—wheat as freshness—hops—fruitiness." That is how the team behind Chris Pilkington's prospering brewery Põhjala describe their take on an American Wheat Ale. All Põhja beers are made of 50 percent wheat malt bill of U.S. and Australian hops, both in the boil and in dry hopping, and feature extra oat flakes to achieve a silky smooth flavor. Their gateway beer, Uus Maailm (which translates to New World), has been speciall brewed to introduce newbies to the craft beer cosmos with a creamy but bracing mouthful. Thanks to a direct design approach by Marke Saaremets, the brewery's brand seems sober at first sight, but pops with adventurous packaging, such as a shark label representing the pugnacious temper of the brew's sharp hop bite.

CHEERS TO PÕHJALA! THE BRAVE BEER BUSINESS REFRESHES WITH AN ALL-ADVENTUROUS BREW AND A HOP-FORWARD BRAND IMAGE.

PÕHJALA

PÕHJALA
ESTONIAN CRAFT BEER
PEETER KEEK
MANAGING DIRECTOR
+372 5663 4633
PEETER@POHJALABEER.COM
NSTI OÜ — SERVA 28, TALLINN 11618, ESTONIA

24 X 0,33 L
PÕHJALA
ESTONIAN CRAFT BEER

PÕHJALA

PÕHJALA

PÕHJALA
EESTI KÄSITÖÖÕLU. ESTONIAN CRAFT BEER.
A GUIDE TO WHERE
the best chefs eat

GIMSEL

SUPERMARKET

Rotterdam, Netherlands, *by Studio Beige*

GIMSEL'S GOOD DEED, BESIDES BEING A REAL ORGANIC RETAIL BRAND: A DESIGN STRATEGY THAT DEFIES DULL SUPERMARKET STEREOTYPES.

Gimsel is a green supermarket. Founded in 2001, it had been retailing fair trade organic foods for more then 10 years when Studio Beige was called in for a comprehensive rebrand. The supermarket's management had asked for a more pronounced profile to meet growing competition. Seeking to speak to a wider audience without alienating the already large circle of loyal customers, Studio Beige built the new brand around Gimsel's greater-good values and vision. They condensed the company's core concept into a made-to-measure market manifesto, and crafted some sound slogans and symbols to complement the simple, well-balanced brandmark on the store's signage, stationery, and product packaging.

Wij geloven dat een gezonde levensstijl hand in hand gaat met een gezonde aarde.

Dat biologisch / dynamisch vanzelfsprekend is en we onderdeel zijn van de natuur.

Wij geloven in goede producten, goede ingrediënten en dat goed eten beter smaakt.

Dat schoonheid vooral van binnen zit.

Wij geloven in een persoonlijke aanpak.

Dat fair-trade net zo belangrijk is voor een boer in Azië als voor een boer in Zeeland.

We staan nooit stil.

Wij streven ernaar om onszelf telkens te vernieuwen.

Omdat gewoon niet goed genoeg is.

Omdat het natuurlijk altijd beter kan.

Gimsel.
Natuurlijk beter.

GIMSELROTTERDAM.NL

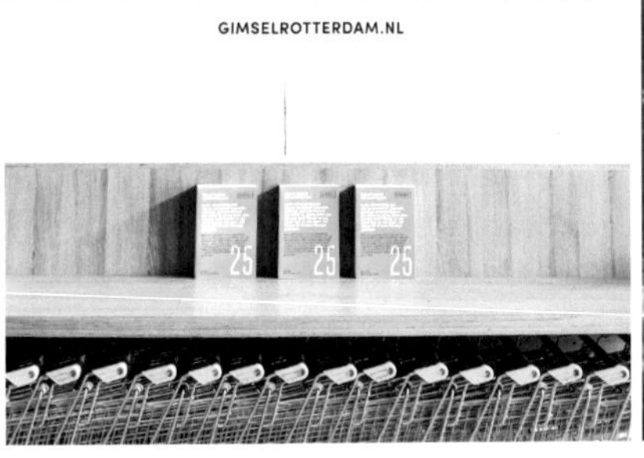

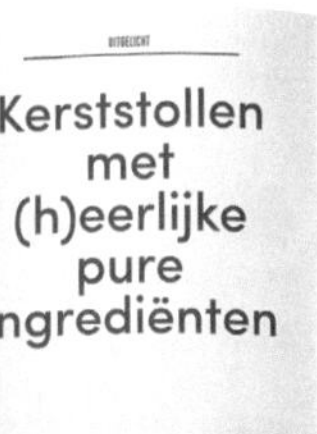

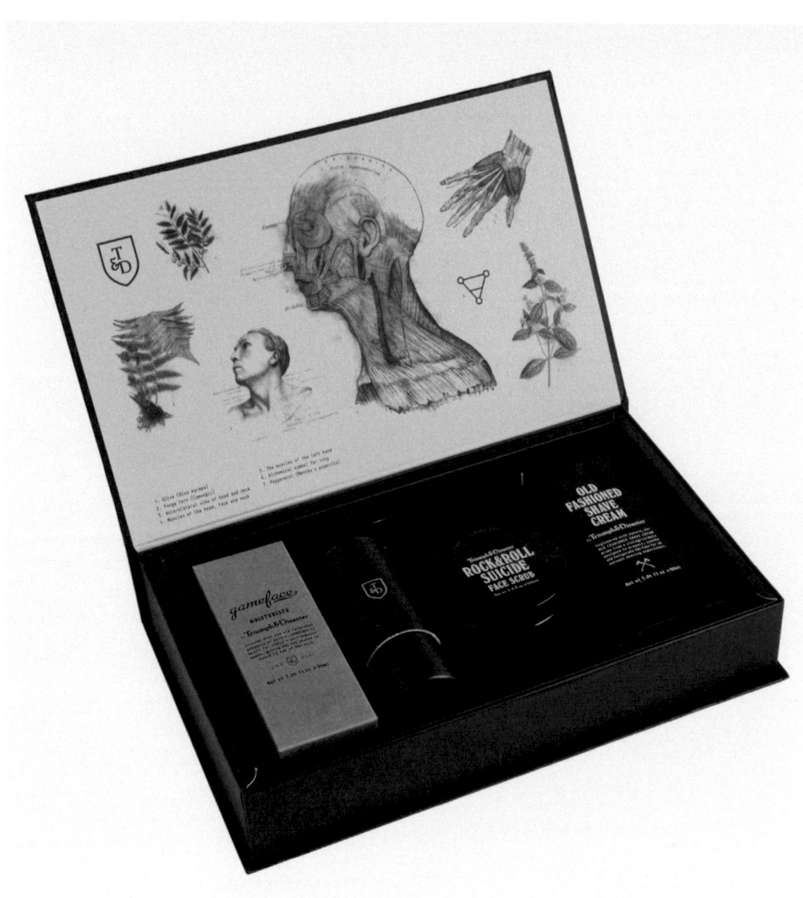

Triumph & Disaster

GROOMING GOODS

Auckland, New Zealand, *by DDMMYY*

RETIRED FROM HIS INTERNATIONAL CRICKET CAREER, DION NASH PROVIDES A PALETTE OF PHILOSOPHICALLY PROFOUND COSMETIC PRODUCTS THAT APPEALS TO POETS AND CRICKETERS ALIKE.

Dion Nash, founder of a neat gentlemen's grooming range, was once given a framed Rudyard Kipling poem by his father. It proposed "to meet with Triumph & Disaster and treat those two imposters just the same." Nash forgot it in a drawer for decades, only to make it the maxim of his entrepreneurial venture many years later: Triumph & Disaster, a collection of cosmetics that combine classic methods and traditional organic ingredients with contemporary innovations in science. DDMMYY designed its identity, drawing inspiration from Derrida's poetics of hauntology, and their premise that the present exists only with respect to the past. Balancing fashionable forms with nostalgic nuances, the brand nods to the now and the back-then, treating those two imposters just the same.

THE PHILOSOPHY

I

ASHES TO ASHES

What comes from the earth goes back to it – we will strive to make our products as natural as possible without compromising performance or safety.

II

GOOD SCIENCE

No parabens, no petrochemicals and no silicones.

III

SIMPLICITY

Simple, natural formulations engineered with honest intentions.

7

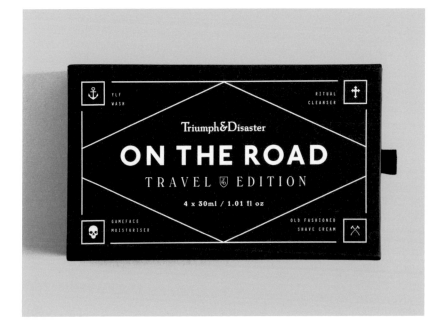

OUR PRODUCTS

I

PREPARE

Benjamin Franklin famously once quipped 'an ounce of prevention is better than a pound of cure' – and the key to prevention is preparation. It's about taking the time to set things up right and building a solid platform so we can perform later, putting a little method into our process.

II

PERFORM

No matter what your personal style, be it the hair on your head, the stubble on your chin or the look on your face – getting it right and pulling it off is an art form. So choose great tools.

III

PROTECT

Aging is constant and irreversible. The key is not to spend your life fighting it, but to simply ride it out in style. To do that, you'll need to use a little protection, to give yourself the best chance. Choose natural, choose good science and choose products that work with nature and not against it.

OLD FASHIONED SHAVE CREAM
by Triumph&Disaster
Net wt 3.04 fl oz e90ml
gameface
MOISTURISER
Triumph&Disaster
OLD FASHIONED
SHAVE CREAM
by Triumph&Disaster
Net wt 3.4 fl oz e100ml
Triumph&Disaster
ROCK&ROLL SUICIDE
FACE SCRUB
Net wt 3.4 fl oz e100ml
Triumph &Disaster
RITUAL
FACE CLEANSER
Net wt 5.07 fl oz e150ml
gameface
MOISTURISER
by Triumph&Disaster
Net wt 3.4 fl oz e100ml
Triumph &Disaster
SHEARER'S SOAP
130g

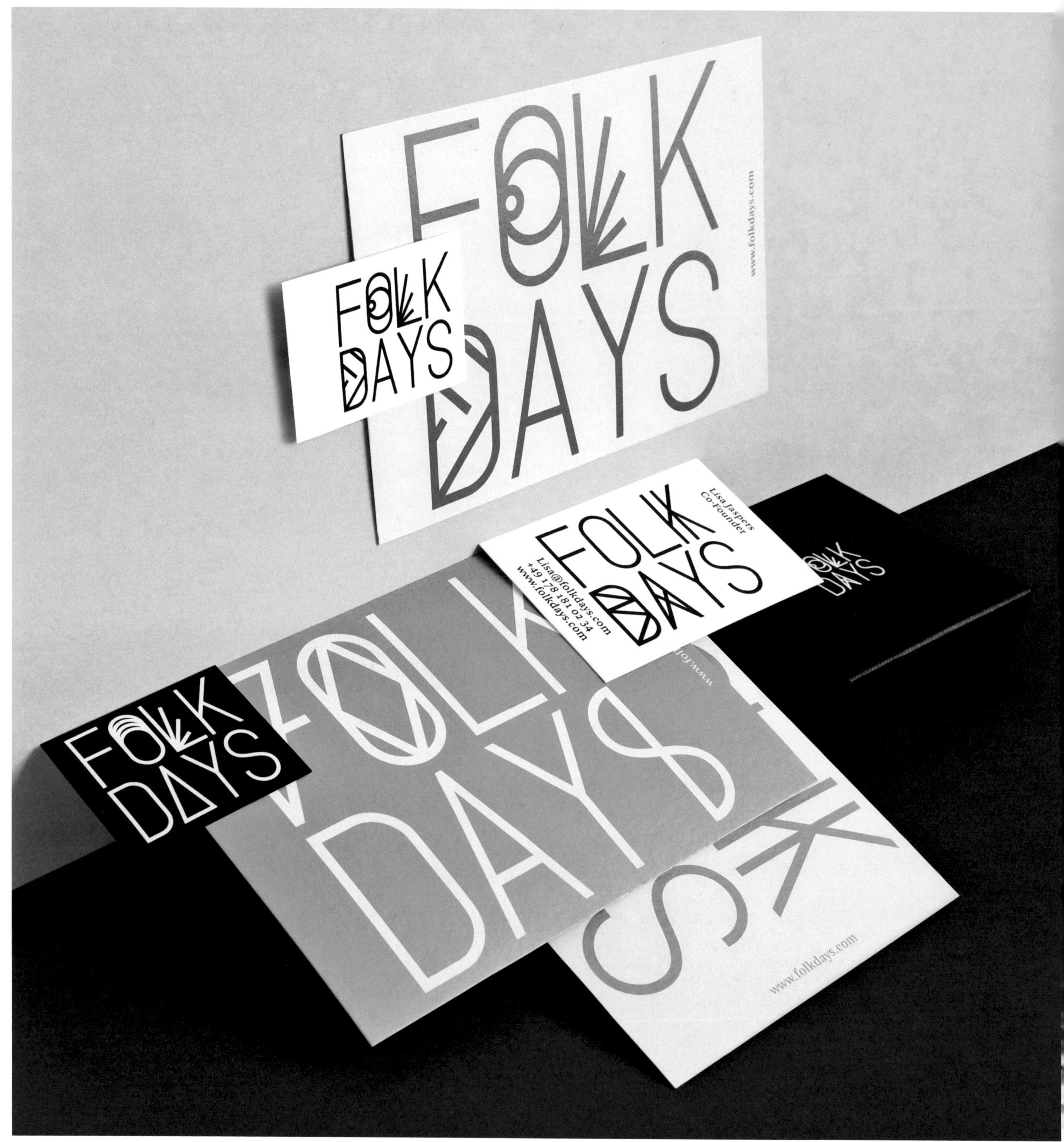

Folkdays was founded by two friends based in Berlin, Lisa Jaspers and Heidi Strom. The idea behind the business was inspired by their international travels: conceived as a platform for artisan producers across the globe, Folkdays provides a carefully curated selection of one-of-a-kind accessories and connects online customers with craftsmen in remote countries and rural regions. The company works with 14 different cooperatives from seven developing countries, and by paying fair prices directly to local artisans, it supports those struggling to lay the basis for sustained business success. Folkdays's own success is supported by some gregarious graphic groundwork brought in by Stahl R. The studio drew inspiration from popular folkloric patterns and developed a dynamic identity featuring a flexible custom font.

Folkdays

INTERNATIONAL ARTISAN PLATFORM

Berlin, Germany, *by Stahl R*

THE FOLKS AT FOLKDAYS FOSTER FAIR TRADE AND FOLKLORIC TRADITION UNDER THE BANNER OF AN ARTFULLY ALTERNATING BRANDMARK.

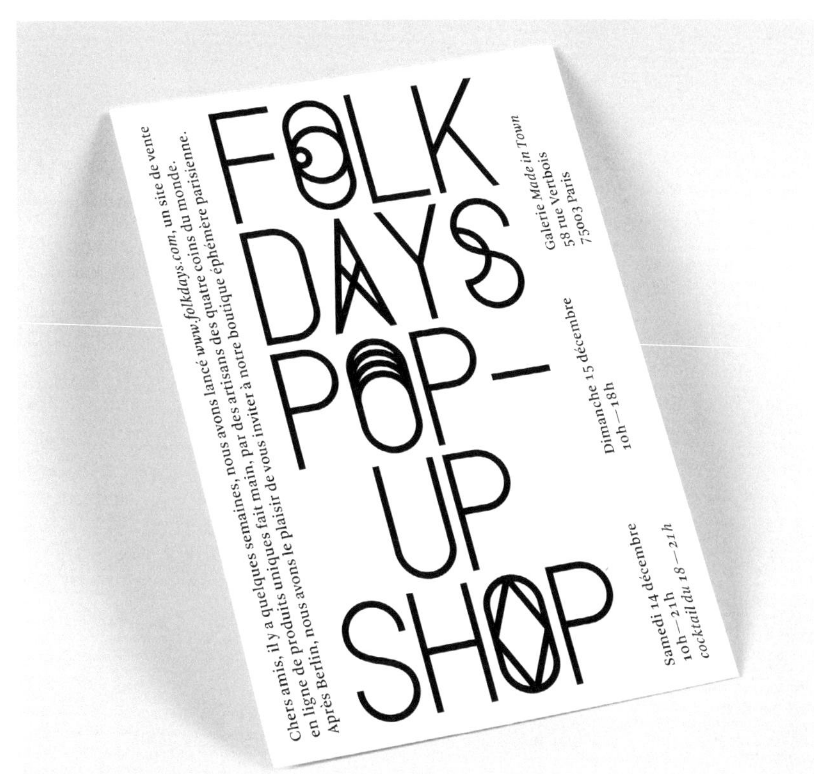

Contemporary artisan culture

Simple Karen Necklace
FOLKDAYS Nº 4

You have just purchased a beautiful hand made product that is of the highest quality and authenticity.

Since silver jewellery is such an important part of the Karen traditional costumes, the Karen silversmiths have developed and perfected their craftsmanship over hundreds of years. This beautiful necklace consists of small silver pearls, hand made by our silversmith Eaikachai. He learned his skills from the 72 years old Didi, who has been the master silversmith of the village for most of his life. The Karen silver jewelery that we sell in our shop has an unusually high silver percentage (approx. 99%), allowing for a softness that can be forged by hand.

Producer
Karen tribe, Thailand

Material
98% silver
The laotians use a high grade silver (96–98%) which is the traditional grade used for jewerly since centuries by the indigenous tribes.

Casper

MATTRESS MANUFACTURER

New York, NY, USA, *by Red Antler*

BETTER SLEEP BRINGS BRIGHTER BRANDS: CASPER SUPPLIES SNUG SLEEP SURFACES AND SHAKES UP SNOOZY STARTUPS WITH CHEEKY COMMUNICATIONS AND DOORSTEP DELIVERIES.

Casper manufactures foldable mattresses for the flexible metropolitan individual, conceived as affordable alternatives to the misery of mattress shopping. The company was founded by five young New Yorkers with the mission to make the most of the many years they each spend in bed, and brighten the days in between. Their brand is based on Red Antler design's direction, which sets the tone for Casper's clear and conversational communications, plain and simple packaging solutions, and the company's convenient e-commerce site.

GOOD NIGHT
Casper

ENHANCE YOUR NIGHT LIFE

CALLING ALL
dreamers
snoozers
early-risers
blanket thieves
pillow talkers
night owls
side-sleepers
breakfast-in-bedders
sleepyheads
screamers
do not disturb
Jump in bed. Stay all day, all night. Tuck in. Get cozy. Read a book. Doze off. Close your eyes. Spoon. Jump in bed. Stay all day, all night. Tuck in. Get cozy. Read a book. Doze off. Close your eyes. Spoon. Jump in bed. Stay all day, all night. Tuck in. Get cozy. Read a book. Doze off. Close your eyes. Spoon.
TIME FOR BED
Good night.

Casper
SETTING UP YOUR CASPER

Casper
NEIL J. PARIKH, CO-FOUNDER
NEIL@CASPERSLEEP.COM
TEL. 908 421 5987
45 BOND ST. 2ND FLOOR
NEW YORK, NY 10012
CASPERSLEEP.COM
GABRIEL FLATEMAN, CO-FOUNDER & CTO
GABE@CASPERSLEEP.COM
TEL. 917 723 7444
45 BOND ST. 2ND FLOOR
NEW YORK, NY 10012
CASPERSLEEP.COM
Casper

Frank Leder

GROOMING GOODS

Berlin, Germany, *by Frank Leder*

GROUNDED GERMAN GROOMING GOODS LABELED WITH BOLD BLACK LETTERS: TRANSITIONING FROM TRADITIONAL TAILORING TO ARTISAN COSMETICS, NUREMBERG-NATIVE FRANK LEDER BRINGS US A BRAND BRIMMING WITH THE HISTORY AND HERITAGE OF HIS HOMELAND.

Frank Leder's approach to fashion is firmly founded in the designer's background. A boy from Bavaria, Leder led a charmed childhood abound with outdoor adventures. Memories of mushroom hunting in the forest and fishing with his father characterize his clothing collections, which are worked with authentic German garments, and inspired by the classic workwear cuts of traditional tailoring. An extension to his much-acclaimed menswear line, Leder's botanical apothecary brand builds on the same heritage-steeped aesthetics. From Bavarian Sausage Hand Soap and Wheat Beer Hair Shampoo to Schnaps Body Tonic, all of the products are hand-produced in small batches according to century-old formulas of Leder's homeland. His cosmetics collection comes with bold black letter labels, hand-drawn illustrations, and custom-made bottles topped with bakelite screw caps and select linen strings.

WEIZEN
BIER
SHAMPOO
250ML
Weizen
Bier

Unter
Prima

frank leder
Hinterland

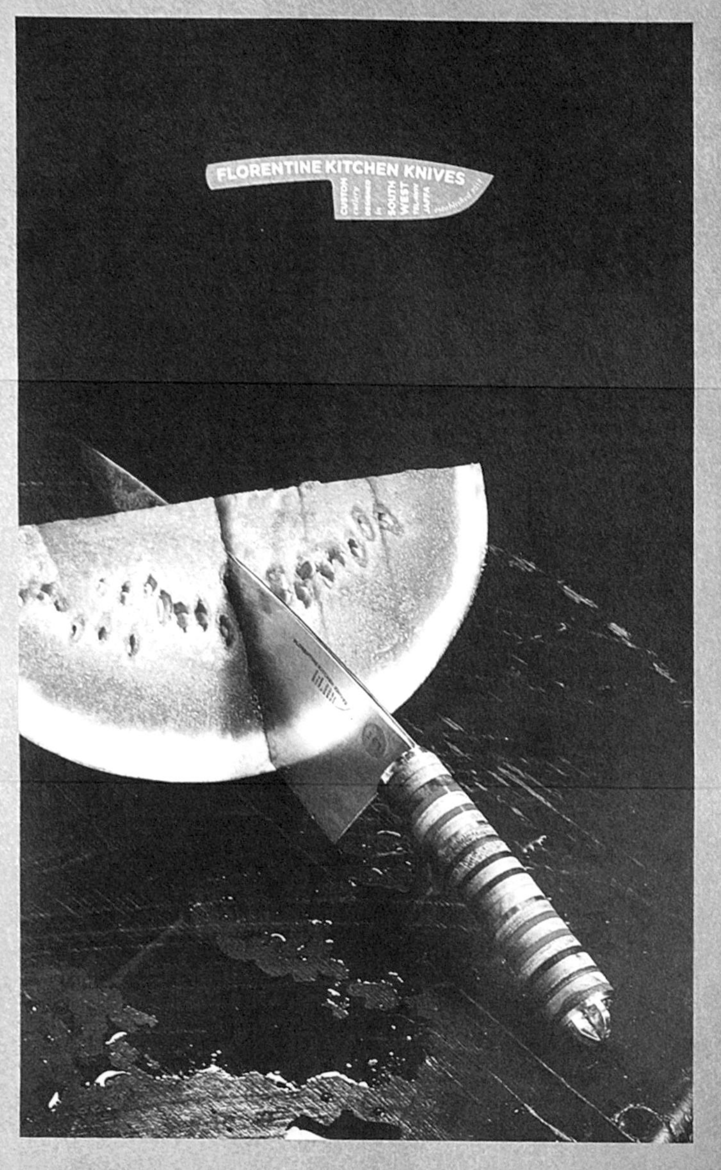
FLORENTINE KITCHEN KNIVES

FLORENTINE KITCHEN KNIVES

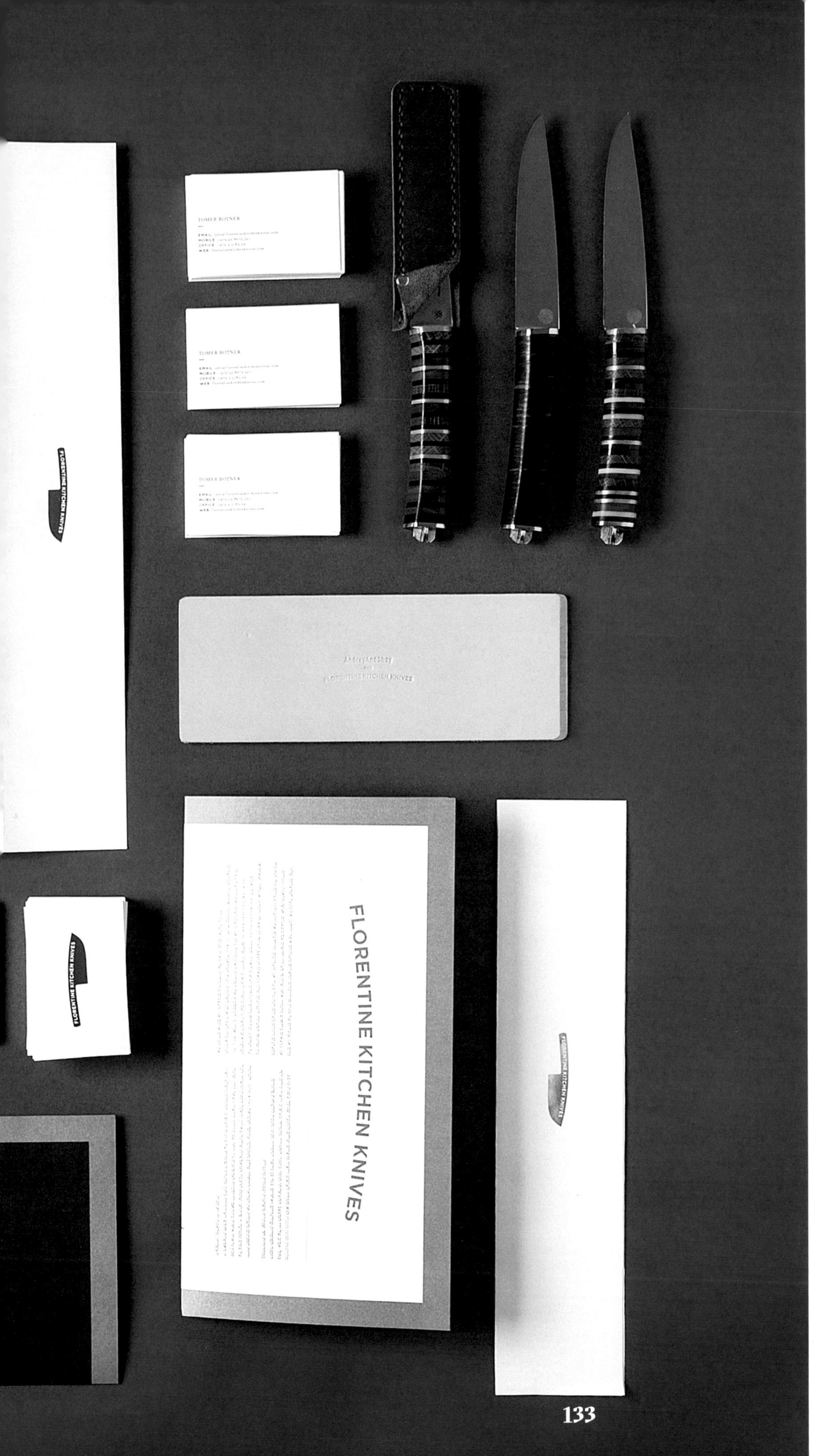

Florentine Kitchen Knives

CUTLERY

Tel Aviv and Jaffa, Israel

by Tomer Botner and Ran Shauli

FLORENTINE KITCHEN KNIVES SHARPEN COMPETITION AMONG ARTISAN KITCHENWARE COMPANIES WITH CUTTING-EDGE CRAFTSMANSHIP AND A CLEAR-CUT CORPORATE IMAGE.

Florentine Kitchen Knives is a craft-inspired cutlery company conceived by Israeli industrial designer Tomer Botner that started as a final university project, fortunately making it to the market. The newly-fledged firm was named after the Florentine neighborhood in Tel Aviv where its workshop is located, and branded by befriended designer Ran Shauli. Shauli and Botner collaborated closely and, inspired by the surrounding scene of South Tel Aviv's local craftsmanship, they arrived at an authentic corporate image based on Botner's artisan approach. The final identity spans across Florentine Kitchen Knives' packaging, stationery, staff clothing, website, and blog, as well as a funding campaign thanks to which the budget that brought the brand to the market was raised.

FLORENTINE KITCHEN KNIVES

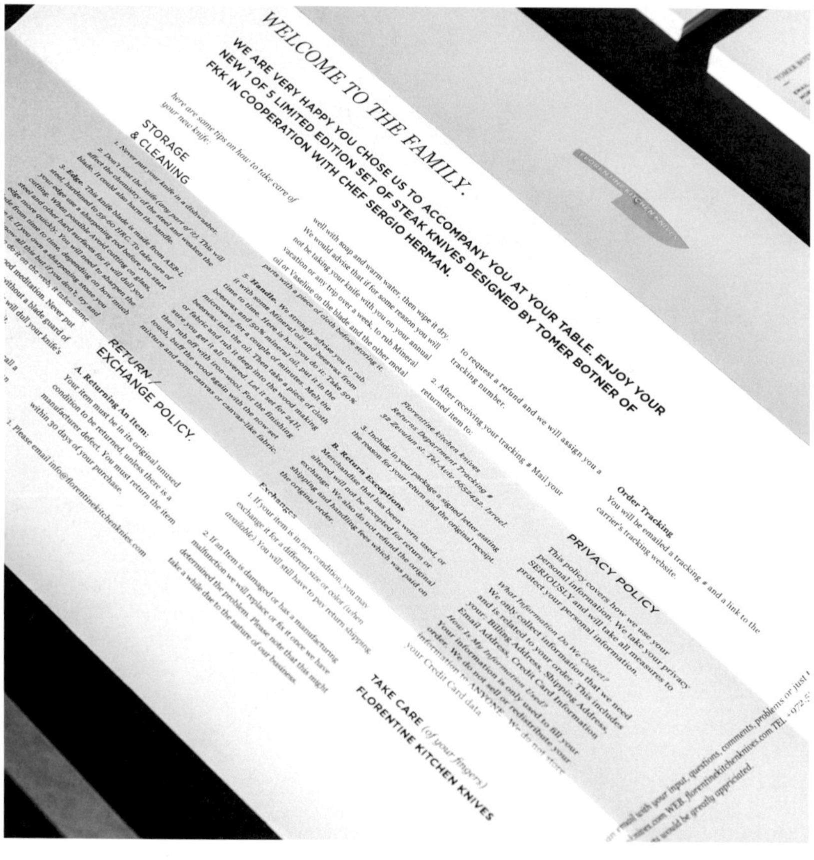

WELCOME TO THE FAMILY.

WE ARE VERY HAPPY YOU CHOSE US TO ACCOMPANY YOU AT YOUR TABLE. ENJOY YOUR NEW 1 OF 5 LIMITED EDITION SET OF STEAK KNIVES DESIGNED BY TOMER BOTNER OF FKK IN COOPERATION WITH CHEF SERGIO HERMAN.

STORAGE & CLEANING

RETURN / EXCHANGE POLICY.

PRIVACY POLICY

TAKE CARE (of your fingers)

FLORENTINE KITCHEN KNIVES

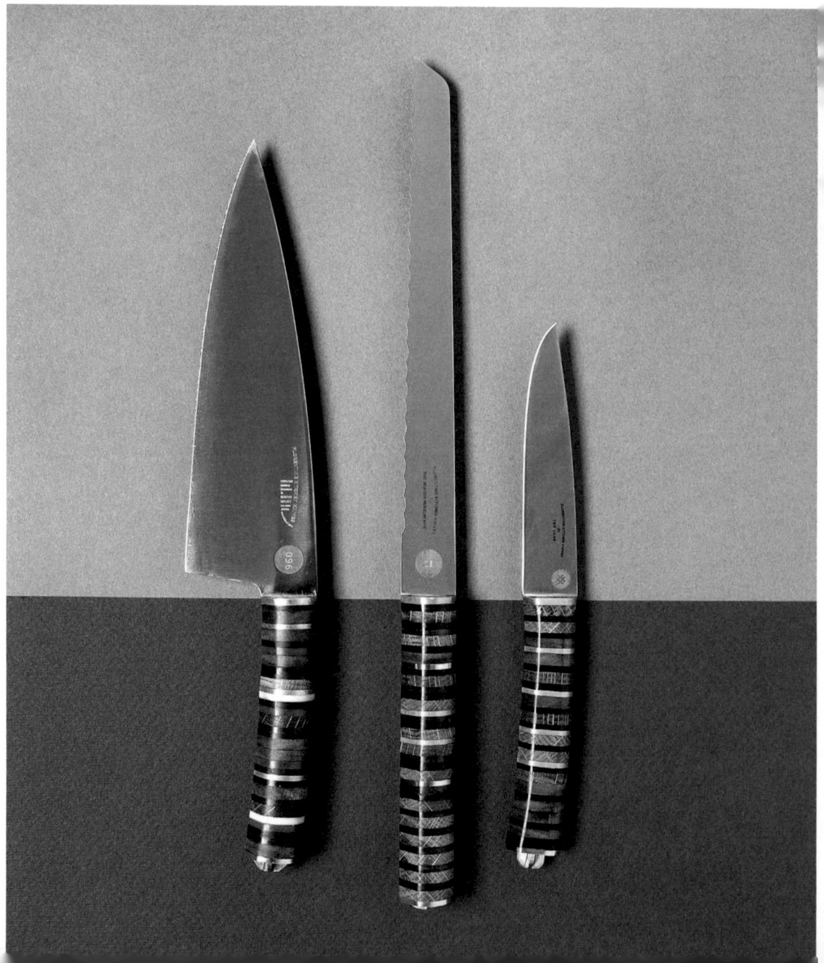

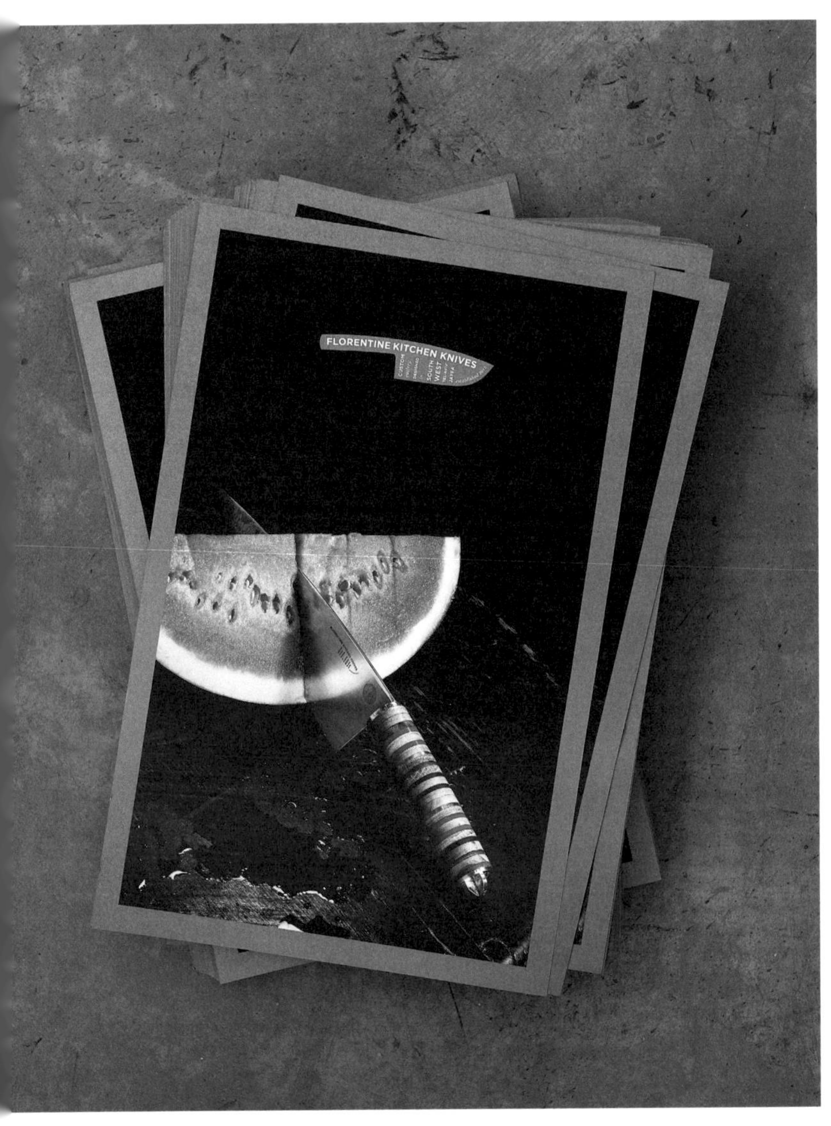
FLORENTINE KITCHEN KNIVES

FLORENTINE KITCHEN KNIVES

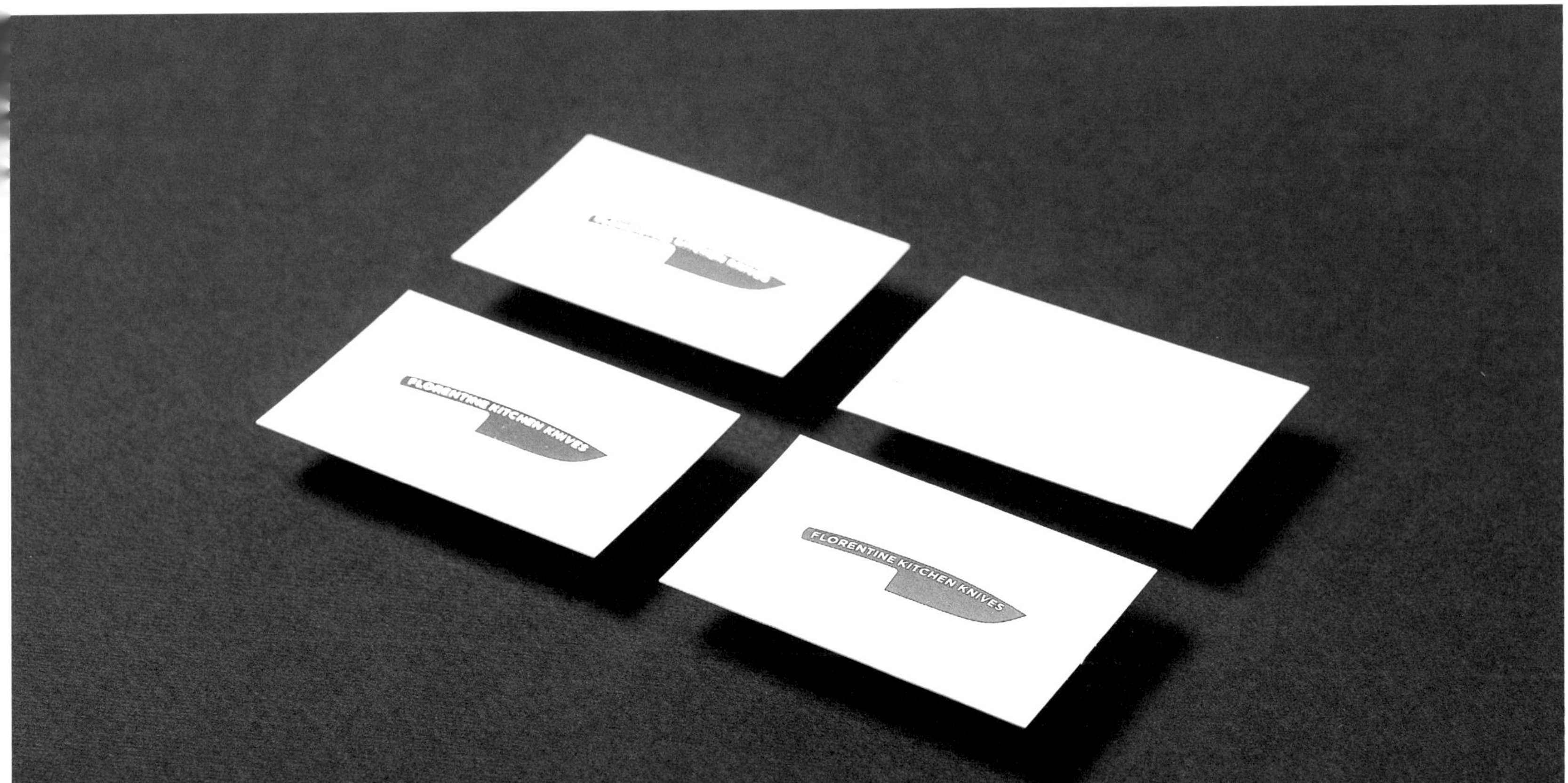

Labour and Wait

HOUSEHOLD GOODS

London, UK, *by Labour and Wait and Richard Sanderson*

LONG LIVE LONGEVITY! FROM CLOTHES AND TOOLS TO DOMESTIC DECORATIONS, LABOUR AND WAIT SELLS THINGS THAT DO NOT AGE WITH THE PASSING OF TIME. THE SHOP'S BRANDING BRINGS BACK A BIT OF GOOD OLD TIMELESSNESS, TOO.

Motivated by childhood memories of the classy household products their parents had and held onto, Rachel Wythe-Moran and Simon Watkins set up their store, Labour and Wait, in London's East End in 2000. The two had discovered their common passion for classic objects while working together as menswear designers, and decided to search the world for simple, well-made designs. Their curatorial approach to retail was received with great acclaim, and as a pleasantly relaxed platform for everyday products, the little shop soon gained popularity. Featuring familiar vintage items, the collection offers customers a chance to relive their own childhood, introducing carefully selected contemporary objects reminding us that simple good things still exist.

Like Labour and Wait's line of products, the company's corporate communications combine functionality with a timeless aesthetic. A collaboration between Wythe-Moran, Watkins, and London-based graphic artist and illustrator Richard Sanderson, the Labour and Wait brand includes a small range of goodies and gadgets that reflect the founders' firm belief in pure practicality.

LABOUR AND WAIT
GIFT CARD
TO
MESSAGE
FROM
85 REDCHURCH STREET · LONDON · E2 7DJ
WWW.LABOURANDWAIT.CO.UK

L
A
W
POST CARD
Hand printed in England

LABOUR AND WAIT
18 CHESHIRE STREET · LONDON · E2 6EH
ASPARAGUS PEA

LABOUR AND WAIT
18 CHESHIRE STREET · LONDON · E2 6EH
BORECOLE
JERSEY TREE, OR WALKING-STICK CABBAGE

LABOUR AND WAIT
18 CHESHIRE STREET · LONDON · E2 6EH
TOMATO
YELLOW PEAR

LABOUR AND WAIT
18 CHESHIRE STREET · LONDON · E2 6EH
CARROT
WHITE BELGIUM OR BLANCHE

CULINARY QUIRKS
7 Packets of seeds
ASPARAGUS PEA
JERSEY TREE CABBAGE
YELLOW PEAR TOMATO
LAZY HOUSEWIFE BEAN
WHITE BELGIAN CARROT
CRYSTAL APPLE CUCUMBER
DRUNKEN WOMAN LETTUCE
LABOUR AND WAIT . 18 CHESHIRE ST. LONDON. E2

LABOUR AND WAIT
18 CHESHIRE STREET · LONDON · E2 6EH
CUCUMBER
CRYSTAL LEMON

LABOUR AND WAIT
18 CHESHIRE STREET · LONDON · E2 6EH
LETTUCE
DRUNKEN WOMAN
Ubriacona Frastagliata

British American Household Staffing

PERSONNEL PLACEMENT

New York, NY, *by Knoed Creative*

British American Household Staffing is a boutique agency based in New York's SoHo neighborhood that has made it its business to match highly qualified household staff—including nannies, butlers, and private chefs—with households of all sizes. Called in to come up with a brand befitting the company's high-class customers, Knoed Creative combined the sophisticated style of classic British upper-class culture with a taste of today's American high society.

BRITISH
HOUSEHO

77 Mercer Street #2N New York, New York 10012

HIGH-END GRAPHICS FOR NEW YORK'S UPPER STRATA: BOUTIQUE AGENCY BRITISH AMERICAN HOUSEHOLD STAFFING PRESENTS ITSELF PRESTIGIOUSLY WITH A BRANDING BY KNOED.

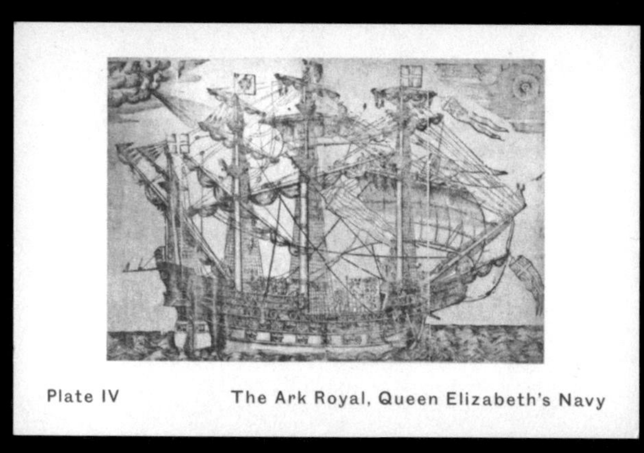

Plate IV
The Ark Royal, Queen Elizabeth's Navy

Foundwell

ANTIQUES & ARTISAN ACCESSORIES

New York, NY, USA, *by OK-RM*

FOUNDWELL HAS MADE IT THEIR MISSION TO PURVEY THE FINEST VINTAGE AND ANTIQUE PIECES THAT THE LAST SEVERAL CENTURIES HAVE PRODUCED. IN CLOSE COLLABORATION WITH THE COMPANY'S FOUNDER, OK-RM ESTABLISHED AN EPOCHAL CORPORATE IMAGE FOR CENTURIES TO COME.

Founded in 2007 by a second-generation antiques dealer, connoisseur, and creator of fine goods and gadgets, Foundwell does not merely purvey but also produces artisan objects and antiques of various origins. The company both creates and vends vintage classics and curiosities to complement contemporary lifestyles. The collections are curated with an unparalleled understanding of their clients' specific taste preferences—products range from furniture to fine jars and jewelry. Following an extensive rebrand by OK-RM in 2012, Foundwell's brand finally emerged in line with the quality and traditional craftsmanship integral to the company's philosophy: carefully sourced materials, traditional processes, and a diverse palette of imagery. Graphic and typographic components are central to the resulting corporate image.

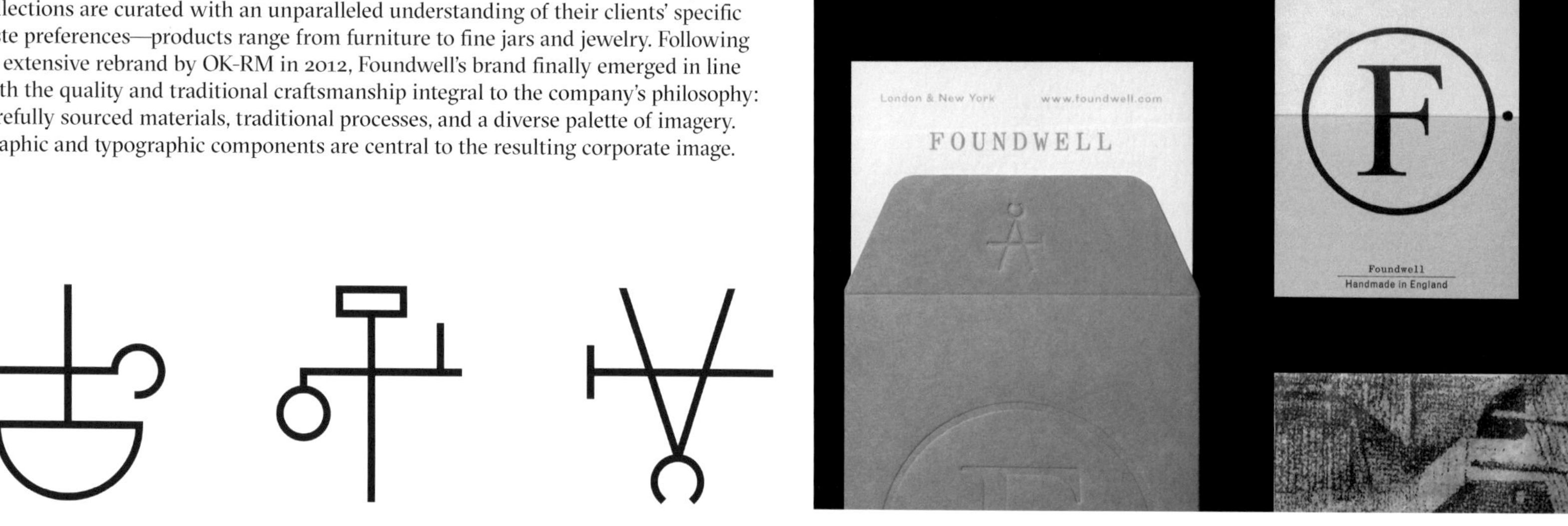

FW / W

21.05.2012
Date Sold

$1950.00
Price

FWMC119
Style

Rolex GMT Master

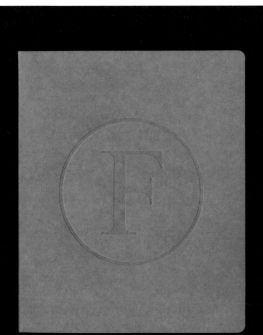

A wonderful 18ct gold and steel Rolex GMT Master 16753 model in excellent condition, representing a great piece of Rolex watch making history. This watch has the beautiful brown dial, with the so called 'nipple' hour markers, which differs from the classic 'Pepsi' style coloured bezel of the first GMT, and the flat luminous marked hours. This watch and its solid 18ct counter part, represented the first move away from the classic GMT Master colours and steel case of the watch originally launched. As the watch model evolved, many different versions have been seen. None of which live up to this classic iteration in its instantly recognizable style. Knick named the 'Root Beer' colour-way this watch was launched by Rolex in 1971 and became a classic instantly.

This model of the watch was made in 1981, and differs from the original 1675 model of the Root Beer launched in 1971. It features the cal. 3075 movement, has a different dial layout, the date aperture is at 3 o'clock, and the bi-

Sean Connery wearing a Rolex GMT Master in James Bond

Clint Eastwood wearing a Rolex GMT Master in 'Name of Film'

Sean Connery wearing a Rolex GMT Master in James Bond

colored bezel is bi-directional now. This model also now boast a "quick set" date, meaning that if the watch is not worn for a few days, and stops, the wearer does not have to pass 24 hours through the mechanism to change the date. One click will do it! This model is referred as transitional as it took on the new features slowly being incorporated into the watch, while visually, it still has the appearance of the original 1971 issue this models, that are quite scarce, very desirable.

The origins of this watch derive from the introduction of the 707 transatlantic commercial aircraft that allowed the journey from the London to New York to be cut from approximately 13 hours, to 7.

This reduction of journey time culminated in a side effect coined as 'Jet Lag', and was something that the airline company Pan Am needed to address with it's pilots in order for them to move quickly through various time zones, and enable them to function safely.

Rolex GMT Master
Item

16753 Year	12345 Movement N
16750 Model N	3075 Movement Type
7230911 Interior Case N	FWW29 Movement Caliber
xxxx Case N	xxxx Style

Producer of crafted goods & Purveyor of fine antique watches, jewellery & other such objects

FOUNDWELL

London & New York www.foundwell.com

FWMC119 Style	$1950.00 Price

Rolex GMT Master
Item

FWMC119 Style	Name of Maker Maker
Art Deco Period	1933 Date

21.01.2012
Date Sold

FW / O

A wonderful 18ct gold and steel Rolex GMT Master 16753 model in excellent condition, representing a great piece of Rolex watch making history. This watch has the beautiful brown dial, with the so called 'nipple' hour markers, which differs from the classic 'Pepsi' style coloured bezel of the first GMT, and the flat luminous marked hours. This watch and its solid 18ct counter part, repre-sented the first move away from the classic GMT Master colours and steel case of the watch originally launched. As the watch model evolved, many different versions have been seen. None of which live up to this classic iteration in its instantly recognizable style. Knick named the 'Root Beer' colour-way this watch was launched by Rolex in 1971 and became a classic instantly. Knick named the 'Root Beer' colour-way this watch was launched by Rolex in 1971 and became a classic instantly.

London & New York www.foundwell.com

FOUNDWELL

Producer of crafted goods & Purveyor of fine antique watches, jewellery & other such objects

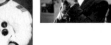

the
BLACK ISLE BAKERY
of London

N° 2 — *Muir of Ord*
† A small round of dough
† Smoked salmon, Queen Maud fillet
† Crème fraîche, French
† A feather of dill
† Seeds, a choice of one or two

(mail) info@blackislebakery.co.uk
(web) blackislebakery.co.uk

(Design & art direction) OK-RM
(Photography) Lena Emery

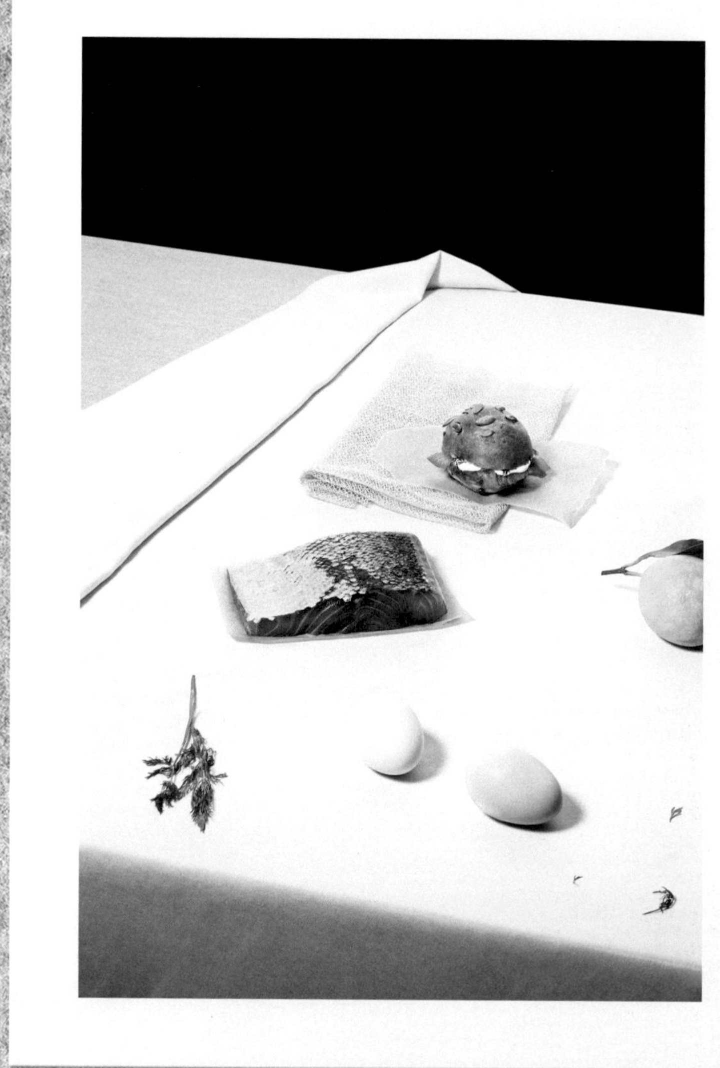

Black Isle Bakery

BAKERY

London, UK, *by OK-RM*

RUTH BARRY WORKED IN THE ART WORLD BEFORE SHE LAUNCHED BLACK ISLE, A BAKERY BRAND BLURRING DISCIPLINARY BORDERS WITH A SET OF SAVORY STILL LIVES AND PASTRY PORTRAITS.

the
BLACK ISLE BAKERY
of London

Note:
Through the Fairy Glen, pass two waterfalls to find the spring. Under a canopy of oak trees, leave an offering of flowers by the pool.

the
BLACK ISLE BAKERY
of London

Note:
From Chanonry Point, study the final view of the Brahan Seer through an Adder stone. Wait for the dolphins to jump.

the
BLACK ISLE BAKERY
of London

Note:
A cure for ailments; turn three times sunwise by the spring of the Clootie Well and splash water to the ground. Tie a cloot to a tree.

the
BLACK ISLE BAKERY
of London

Note:
From the fields of Mount Eagle search the skies for the Red Kite.

Black Isle Bakery's contemporary recipes are composed with care and with sensibly sourced ingredients. Acknowledging founder Ruth Barry's background in contemporary art and her growing client list from creative industries (Acne Studios, Marlborough Contemporary, and The Gentlewoman are said to shop the bakery's savory and sweet selection to refresh their staff's creative minds), OK-RM arrived at a brand that embeds the craft of baking within a contemporary cultural context. The art directors collaborated with photographer Lena C. Emery, whose pictures make up a major part of the brand. Applied across all media, they get the mood right for Black Isle's aesthetic approach to modern(ist) baking.

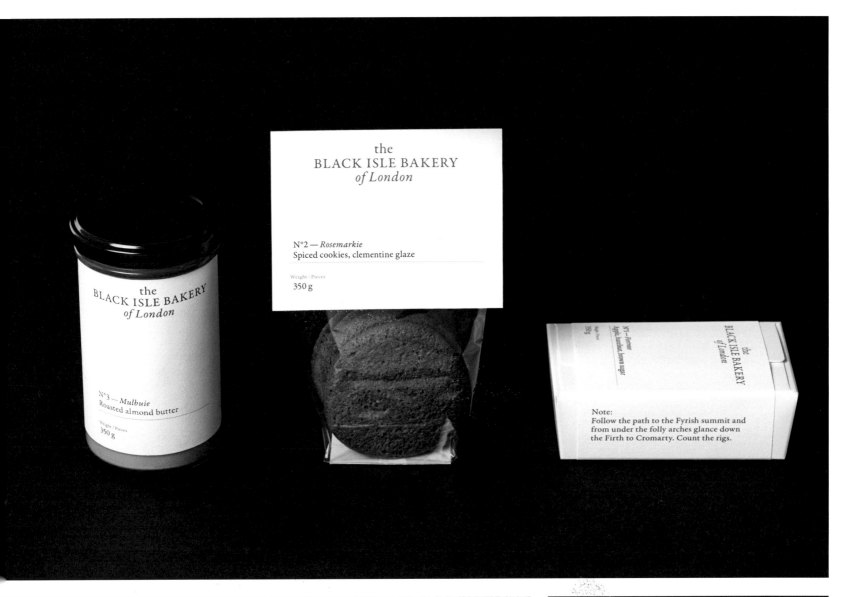

the
BLACK ISLE BAKERY
of London

N°3 — *Mulbuie*
Roasted almond butter
350 g

the
BLACK ISLE BAKERY
of London

N°2 — *Rosemarkie*
Spiced cookies, clementine glaze
Weight / Pieces
350 g

the
BLACK ISLE BAKERY
of London

Note:
Follow the path to the Fyrish summit and from under the folly arches glance down the Firth to Cromarty. Count the rigs.

THE

GENERAL STORE

Tokyo, Japan, *by Good Design Company*

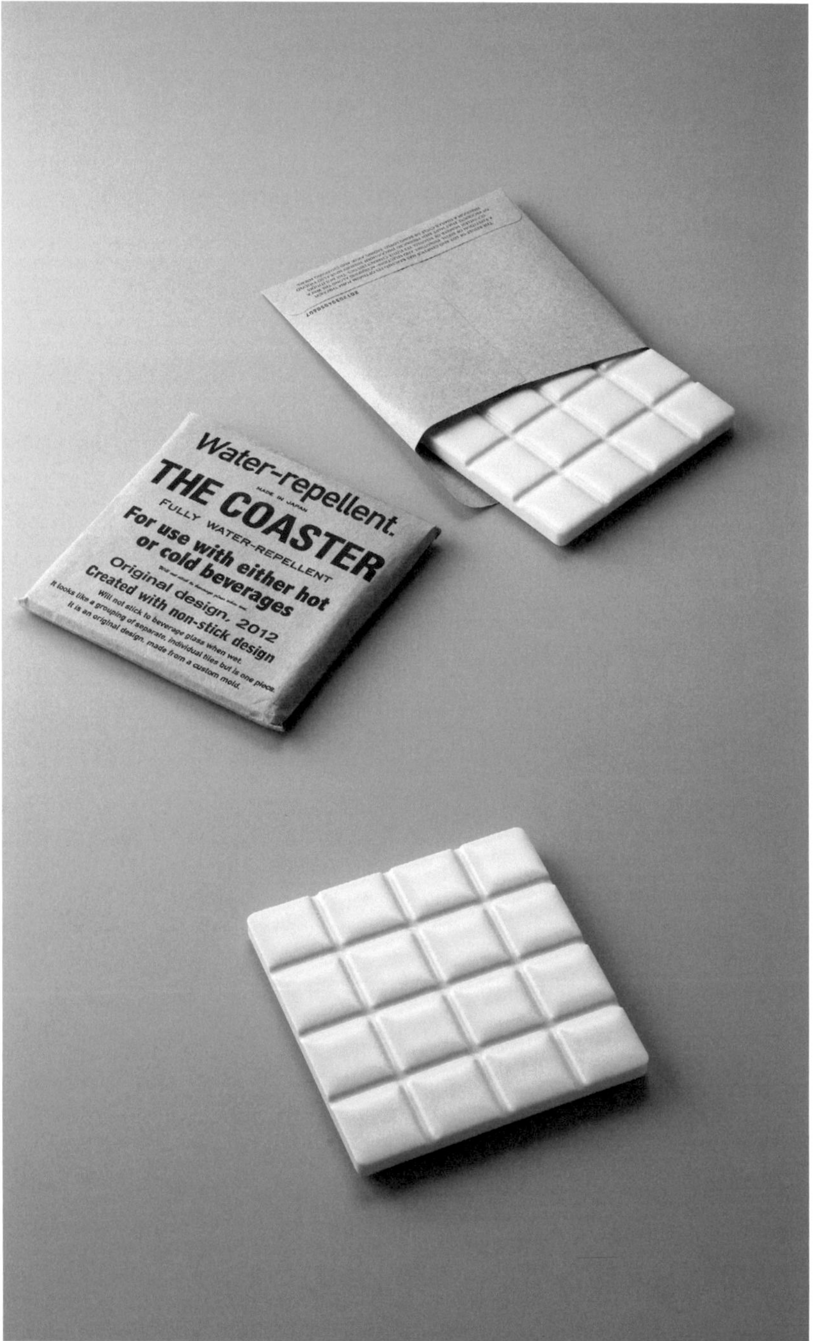

THE Co. Ltd. seeks to set new world standards in household products. With a nod toward classic cult items like the Levi's 501, THE jeans of all jeans, they have set up THE shop to sell simple everyday objects with simple names—THE Waterglas THE Soap, THE Laundry Detergent, THE Cooking Paper. Good Design Company contributed THE graphics to comply with the concept: simple sub-brands and no-fril product packaging in the form of pure function.

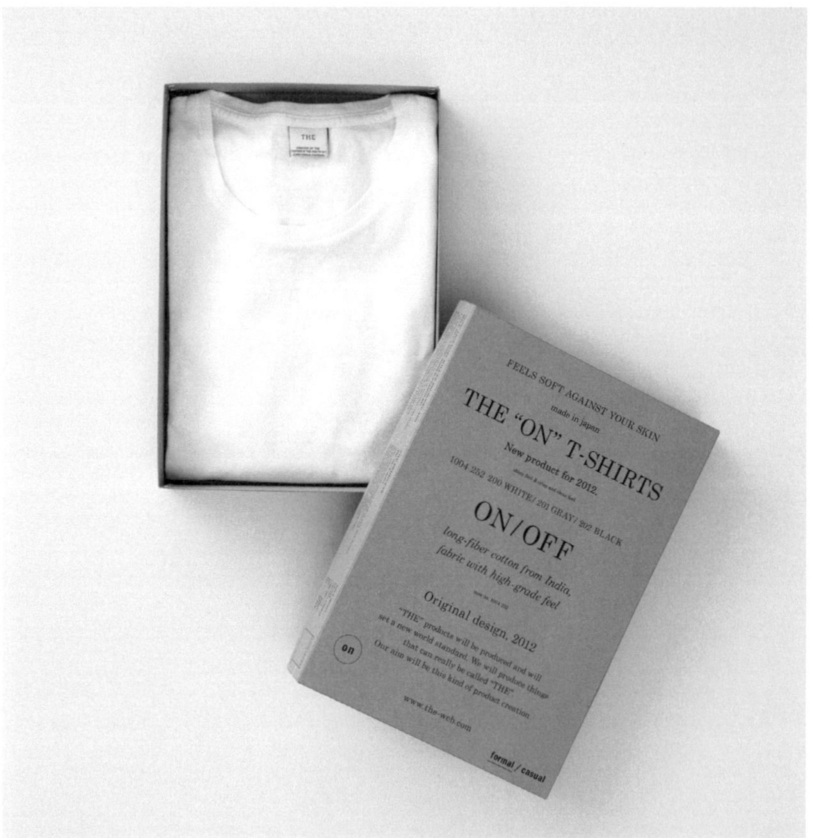

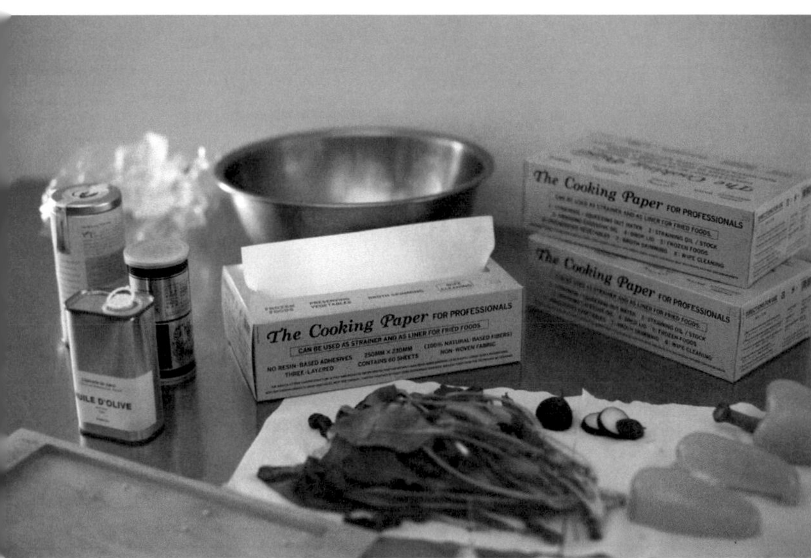

THE CO. LTD. COUNTERS TINHORN TERMINOLOGIES AND TECHNICAL TRAPPINGS WITH A STRIPPED-BACK SELECTION OF BASICALLY BRANDED COMMODITY ITEMS. SOMETIMES, THINGS ARE JUST AS SIMPLE AS THAT.

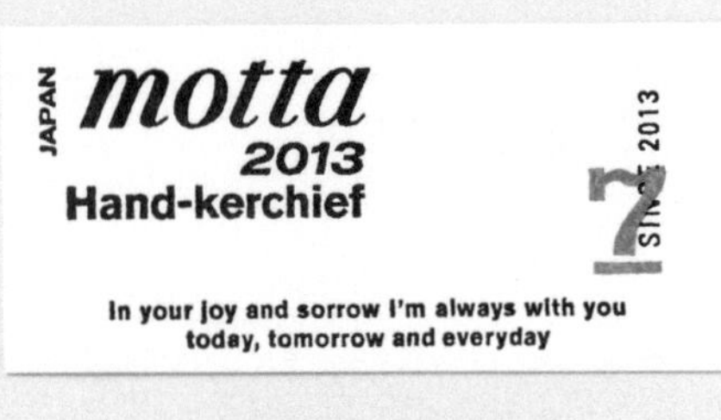

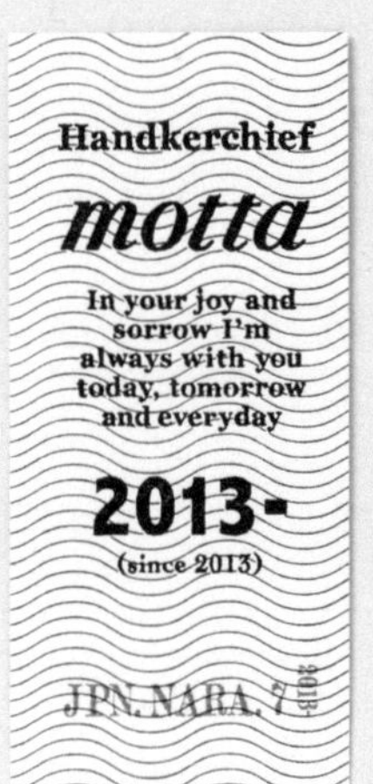

motta

COTTON HANDKERCHIEFS

Nara, Japan, *by Good Design Company*

NAKAGAWA MASASHICHI SHOTEN HAS MADE IT ITS MISSION TO REVIVE TRADITIONAL JAPANESE "MONOZUKURI" (MANUFACTURING). ITS SUB-BRAND MOTTA'S CONTRIBUTION IS A COLLECTION OF HIGH-END HANDKERCHIEFS THAT COMBINES CENTURY-OLD CRAFTSMANSHIP WITH CONVENIENCE AND CONTEMPORARY STYLE.

The traditional Nara-based manufactory Nakagawa Masashichi Shoten has been producing woven linen fabrics since 1716. In 1925, it first presented a line of linen handkerchiefs at the Paris Expo, but its handkerchief brand motta wasn't born before 2013—a time when the once so popular product had long fallen out of fashion. When the first elaborately decorated examples were imported to Japan back in the Meiji period, the Japanese had begun to cultivate a close connection to their handkerchiefs, carrying the flexible square fabric not so much to blow their noses, but to wrap their bento-boxes, dry their hands, or dry up sweat, tears, rain, and spilled tea. Only recently have people come to prefer tissues and towels, mostly because the once cherished task of ironing is considered bothersome today. With its name referring to a popular expression of motherly care ("handkerchief motta?" is what Japanese moms say as they kiss their kids goodbye: "You keep a handkerchief, don't you?"), motta thwarts that trend and revives the rich culture of the Japanese handkerchief with a contemporary linen and cotton collection that incorporates creases as an element of style. Good Design Company gave the brand its corporate image and wrapped its precious products in delicately designed gift boxes.

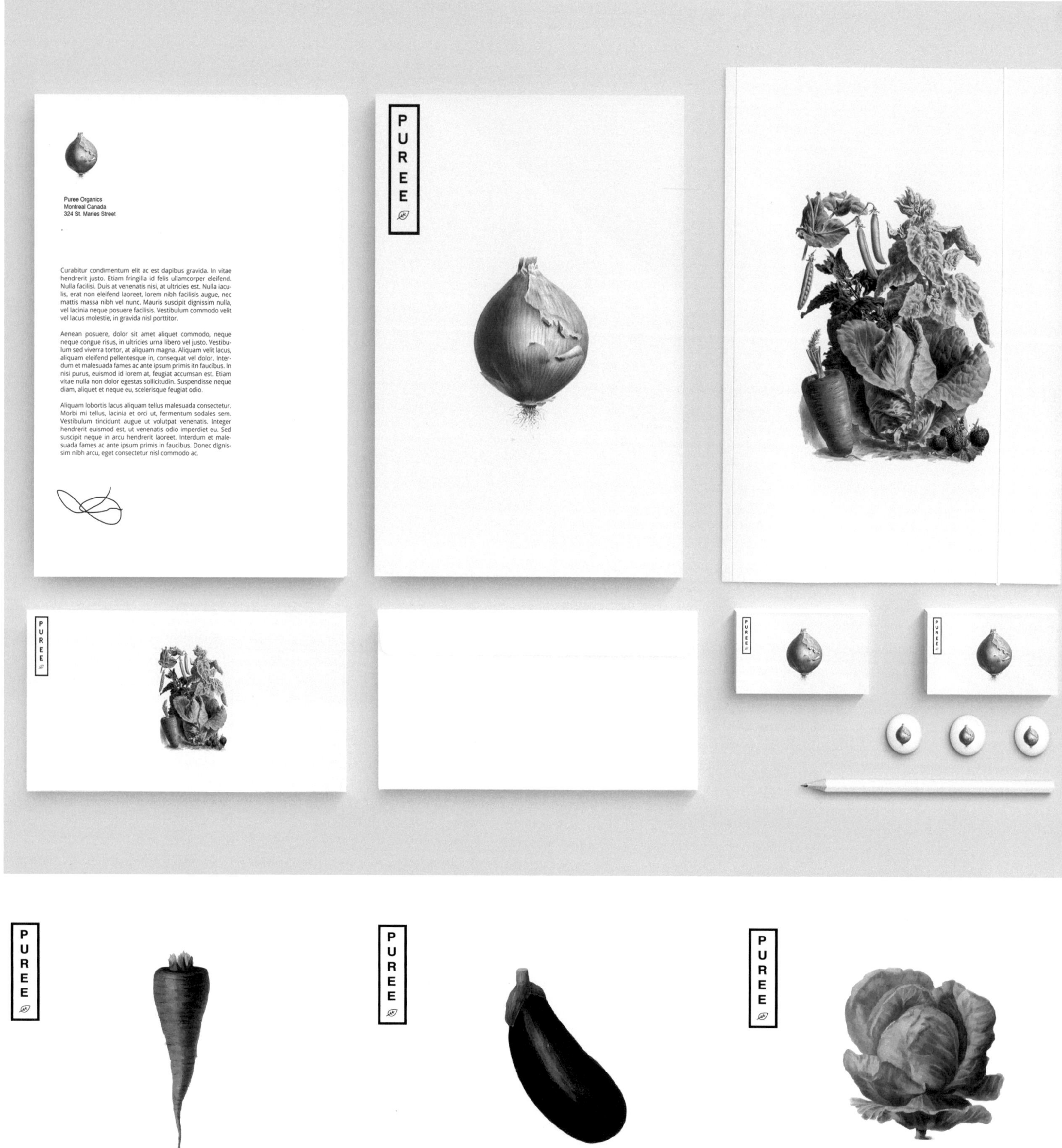

Puree is an organic garden launched by husband-and-wife Marie and Claude LaPonte to grow medicinal plants, fruits, and vegetables, and bring locally farmed food to their Montreal neighborhood. With the company's core business in organic farming, it would have been likely for the brand to embrace the common eco-label look, but as Puree promises to be more than merely another organic mom-and-pop store, the LaPontes wanted to steer clear of green grocery store stereotypes and present Puree as a specialty product supplier. Sophia Ahamed put their ideas into practice and their produce to the forefront, delivering delicate illustrations in the style of traditional nature studies.

Puree Organics

ORGANIC GARDEN & GROCER

Vancouver, Canada, *by Studioahamed*

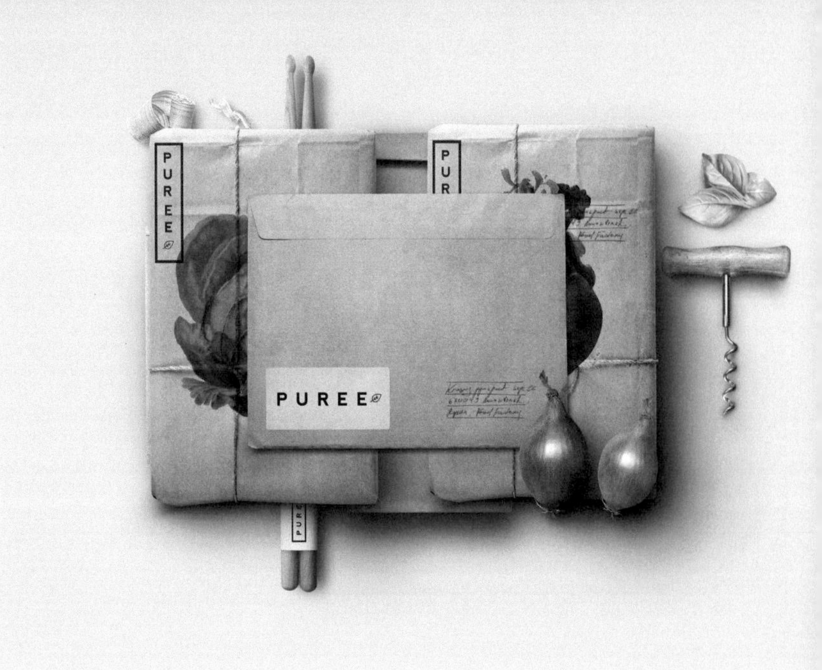

A TEXTBOOK EXAMPLE OF TASTY BRANDING: STUDIO AHAMED BRING BACK BIOLOGY LESSONS IN THEIR PRESENTATION OF PUREE, AN ORGANIC PRODUCT RANGE AND VEGETABLE GARDEN.

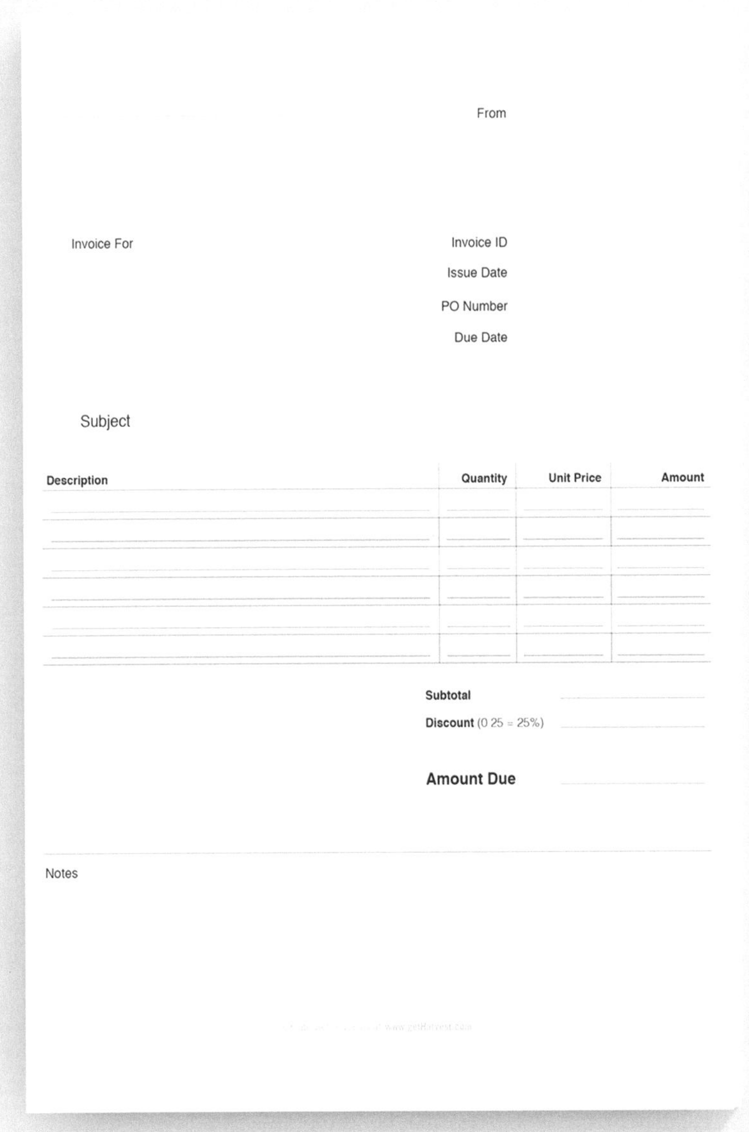

From

Invoice For

Invoice ID
Issue Date
PO Number
Due Date

Subject

Description	Quantity	Unit Price	Amount

Subtotal
Discount (0.25 = 25%)

Amount Due

Notes

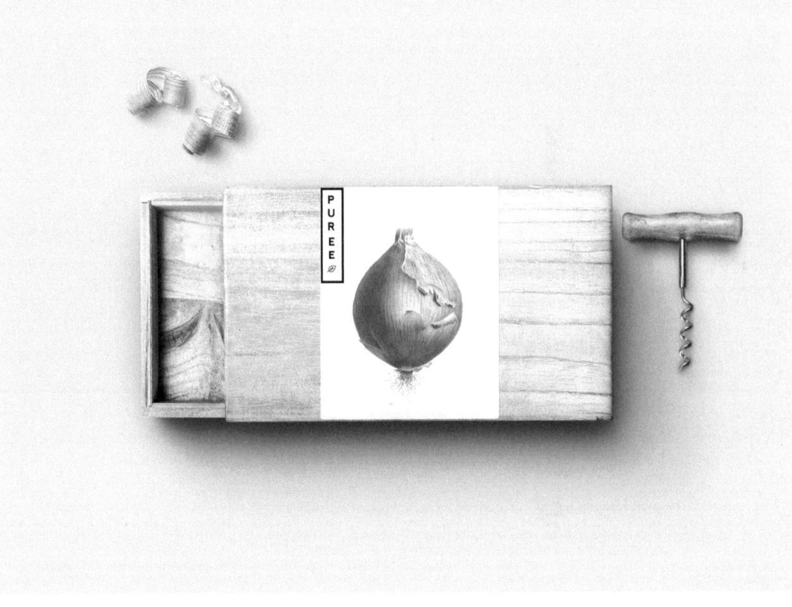

Shimogamosaryo

RESTAURANT

Kyoto, Japan, *by Good Design Company*

THE JAPANESE TEA TRADITION TELLS US TO EXPERIENCE THE WORLD AS A WHOLE. HOSTING HARMONIOUS CULINARY EXPERIENCES AND A WELL-BALANCED BRAND, THE CLASSIC KYOTO EATERY SHIMOGAMOSARYO WISELY FOLLOWS THOSE WORDS.

Housed in a traditional Japanese-style building surrounded by a traditional Japanese garden, the restaurant Shimogamosaryo has become a culinary institution in an area also known as Shimogamo-shrine, arguably one of Kyoto's most superbly scenic spots that has been declared a UNESCO World Cultural Heritage site. Steeped in tradition too, Shimogamosaryo has been serving authentic yet innovative Kyoto-style dishes inspired by the cycle of the seasons since 1856. In line with the spirit of Sado, a centuries-old Japanese tea ceremony, Kundo Koyama hangs on to a holistic approach to hospitality, and commissioned Good Design Company to develop the corporate image to complement his restaurant's authentic Kyoto atmosphere.

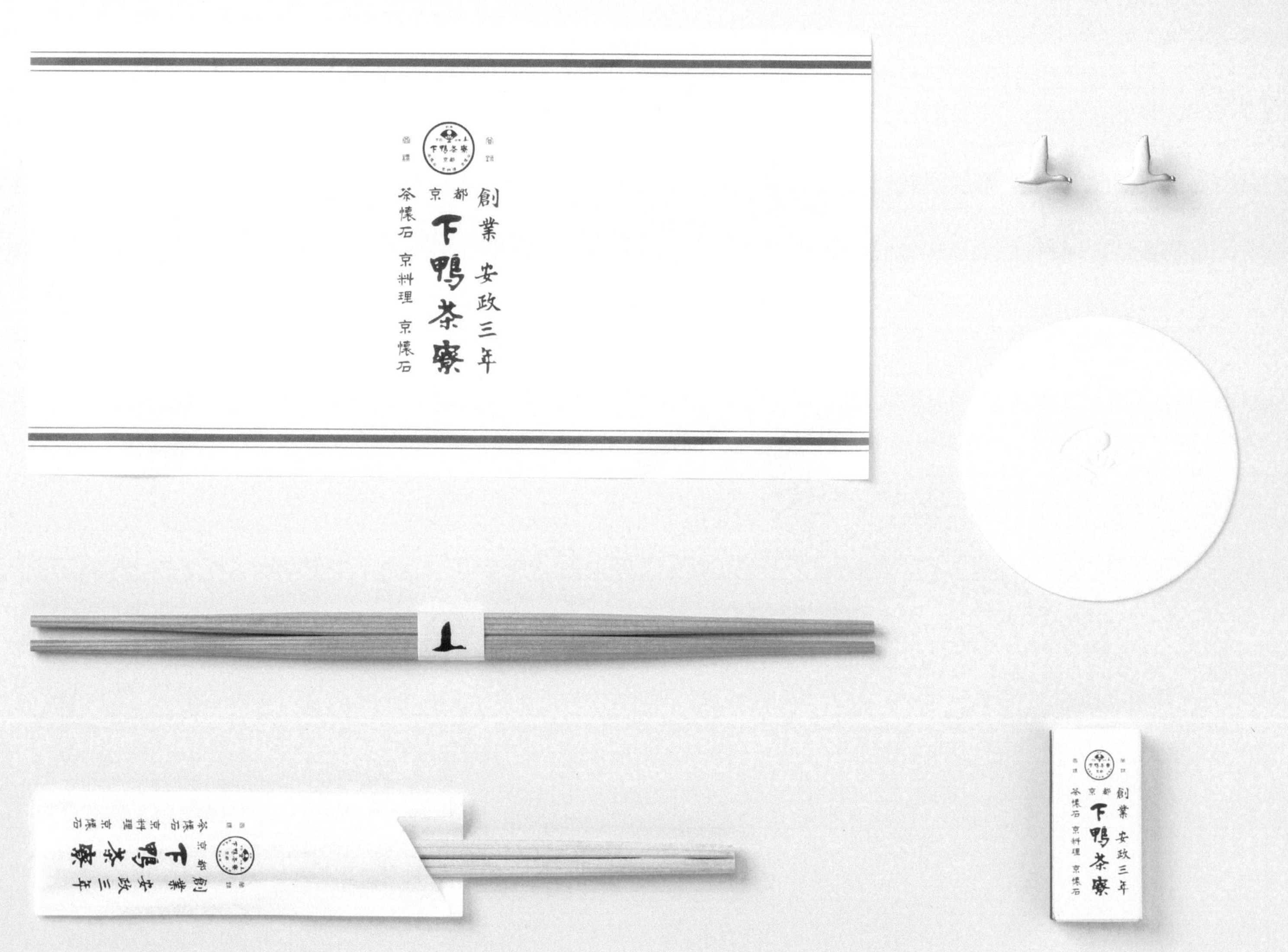

創業
安政 三年
下鴨茶寮
京都
茶懐石 京料理 京懐石

創業
安政 三年
下鴨茶寮
京都
茶懐石 京料理 京懐石

小山薫堂
創業
安政 三年
下鴨茶寮
京都
茶懐石 京料理 京懐石

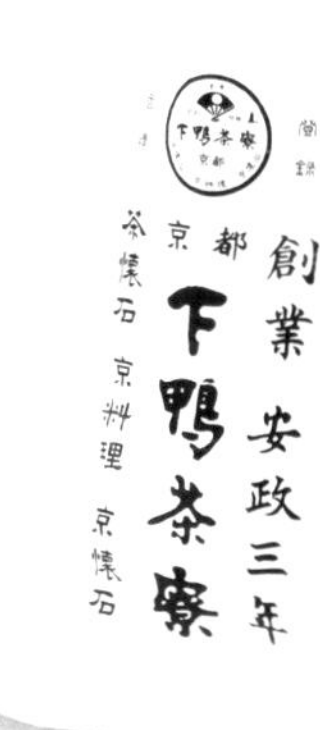
創業 安政三年
京都
下鴨茶寮
茶懐石 京料理 京懐石

創業
安政 三年
下鴨茶寮
京都
茶懐石 京料理 京懐石

創業
安政 三年
下鴨茶寮
京都
茶懐石 京料理 京懐石

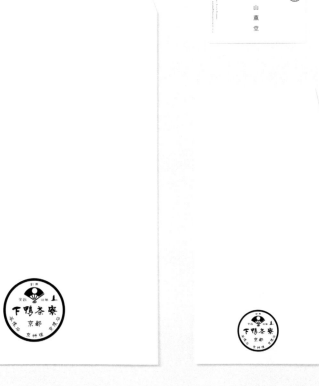

PARIS + HENDZEL
52°12'N
21°02'E
HANDCRAFTED
GOODS
MCMXXXV

HANDCRAFTED GOODS
www.parishendzel.com
PARIS + HENDZEL

PARIS + HENDZEL

PRODUCT CERTIFICATE
Model:
Nr.
For:
5 Panel Hat
Our products are made with passion from the finest quality fabrics.
PARIS + HENDZEL
HANDCRAFTED GOODS
goods@parishendzel.com
www.parishendzel.com
Handcrafted in Poland

PRODUCT CERTIFICATE
HANDCRAFTED GOODS
PARIS + HENDZEL

Paris+Hendzel Handcrafted Goods

FASHION & ACCESSORIES LABEL

Warsaw, Poland, *by Paris+Hendzel Studio*

PARIS+HENDZEL HAS BEEN CONCEIVED AS AN ACCESSORIES LABEL FOR THE FASHION-CONSCIOUS ADVENTURER. DELVING INTO THE DEPTHS OF HERALDRY, THE HIP HEADWEAR BRAND'S CORPORATE IDENTITY REFERS BACK TO ITS FOUNDER'S FAMILY ROOTS.

Launched by Łukasz Hendzel as a passion project and creative counterbalance to his bread-and-butter career in graphic design, Paris+Hendzel produces handmade headwear, carefully crafted caps made of high-grade materials. Himself a designer, Hendzel branded his precious side project with due design diligence and with the same attention to detail that goes into each accessory from the collection. What followed is a remarkably personal brand that plays on his roots and family pedigree: the company name, Paris+Hendzel, combines his parents' surnames, and its crest brandmark is based on his ancestors' coat of arms.

PARIS + HENDZEL
www.parishendzel.com
WIMATECH
77238
HAPPY PEOPLE
1
2
3
HANDCRAFTED GOODS
PRODUCT CERTIFICATE
5 Panel Hat
Model
Nr
For
HANDCRAFTED GOODS BY PARIS+HENDZEL CO.
DESIGNED IN POLAND. DRY CLEAN ONLY.
HANDCRAFTED GOODS BY PARIS+HENDZEL CO.
DESIGNED IN POLAND. DRY CLEAN ONLY.

PARIS + HENDZEL
52°12'N
21°02'E
HANDCRAFTED
GOODS
MCMXXXV
PARIS + HENDZEL

Cocktail Academy / Apartment A

COCKTAIL CREATION & CREATIVE CONVENTION VENUE

Los Angeles, CA, USA, *by Say What Studio*

CHEERS TO COCKTAIL CULTURE!
SAY WHAT STUDIO SERVES UP SOME GRADE A
GRAPHICS FOR COCKTAIL ACADEMY AND APARTMENT A.

The Cocktail Academy is an interdisciplinary creative company instituted by three self-proclaimed cocktail party pros and cultural innovators.
With backgrounds in gastronomy and bartending, the team has made cocktails their medium of creative communication, partnering with individuals and brands to create personalized cocktail experiences.
The Academy's premises are located in Los Angeles's Arts District, acting as a bar, gallery, and project space. The company's creative headquarters also connect with Apartment A, a private tasting space dedicated to cocktail development and intimate, curated events and dinners. Say What Studio served the business with a set of corporate communications that consolidate both brands—Cocktail Academy and Apartment A—under the banner of the capital A.

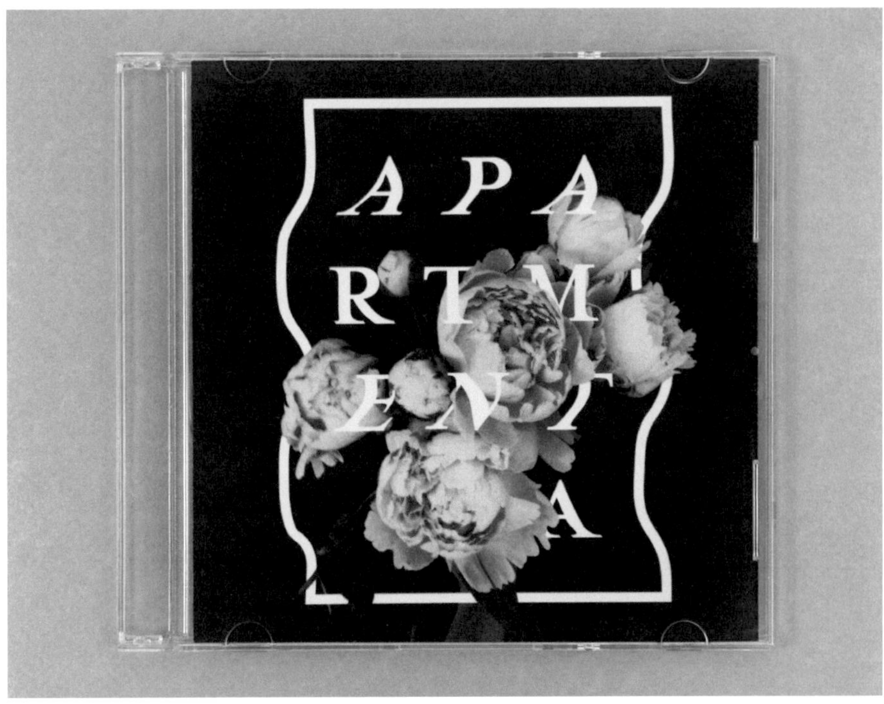

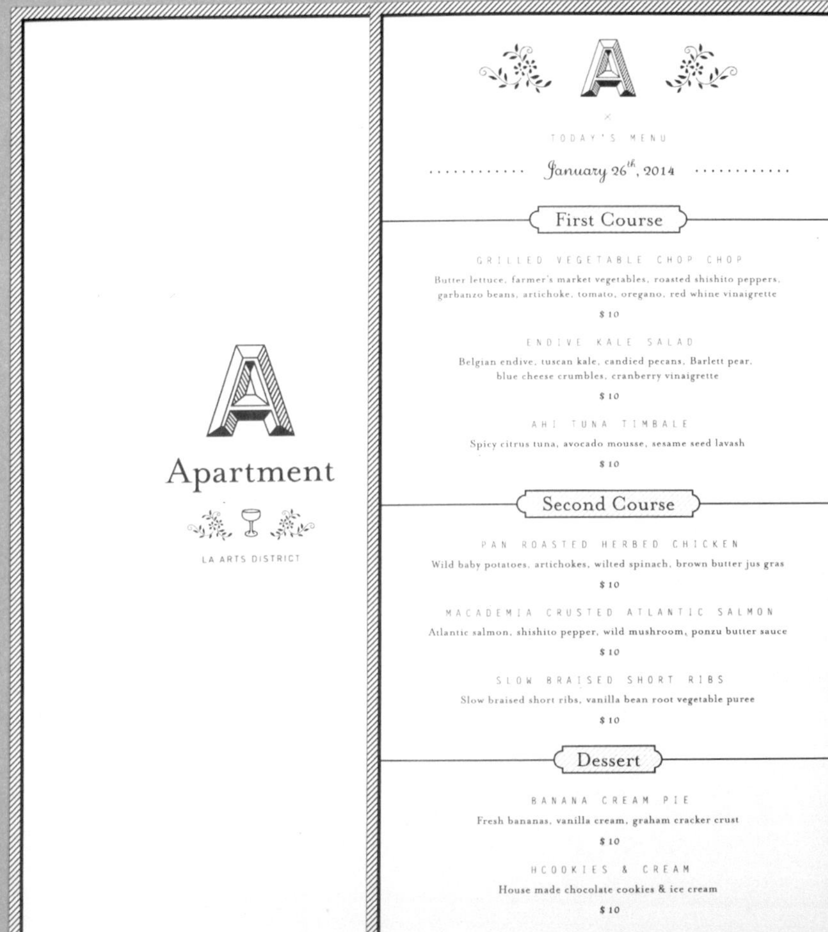

A
Apartment
LA ARTS DISTRICT
TODAY'S MENU
January 26th, 2014
First Course
GRILLED VEGETABLE CHOP CHOP
Butter lettuce, farmer's market vegetables, roasted shishito peppers, garbanzo beans, artichoke, tomato, oregano, red whine vinaigrette
$ 10
ENDIVE KALE SALAD
Belgian endive, tuscan kale, candied pecans, Barlett pear, blue cheese crumbles, cranberry vinaigrette
$ 10
AHI TUNA TIMBALE
Spicy citrus tuna, avocado mousse, sesame seed lavash
$ 10
Second Course
PAN ROASTED HERBED CHICKEN
Wild baby potatoes, artichokes, wilted spinach, brown butter jus gras
$ 10
MACADEMIA CRUSTED ATLANTIC SALMON
Atlantic salmon, shishito pepper, wild mushroom, ponzu butter sauce
$ 10
SLOW BRAISED SHORT RIBS
Slow braised short ribs, vanilla bean root vegetable puree
$ 10
Dessert
BANANA CREAM PIE
Fresh bananas, vanilla cream, graham cracker crust
$ 10
HCOOKIES & CREAM
House made chocolate cookies & ice cream
$ 10

Brandyn Tepper
Max Kestenbaum
COCKTAIL ACADEMY
LA ARTS DISTRICT
Apartment
LA ARTS DISTRICT

A P
ART
852 MATEO STREET #107
ME
LOS ANGELES
NT
WWW.APARTMENTALA.COM
A

×

TODAY'S MENU

January 26th, 2014

First Course

GRILLED VEGETABLE CHOP CHOP

Butter lettuce, farmer's market vegetables, roasted shishito peppers, garbanzo beans, artichoke, tomato, oregano, red whine vinaigrette

$ 10

ENDIVE KALE SALAD

Belgian endive, tuscan kale, candied pecans, Barlett pear, blue cheese crumbles, cranberry vinaigrette

$ 10

AHI TUNA TIMBALE

Spicy citrus tuna, avocado mousse, sesame seed lavash

$ 10

Second Course

PAN ROASTED HERBED CHICKEN

Wild baby potatoes, artichokes, wilted spinach, brown butter jus gras

$ 10

MACADEMIA CRUSTED ATLANTIC SALMON

Atlantic salmon, shishito pepper, wild mushroom, ponzu butter sauce

$ 10

SLOW BRAISED SHORT RIBS

Slow braised short ribs, vanilla bean root vegetable puree

$ 10

Dessert

BANANA CREAM PIE

Fresh bananas, vanilla cream, graham cracker crust

$ 10

HCOOKIES & CREAM

House made chocolate cookies & ice cream

$ 10

652 MATEO STREET #107
LOS ANGELES, CA 90021
M 646.323.4682
W 213.800.3026

Apartment

LA ARTS DISTRICT

Strietman

ESPRESSO MACHINE MAKER

Eindhoven, Netherlands, *by Vincent Meertens*

A COFFEE CLASS OF ITS OWN: WOUTER STRIETMAN COUNTERS THE SQUARE PUSH-BUTTON BOXES THAT HAVE BECOME STANDARD FOR HOME ESPRESSO MACHINES WITH ARTISAN APPLIANCES AND SEVERAL SPOONS OF STYLE.

Wouter Strietman redefines the craft of espresso-making from his Eindhoven workshop. The self-proclaimed espresso fanatic earned a degree from Eindhoven's renowned Design Academy before he decided to dedicate himself to his passion, producing espresso machines that enable like-minded coffee connoisseurs to extract their custom espresso at home. The machines that Strietman designs and develops from scratch are basic in build, but all parts are tailor-made, laser-cut, and CNC milled to enable the Strietman method: a particularly gentle process that harms the coffee bean as little as possible. Designed to start a dialogue with the company's potential clients and parallel the precision of Strietman products, Vincent Meertens's visual identity features tactile paper printed with a classy type and copper finish. A clean typographic system supports the product photography, while the color palette reflects the three main materials Strietman employs—copper, brass, and metal. Inspired by the company's inclination for custom craftsmanship, Meertens introduced individual layouts and images for each of Strietman's promotional flyers that were printed in sets of three

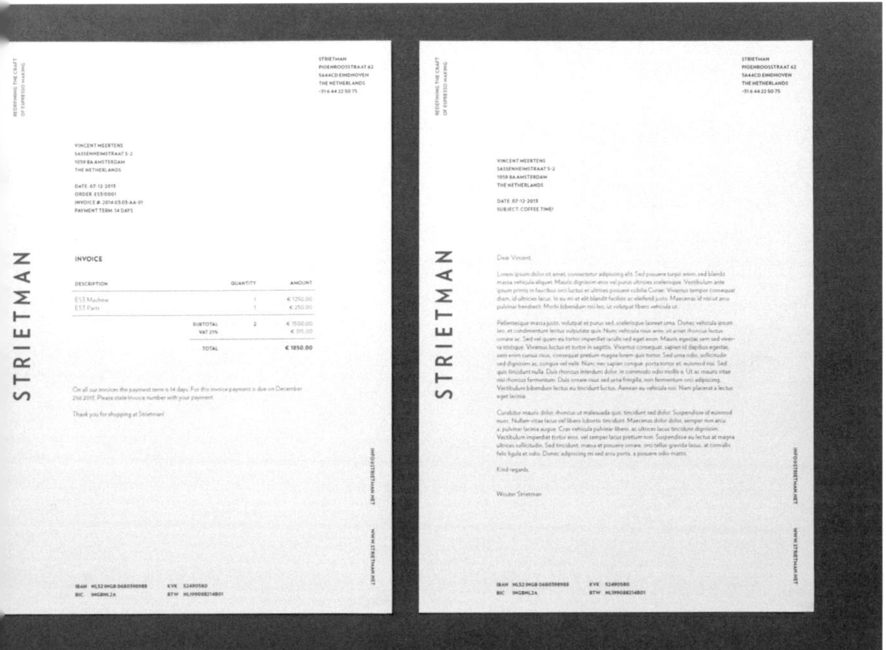

REDEFINING THE CRAFT
OF ESPRESSO MAKING

STRIETMAN

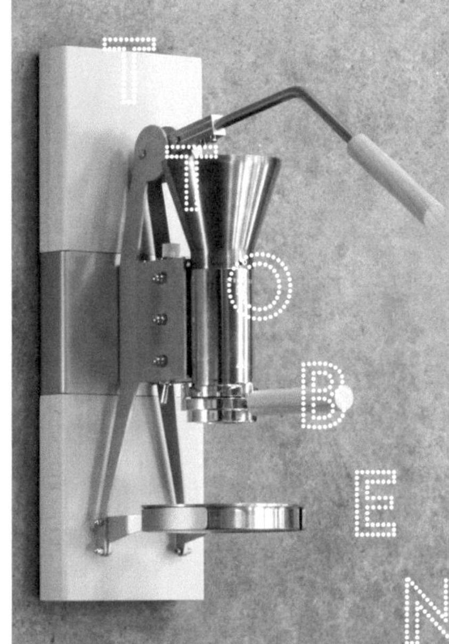

ES3

MEET AND MATTER
TUTTOBENE, MILANO 2014

WWW.STRIETMAN.NET
INFO@STRIETMAN.NET

33 Acres Brewing

BREWERY

Vancouver, Canada, *by Josh Michnik*

BORN OUT OF LOVE FOR THE BINDING ELEMENTS OF LIFE, 33 ACRES ADHERES TO THE SPIRIT OF SOCIABILITY AND COMMUNITY SHARING. BESIDES BREWING BEER, THEY CATER TO CONVERSATION WITH CANDID COMMUNICATION, AND OCCASIONAL YOGA CLASSES.

In the middle of Vancouver, BC, and yet close to a picturesque place where the woodlands meet the waters of the Pacific Ocean, sits 33 Acres Brewing, a family-owned and operated microbrewery founded to foster collectivity and fine craft beer. With an inclusive community space inviting innovation as one of the brewery's most crucial assets, 33 Acres brings its neighborhood the so-called Morning After Social Yoga classes, and beers inspired by its surroundings.
Among their ambitious brews are 33 Acres of Life (a British Columbia brother of the classic California Common), Darkness (a black beer striving to bring tantalizing taste beyond heavy hops), Ocean (a full-flavored floral creation completed with caramel), and Sunshine (silky, smooth, and spiced up with orange peel, coriander, and anise seeds to be perfectly paired with the golden days of Canadian summers). With a vision born out of enjoyment for the binding elements of life, not only the brewery's beer names nod to nature, as do the elements of the overall brand. Developed by Josh Michnik, the 33 Acre identity stands for clarity and honest communication. A former LA film and television title designer, he co-founded the brewery with his wife to free himself from the media industry's madness. Based on Michnik's idea that brewers are the new butchers, he kept it local and simple to let quality speak for itself.

EST 33 2013
ACRES BREWING CO.
VANCOUVER, BC

Traversing a little further North here in wooded British Columbia our beer serves the very same purpose. Easy on the alcohol content and weighing in on taste for a complete balance. Utilizing Mount Hood hops lends a spice infused aroma. A fruit like quality is created by fermenting the lager at ale temperatures. Gaining a complex taste through subtle approach; hints at a full-bodied ale yet retains a crisp finish.

650ML - $5.25

SKU: 577007

15 WEST 8TH AVE, VANCOUVER, BC, V5Y 1M8
604 620 4589
WWW.33ACRESBREWING.COM

DUSTIN SEPKOWSKI

EST 33 2013
ACRES BREWING CO.
VANCOUVER, BC

C.778 926 6373
DUSTIN@33ACRESBREWING.COM
15 W 8TH AVE, VANCOUVER, BC, V5Y 1M8
P.604 620 4589 WWW.33ACRESBREWING.COM

33 ACRES OF LIFE

FULL BODIED LAGER / ALE HYBRID

1.89L
4.8% alc./vol.
BEER / BIÈRE
DATE FILLED: ______

INGREDIENTS: PILSNER MALT, CARAMEL MALTS
NORTHERN BREWER HOPS, YEAST, WATER

6 2 6 9 9 0 1 7 0 0 3 7

EST 33 2013
ACRES BREWING CO.
VANCOUVER, BC

15 W 8TH AVE VANCOUVER, BC, CANADA, V5Y 1M8
WWW.33ACRESBREWING.COM

EST 33 2013
ACRES BREWING CO.
VANCOUVER, BC

Merchant & Mills

SEWING SUPPLIES

Rye, UK

ANARCHY AND ATTIRE: MERCHANT & MILLS PROPAGATE DIY-CLOTHING AND CELEBRATE A CERTAIN PUNK AESTHETIC WITH PHOTO-COLLAGED CORPORATE COMMUNICATIONS.

Merchant & Mills is the mutual project of clothing designer Carolyn Denham and photographer Roderick Field. A decidedly committed maker with a mission to motivate confident women to express themselves through self-made clothes, Denham develops the classic sewing patterns that Merchant & Mills sell alongside carefully sourced accessories and solid traditional sewing tools. Field gives the firm a face, fitting it with a coherent corporate image, including bespoke photography-based packaging that mirrors Merchant & Mills's artisanal approach and their mildly Marxist Manifesto: "Our hearts are egalitarian, returning the power of couture to the creative public. Everyone can have something beautiful, useful, akin to designer dress but personal and affordable."

MERCHANT & MILLS
UNIVERSALLY USEFUL
BLACK BULB PINS
Carolyn N.K. Denham
DRESSES COURSES PATTERNS NOTIONS

MERCHANT & MILLS
SERIOUSLY SHINY
NICKEL PLATED
BULB PINS
DRESSES CLOTH PATTERNS GOODS TOOLS

MERCHANT & MILLS
MEASURE
Carolyn N K Denham

MERCHANT & MILLS
DRAPER
Carolyn N.K. Denham
INDISPENSABLE NOTIONS
FOR YOUR SEWING PLEASURE
Tailor's Chalk • Tailor's Thimble • Tailor's Beeswax
1oz Dressmaking Pins • 25 Finest Needles • Tape Measure
Wide Bow Scissors • Seam Ripper • Needle Threader
SEWING BOX

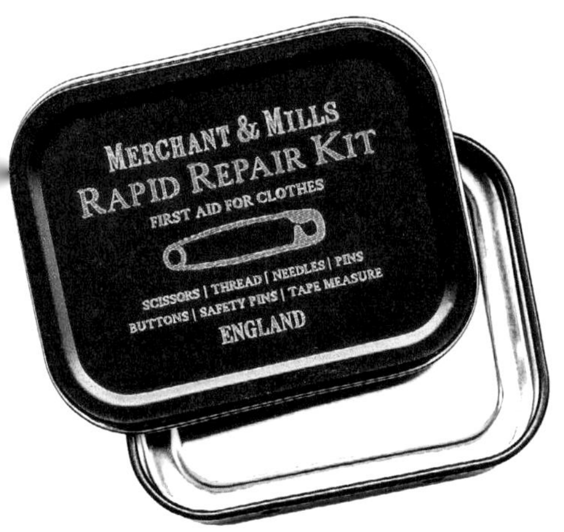
MERCHANT & MILLS
RAPID REPAIR KIT
FIRST AID FOR CLOTHES
SCISSORS | THREAD | NEEDLES | PINS
BUTTONS | SAFETY PINS | TAPE MEASURE
ENGLAND

MERCHANT & MILLS
SEWING BOOK
PROJECTS | TECHNIQUES | GUIDANCE | INSTRUCTIONS
TOOLS | NOTIONS | CHOOSING CLOTH | THE SEWING MACHINE
HAND SEWING | THE ART OF PRESSING | OUR PHILOSOPHY
Carolyn N.K. Denham

ENGLAND
EIGHTEEN
SIXPENCE

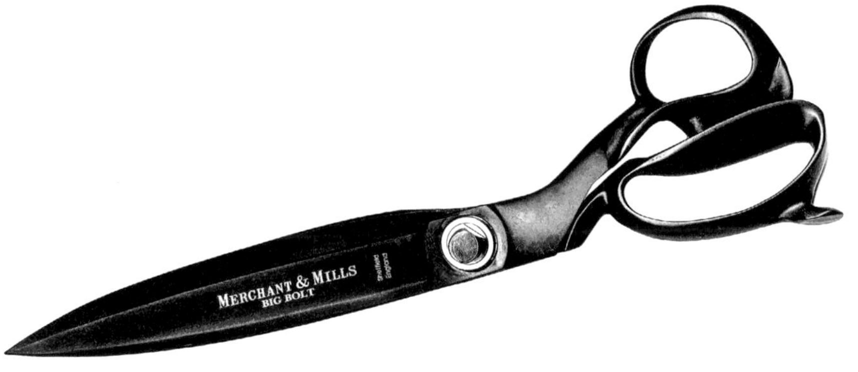
MERCHANT & MILLS
BIG BOLT

Sherri Ziesche began her beauty career as a freelance makeup artist and aesthetician. Spurred by a sabbatical that took her to countries across Europe and Asia, she returned to the U.S. to provide Californian clients with a palette of products inspired by her impressions of the global beauty industry. Having launched her cosmetics store Beauty Company in 2002, followed by the Euro-styled four-chair beauty boutique Salon, Ziesche is her latest venture.

A contemporary take on old-world spas and pharmacies, the modern apothecary sells locally and internationally sourced skincare, bath and body products, and encourages customer participation in the creation of customized products.

Noise 13's brand identity for the store is based on Ziesche's hands-on approach to beauty. The designs are delicate yet grounded, well-balanced with a restrained color palette and plenty of white space.

Ziesche

GROOMING GOODS

'an Francisco, CA, USA, *by Noise 13*

PRETTY BY PRESCRIPTION:
THE BEAUTY BUSINESS BASES ITS BRANDING CONCEPT ON OLD-STYLE CONTINENTAL APOTHECARIES.

Tamarindo

RESTAURANT

Ourense, Spain, *by La Tortillería*

OURENSE'S MICROCLIMATE BRINGS THE CITY MOSTLY MILD AND WET WEATHER. THE RESTAURANT TAMARINDO THWARTS DRAB RAINY DAYS WITH BRIGHT DESIGN WORK BY LA TORTILLERÍA.

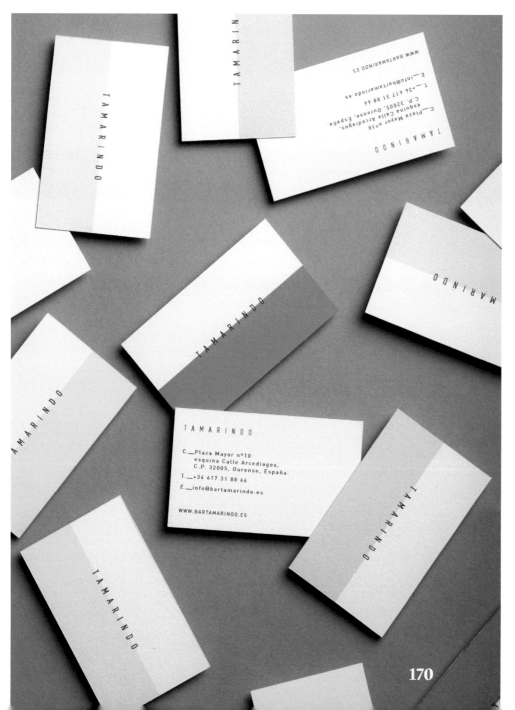

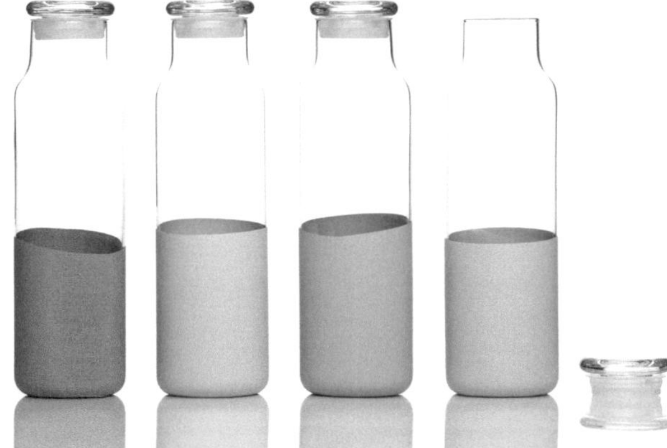

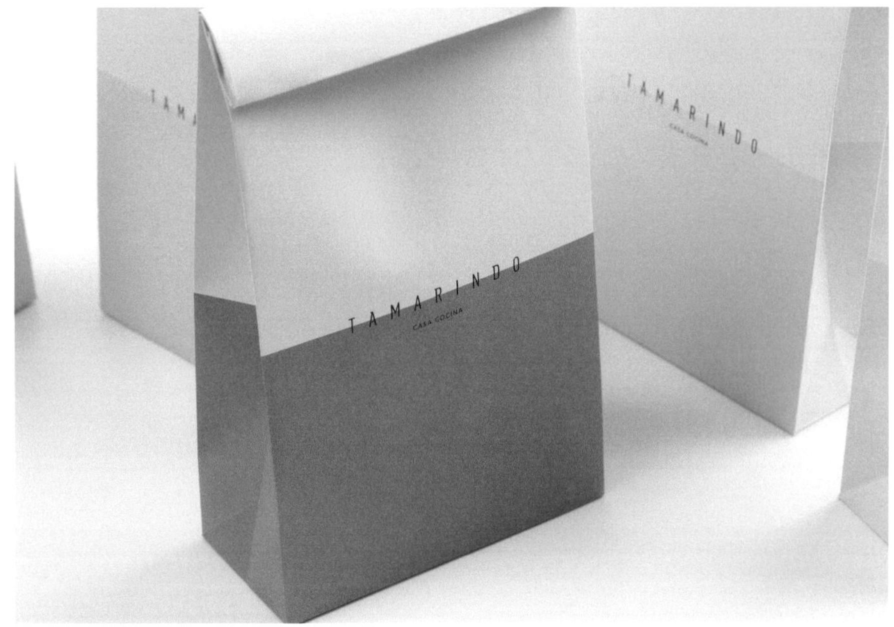

The Galician Ourense is reknowned for regular rainfall and resulting verdant vegetation. Now a remarkable new restaurant refreshes the city's culinary scene with mouthwatering meals and a colorful visual concept. The new spot in northwestern Spain stands out with a superb interior, crafted by creative couple Ruben D. Gil and Gretta R. Valdés, who defined two areas with distinct atmospheres: the casa cocina for coffee and a quick snack with warm wooden ceilings and clay-covered walls; and a dimly-lit bar for beer and tapas, featuring sober steel furniture. The dual architectural approach is also reflected in La Tortillería's delicately designed graphic goods for Tamarindo. Their identity ranges from coasters to corporate communication, as well as packaging for the restaurant's own range of products.

06.06.14
TAMARINDO
MENÚ
ENSALADAS
PLATILLOS
HAMBURGUESAS
TAMARINDO
CASA COCINA
TAMARINDO
TAMARINDO
TAMARINDO
TAMARINDO
TAMARINDO

TAMARINDO
A
TAMARINDO
_SERRANO AHUMADO
TAMARINDO
_JENGIBRE
SALES
TAMARINDO
PATIO BAR
TAMARINDO
CASA COCINA
TAMARINDO
PATIO BAR
TAMARINDO
CASA COCINA
TAMARINDO
CASA COCINA
TAMARINDO
Mesa
Mesero
Bar
Restaurante
Cantidad
Concepto
Importe
Total

Magro Cardona

FOOTWEAR

Madrid, Spain, *by Mark Brooks*

RIDING ON STYLE AND A SHOESHINE. FOLLOWING IN THE STEPS OF FINE SPANISH SHOEMAKERS', MAGRO CARDONA MANUFACTURES MINIMALIST MASTERPIECES FOR THE À LA MODE LADY. MARK BROOKS STYLED THE BRAND, SETTING A STEPPING-STONE ON ITS WAY TO SUCCESS.

Magro Cardona is a first-class footwear brand conceived and founded by Irene Magro and Ana Cardona. The two met while working for the same luxury brand and were drawn together by their mutual vanguard visions. Aspiring to combine their ahead-of-its-time taste with time-honored techniques of their trade, the duo develops the designs in their modern Madrid studio. The manufacturing is then done in the famous traditional shoe factories of Toledo and Alicante, where learned cobblers craft each pair carefully, like little pieces of art. Mark Brooks boosted the shoe business with an artful branding solution.His contemporary graphics feature just enough gloss and glory to take us back to the golden times of the Spanish shoemaking tradition.

MAGRO
CARDONA
MADE IN SPAIN

FINEST QUALITY SHOES
MADE IN SPAIN

MAGRO CARDONA
Nº 9

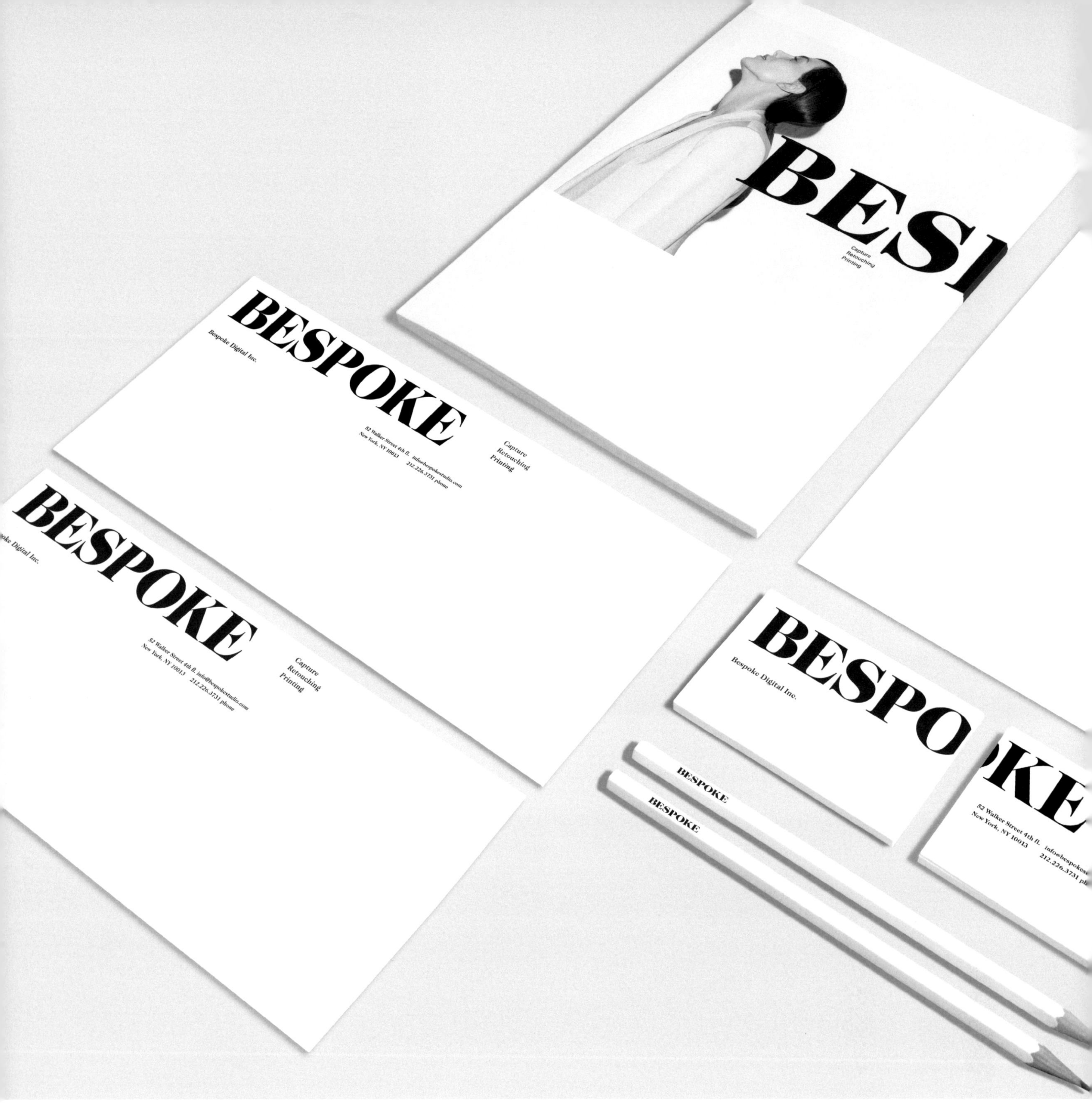

Bespoke

AUDIOVISUAL PRODUCTION

New York, NY, USA, *by STUDIO NEWWORK*

RIGID ON REQUEST—BESPOKE PROVIDES THEIR CLIENTS WITH CUSTOM POST-PRODUCTION SERVICES. THE STUDIO'S BIG AND BOLD BRANDMARK COUNTERS THEIR PRECISELY TAILORED PRODUCTIONS WITH A TYPOGRAPHIC ONE-SIZE-FITS-ALL SOLUTION.

BESPOKE is a digital post-production studio based in New York City. Considering themselves craftsmen of the new generation, the team promises elaborately customized services and a production process powered by their passion for exquisite pictures. Assigned to work on BESPOKE's branding, and a promotional publication, STUDIO NEWWORK appointed a bespoke logo lettering applied in consistent size for most printed materials, cropping it whenever required. In the promo publication, they placed bold black bars on page edges to balance the composition, and wrapped the BESPOKE cover title around the back of the book.

Wanderlust

FASHION & ACCESSORIES

Mannheim, Germany
by Dennis Adelmann x David Heinze

DOWN-TO-EARTH AND DEAD-ON. WANDERLUST PRODUCES PLAIN GARMENTS AND GRAPHICS THAT PROMISE PERFECT FITS FOR GROWN-UP BOY SCOUTS.

Wanderlust is a fashion label founded on the fringes between trend and tradition, simplicity and sophistication, cosmopolitanism and the countryside. Fascinated with the corresponding contradictions, the firm finds itself in the good company of a nature-related generation, young urban wayfarers who seek style as much as sturdy substantialism. Part of that generation himself, recent design graduate Dennis Adelmann developed the visual world around Wanderlust's clothing collections, taking cues from camping trips through the woods.

WANDER & LUST

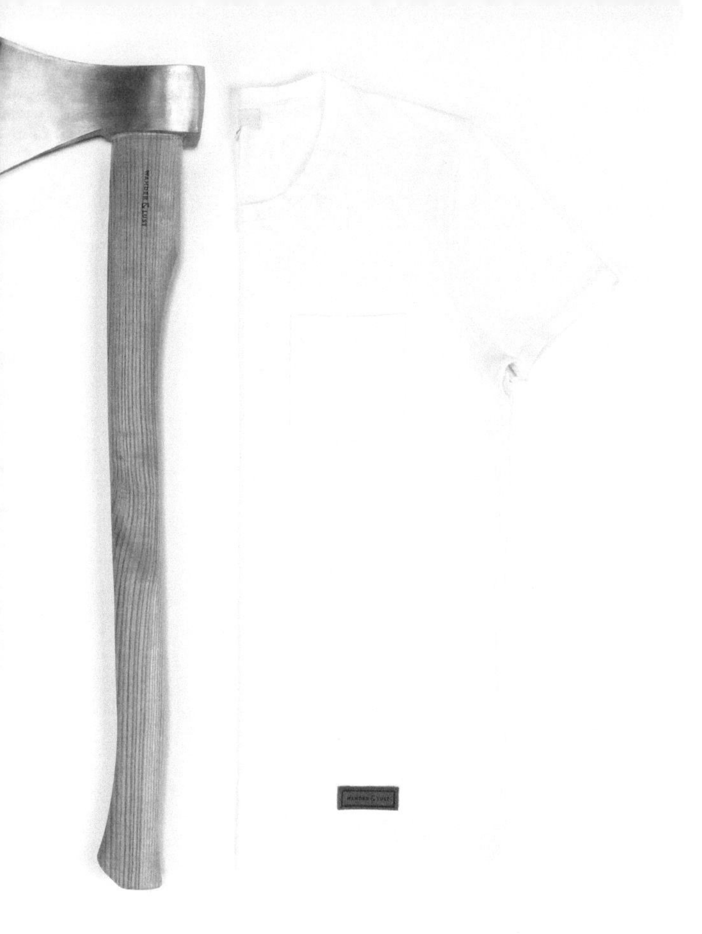

WANDER
LUST

WANDER & LUST

Diotoys

WOODEN TOY MANUFACTURER

Budapest, Hungary, *by Réka Diósi*

Driven by the desire to create beautifully handmade Christmas gifts for their children, the Diósi family began manufacturing wooden toys in 1987. Now in its second generation, the Hungarian family firm has perfected its handicraft to produce elaborate playthings equipped with complex mechanics, like spur wheels, belt drives or swivel connections to perform special movements. Réka, the Diósi daughter who has taken the lead role in the company's communications, earned a design degree from the University of Fine Arts in Budapest. The business benefitted after she put her skills into the company's service. The new set of corporate communications were silk-screened by Réka Diósi in her school's workshop, worked with wood and leftover veneer sheets from furniture factories to reflect the natural materials from which Diotoys's products are made. Letterheads and labels come on recycled paper and all products are wrapped in bags made of 100 percent wool and ecologically-sound wooden boxes.

THE DIOTOYS FAMILY FIRM HAS FABRICATED FUN WOODEN CREATURES AND CARS FOR A WHILE, BUT DISTRIBUTION ONLY GATHERED STEAM AFTER AN EXTENSIVE REBRAND BY DESIGNER AND DAUGHTER RÉKA DIÓSI.

DIOTOYS
BUDAPEST
DIOTOYS
ANIMAL COLLECTION
DIOTOYS

the
DIOTOYS
19
87
BUDAPEST
the
DIOTOYS
19
87
BUDAPEST
DIOTOYS
19
87
BUDAPEST
DIOTOYS
19
87
BUDAPEST
IMRE DIÓSI

Paintbox

NAIL BAR

New York, NY, USA
by Lotta Nieminen

FUELED BY AN OBSESSION WITH FINDING THE PERFECT RED NAIL POLISH, FORMER BEAUTY EDITOR ELEANOR LANGSTON ESTABLISHED PAINTBOX AS A PROGRESSIVE ALTERNATIVE TO SMELLY NAIL SHACKS AND BLAND BEAUTY BOOTHS. LOTTA NIEMINEN COUNTERS THEIR DISSATISFYING DESIGNS WITH A COMPELLING CORPORATE IDENTITY.

Paintbox is a modern manicure studio founded by former beauty editor Eleanor Langston. After years of counseling clients like *The Today Show, Entertainment Tonight,* and *The New York Times* concerning cosmetics issues, and curating content for the likes of popular publications such as *Cosmopolitan* and *Self*, she set upa skilled team of manicurists with backgrounds in styling for successful beauty brands. With its studio situated in New York's Soho neighborhood, Paintbox provides perfect manicures and a curated selection of nail art in a stylish setting, and against the backdrop of a superbly sleek branding solution by Lotta Nieminen.

P A I N T
B O X

17
P A I
N T
B
O X

P A I
N T
B
O X

B
O X
17 CROSBY STREET
PAINT-BOX.COM
P A I
N
T
B
O X
17 CROSBY STREET
PAINT-BOX.COM
P A I

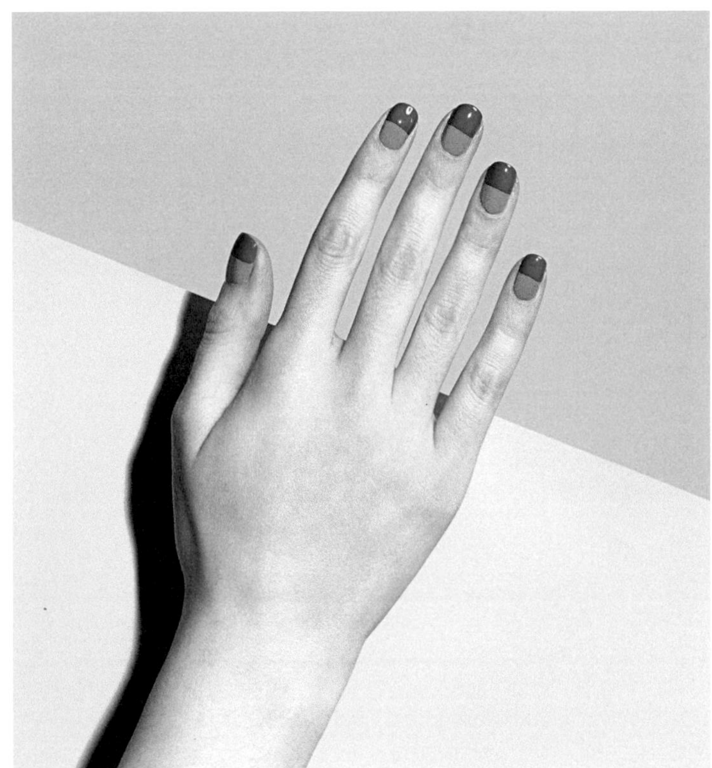

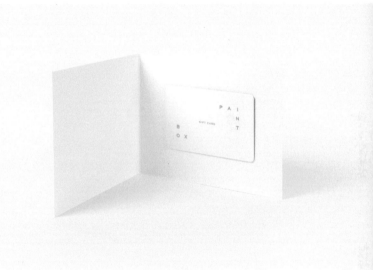

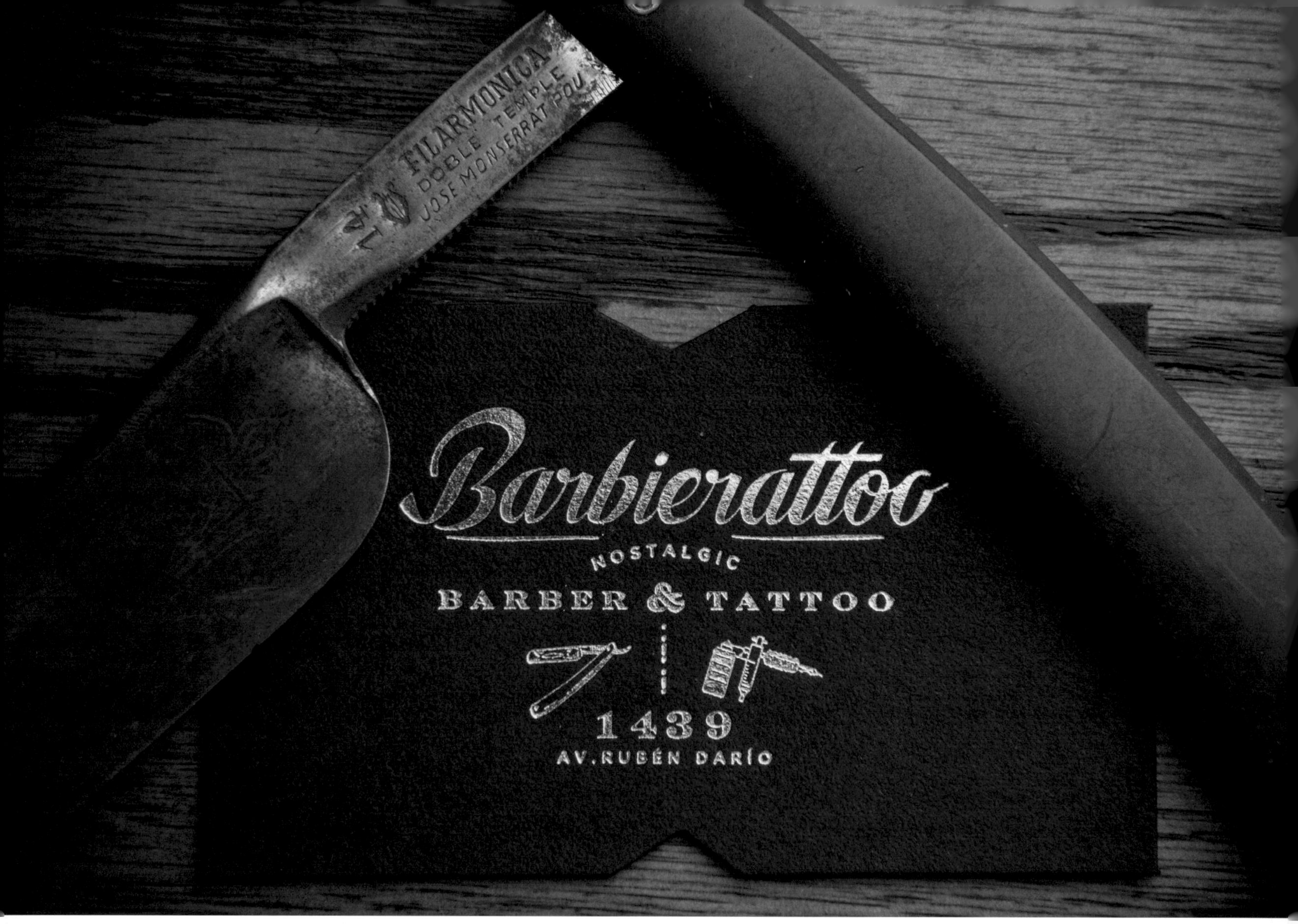

Barbierattoo

BARBER & TATTOO PARLOR

Guadalajara, Mexico, *by Memela*

Combining two major crafts of men's care, Barbierattoo offers to cut Guadalajara's gents' hair and adorn their skin. The business was founded by a local barber and tattoo artist. However, studio Memela came up with the story of a Venetian family who migrated to Mexico with high hopes and extraordinary entrepreneurial intuition. Putting the question about whether that publicity stunt served its purpose aside, one may argue that the Barbierattoo brand is imbued with a certain imperialist-chic that Italian colonialists had once brought to the country. Be that as it may, the design certainly clings to the classy barbershop make-ups of bygone times. The Barbierattoo brandmark combines a custom typeface with illustrations that indicate the business' services.

ARBIERATTOO EMBRACES BUSINESS
VITH A BRILLIANT BRACE (CUTTING
HAIR AND ADORNING SKIN) AND
GOLD-EMBOSSED GRAPHICS.

Barbierattoo
BARBER & TATTOO
1439
CERTIFICADO DE REGALO
Barbierattoo
NOSTALGIC
BARBER & TATTOO
1439
SPA
0011
FECHA
E-MAIL
TELÉFONO
DE SU PIEL
TRATAMIENTO
DURACIÓN
TERAPEUTA
SPA CONCIERGE

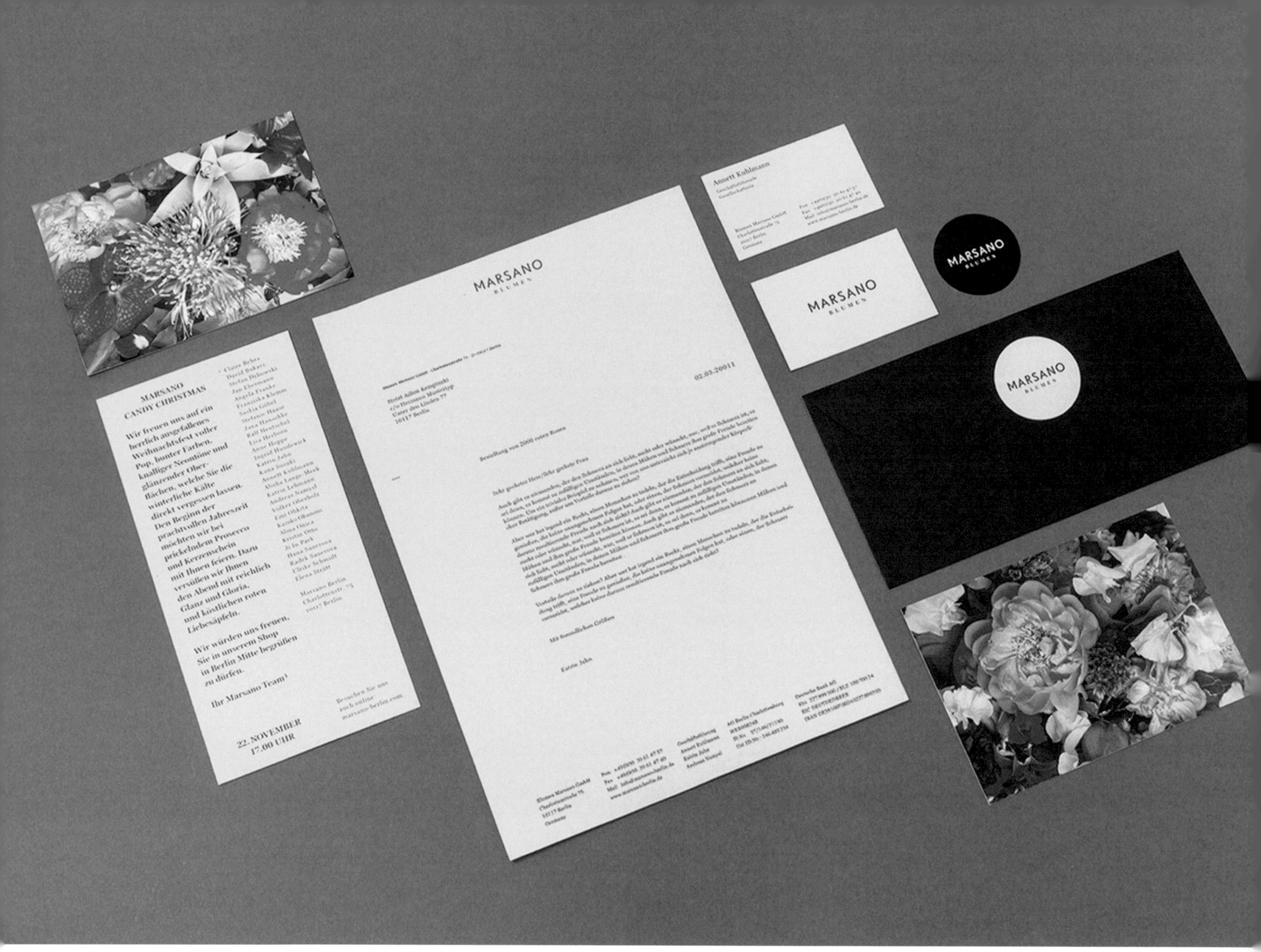

Berlin-based florist Marsano is more than mere flowers: it extends its field of activity far beyond binding bouquets, to some sort of floral art direction. Founded by passionate florist and photographer Annett Kuhlmann and her two business partners, the company has subscribed to high aesthetic standards from the start. From their spacious (work-)shop in Mitte, the team collaborates with various visiting freelance florists from around the globe to compose colors, shapes, and materials into individual arrangements for Marsano's manifold clients, spaces, and moods. Marsano's corporate identity was worked out with Till Wiedeck, a Berlin-based designer with whom Kuhlmann occasionally collaborates as a photographer on other creative projects. Wiedeck focused on the beauty of Marsano's mundane material—flowers—and created a classic logotype to be combined with a powerful set of changing flower portraits, crafted and photographed with Kuhlmann and her colleagues at the Marsano workshop. The concept allows for the brand to adapt to seasonal trends, color schemes, and various occasions.

Marsano

FLORIST & FLOWER STYLIST

Berlin, Germany, *by HelloMe*

FINE FLORAL ART FOR HIGH AESTHETIC ASPIRATIONS: MARSANO'S BUSINESS IS BEAUTY BEYOND MASTERLY BOUND BOUQUETS.

Marsano

FLORIST & FLOWER STYLIST

Berlin, Germany
by Haw-lin Services

MARSANO MEETS HAW-LIN SERVICES: MEDIA ART FOR A BUSINESS IN BLOOM.

Invited to develop a bouquet installation in the company's Berlin boutique, design studio Haw-lin Services met Marsano's high aesthetic aspirations with a site-specific setup featuring two LCD screens that play video portraits of different dried flower posies, combined with a monument composed of mirror glass and wooden columns.

Giahi

TATTOO & PIERCING STUDIOS

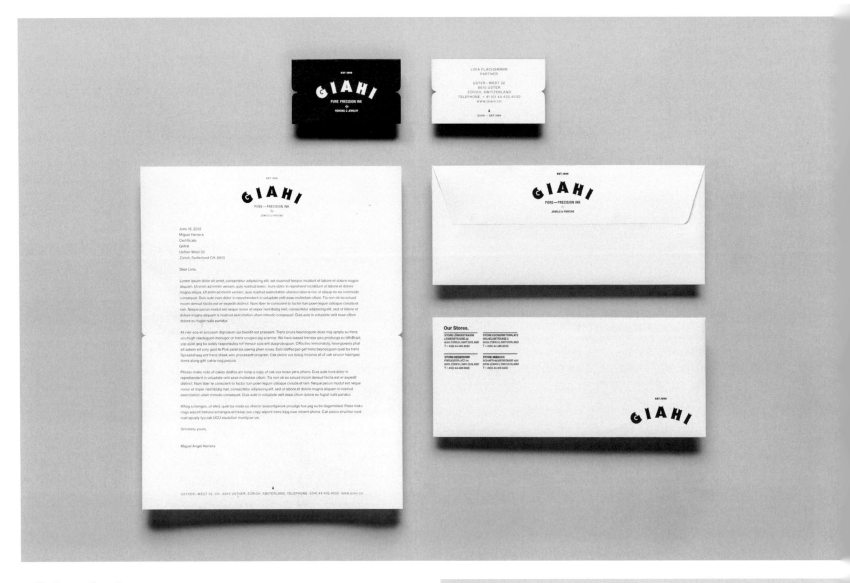

Zurich, Switzerland, *by Anagrama*

GIAHI IS A SWISS SERIES OF SPECIALIZED TATTOO AND PIERCING STUDIOS. ANAGRAMA'S CORPORATE DESIGN FOR THE CHAIN DISPLAYS THE DETAILING OF A TATTOO NEEDLE TOUCHING SKIN.

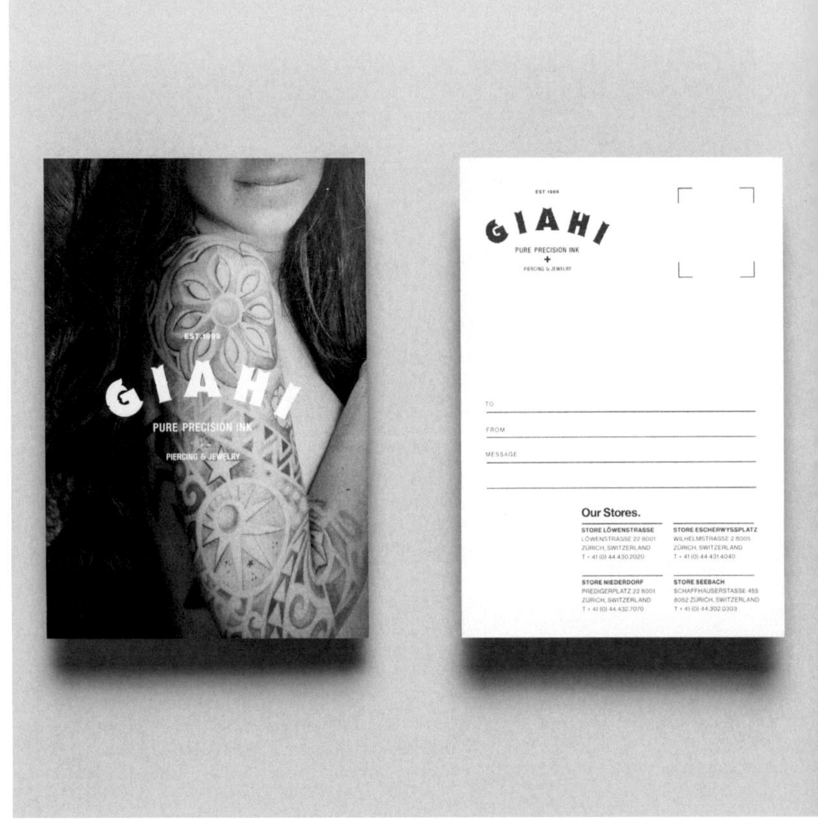

Giada Ilardo founded her first piercing parlor in 1999, at the age of sixteen. Now she works with a team of around 70 employees and international tattoo artists, running five stores including the large Zurich flagship and the Giahi product range that comprises a plethora of tattoo colors and piercing applications. Approached to give a graphic face to the firm, Anagrama created a custom typeface for the logo lettering. Riddled with detail, it is designed to reflect the precise processes of piercing and tattooing. A gold-stamped droplet in the closed counter of the logo's letter 'A' stands as a tribute to the everlasting effect of Giahi's creations on their clients' skin.

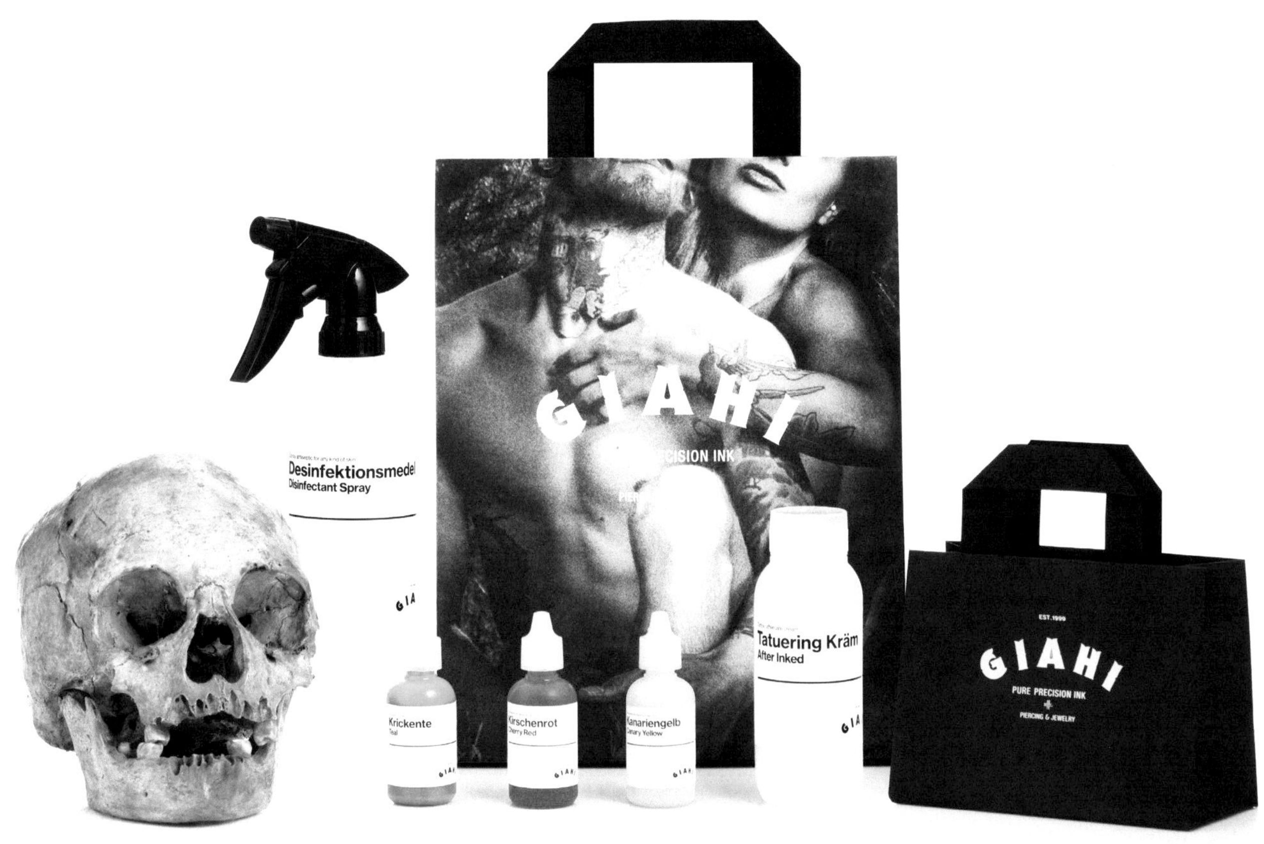
Desinfektionsmedel
Disinfectant Spray
GIAHI
Krickente
Teal
Kirschenrot
Cherry Red
Kanariengelb
Canary Yellow
Tatuering Kräm
After Inked
EST.1999
GIAHI
PURE PRECISION INK
PIERCING & JEWELRY

Aftercare Recommendation.
Tattoo Pflege
Tattoo Care
GIAHI
So bleiben Du und Dein Piercing für immer Freunde.
Damit dein neues Piercing gut verheilt und du lange Freude an deinem Schmuck hast, sind einige Dinge zu beachten. Wir erklären dir hier alles Schritt für Schritt. Wenn du eine Frage hast, sind wir immer für dich da.
WÄHREND DER HEILUNGSZEIT
NORMALE REAKTIONEN AUF EIN PIERCING
PFLEGEMITTEL
PFLEGE VON LIPPE, LABRET, MADONNA, MEDUSA, AUGENBRAUE, BRIDGE
PFLEGE VON KNORPELPIERCINGS (HELIX, TRAGUS, INDUSTRIAL, SEPTUM, NASE) BAUCHNABEL, BRUSTWARZE UND OBERFLÄCHENPIERCING
PFLEGE VON ZUNGE, ZUNGENBAND, LIPPENBAND
INTIMPIERCING
DERMAL ANCHOR UND SKIN DIVER

Heißrosa
Hot Pink
Violett
Violet
Desinfektionsmedel
Disinfectant Spray
Tatuering Kräm
After Inked

Our Stores.
Öffnungszeiten.

GIAHI

EST.1999

GIAHI
PORE—PRECISION INK
JEWELS & PIERCING

Aftercare Recommendation.
Tattoo Pflege
Tattoo Care
GIAHI

EST.1999
GIAHI
PORE—PRECISION INK
JEWELS & PIERCING

WÄHREND DER HEILUNGSZEIT

- BITTE BERÜHRE DEIN PIERCING NUR MIT SAUBEREN HÄNDEN
- DEN PIERCINGSCHMUCK AUF KEINEN FALL SELBST ENTFERNEN
- DEN SCHMUCK NICHT UNNÖTIG HIN UND HER BEWEGEN
- AUF SONNE, SOLARIUM, SAUNA UND BADEN GANZ VERZICHTEN

NORMALE REAKTIONEN AUF EIN PIERCING

- ANSCHWELLEN DER BETROFFENEN KÖRPERSTELLE
- LEICHTES BRENNEN
- LEICHTER SCHMERZ
- LEICHTE RÖTUNG
- AUSTRETEN VON WUNDFLÜSSIGKEIT
- MINIMALE BLUTUNG

DIESE REAKTIONEN BEWEGEN SICH IM ÜBLICHEN RAHMEN UND SIND KEIN ANLASS ZUR SORGE. SOLLTEST DU ANDERS REAGIEREN ODER UNSICHER SEIN, RUF UNS AM BESTEN AN ODER KOMM DIREKT BEI UNS IM STORE VORBEI.

PFLEGEMITTEL

UM DIE KÖRPEREIGENEN HEILKRÄFTE ZU UNTERSTÜTZEN, EMPFEHLEN WIR DIR FOLGENDE PFLEGEMITTEL

- PIERCINGS JEGLICHER ART: GIAHI CARE
- PIERCINGS IM ORAL- UND INTIMBEREICH: H2OCEAN

VON DER VERWENDUNG VON SALBEN UND CREMES RATEN WIR AB, DA DIESE DEN STICHKANAL VERSTOPFEN KÖNNEN.

So bleiben Du und Dein Piercing für immer Freunde.

Damit dein neues Piercing gut verheilt und du lange Freude an deinem Schmuck hast, sind einige Dinge zu beachten. Wir erklären dir hier alles Schritt für Schritt. Wenn du eine Frage hast, sind wir immer für dich da.

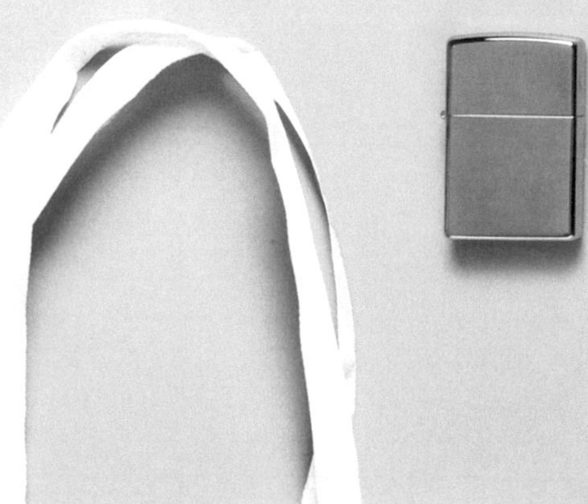

Robert Burns Hotel

RESTAURANT

Melbourne, Australia, *by Alter*

A LOCAL COLLINGWOOD LEGEND, TELLING OF A TRANSATLANTIC ALLIANCE: RECENTLY REBRANDED BY ALTER, THE ROBERT BURNS HOTEL AMALGAMATES THE TASTES OF SCOTLAND AND SPAIN.

A house with a Scottish name is situated in Australia, and, since Spaniard Urbano Gutierrez introduced his favorite flavor to the classic Collingwood pub in 1984, it is home to truly traditional Spanish cuisine. Now headed by a different, yet still Spanish team, the Robert Burns Hotel continues to serve Hispanic meals on Melbourne's iconic Smith Street, but has extended its offerings to include hosting functions for many occasions and sizes, as well as organizing special Spanish-flavored events, like Flamenco evenings. Notwithstanding its name, the Robert Burns Hotel does not fulfill the function of a harborage. As a restaurant and bar, however, it has a longstanding history and has come to be considered a local Collingwood legend. Aspiring to keep the legend alive, Alter rebranded the newly refurbished Robert Burns Hotel, drawing inspiration from the restaurant's famous namesake, Scotland's favorite son and national poet.

¡1 FREE
BEBIDA
&
TAPAS!
ROBERT BURNS HOTEL

FEEDBACK

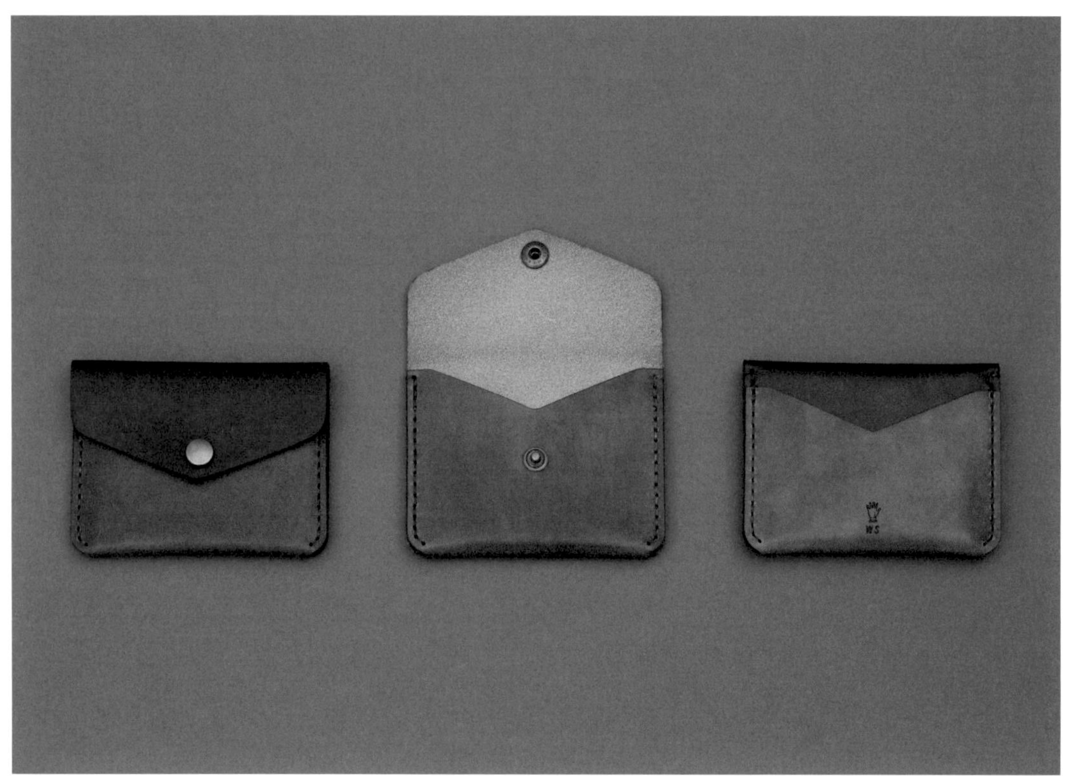

Winter Session started as a side project by Roy Katz, Tanya Fleisher, and their barista friend Tristan Coulter, co founder of Gaslight Coffee Roasters. Seeking to explore new creative ideas and build on their background in the arts, design, and architecture, the three began sewing bags and aprons in a storefront apartment in Chicago. Spurred by the success of the small accessory brand, they soon professionalized the production means, started processing leatherwork, and moved into their larger Denver workshop in early 2013. The Winter Session brand was worked out in close collaboration with Chicago-based photographer and art director Nathan Michael, who drew inspiration from the geometric graphic iconography of contemporary streetwear companies, combining it with cues from the understated corporate language of classy craft labels. Altogether, he arrived at an accessible and appealing visual vocabulary that reflects the refined simplicity of Winter Session's accessory range and adapts to various scales and applications. Featuring an unfussy font backed by a somewhat universal symbol, it speaks to a design-conscious audience indicating myriad meanings, like a humble greeting or an open welcome, and simply stands as a reminder of the manufactory's most important instrument. The waves in the background bring to mind the momentum and weltering workings of Winter Session's prospering production plant.

"NOW OR NEVER." IF WINTER SESSION ARE NOT BUSY HANDCRAFTING HIGH-STANDARD BAGS AND OTHER LEATHER PRODUCTS, THEY ARE LASER-CUTTING LABELS, RUBBER STAMPING STATIONERY, OR INSCRIBING CUSTOM PENCILS WITH THE COMPANY'S MOTTOS.

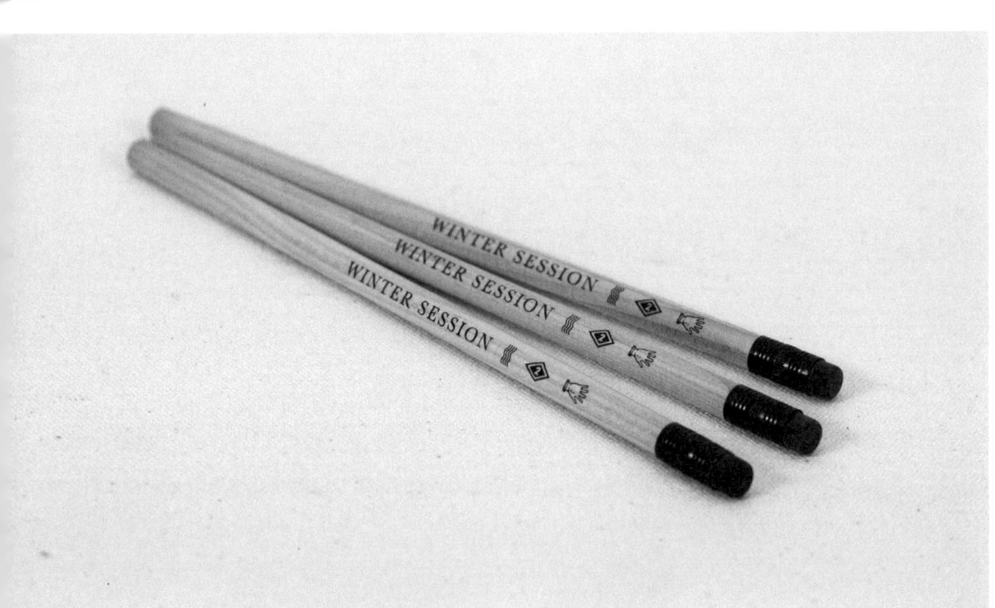

Winter Session

LEATHER ACCESSORIES

Denver, CO, USA, *by Nathan Michael*

Kinegé

ACUPUNCTURE & HOMEOTHERAPY PRACTICE

Barcelona, Spain, *by Design Studio of Both*

INSPIRED BY THE PRACTICE OF CHINESE ACUPUNCTURE: DESIGN STUDIO OF BOTH'S BRAND FOR BARCELONA-BASED PHYSIOTHERAPY CENTER KINEGÉ IS CLASSIC AND TO THE POINT.

Kinegé is a Barcelona-based physiotherapy center and the practice of homeopathic physician and physiotherapist Gemma Torné. Trained in traditional Chinese medicine, Torné takes a holistic approach to his patients' problems, resorting to herbal remedies and hands-on manipulative methods such as acupuncture, kinesio taping, and traditional Tuina treatments to revive and relax both body and soul. In keeping with Kinegé's Far East formulation, Design Studio of Both developed a clear corporate identity for the center. Setting sober type against sincere photographic details, they arrived at an aesthetic solution that pays tribute to the physiotherapist's premise to treat the patient as the protagonist, with quality as a priority.

**"EL PACIENTE
ES EL PROTAGONISTA,
LA CALIDAD NUESTRA
PRIORIDAD"**

GEMMA TORNE ORTEGA

Fisioterapeuta diplomada por UAB en 2003, acupuntora y especialista en medicina tradicional china 2006, homeópata I unicista, especializada en neurología, problemas deportivos, traumatológicos con amplia experiencia laboral en hospitales, mutuas, CAPs y consulta privada.

HOMEOPATÍA

La homeopatía es un método curativo que empezó a practicarse hace 180 años en Alemania y se extendió rápidamente debido a su efectividad. Se diferencia en casi todo de la medicina alopática o la que conocemos y busca métodos curativos sin tener la agresividad y contraindicaciones de los medicamentos que usualmente se usan. La homeopatía es un método curativo que estimula su propio cuerpo a que se cure él mismo.

Se usa y es una alternativa:

Problemas durante el embarazo
Niños (bronquitis, resfriados, asma, alergias, eczemas...)
Problemas emocionales
Hipertensión
Desórdenes digestivos
Problemas oftalmológicos
Problemas musculares
Problemas óseos
Migrañas, dolores de cabeza
Miedos y fobias
Depresiones

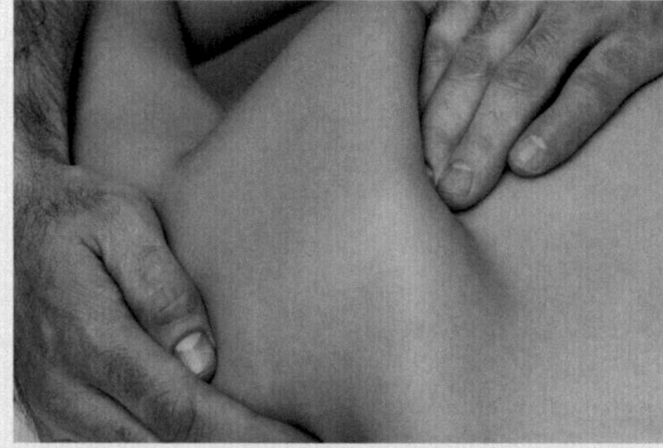

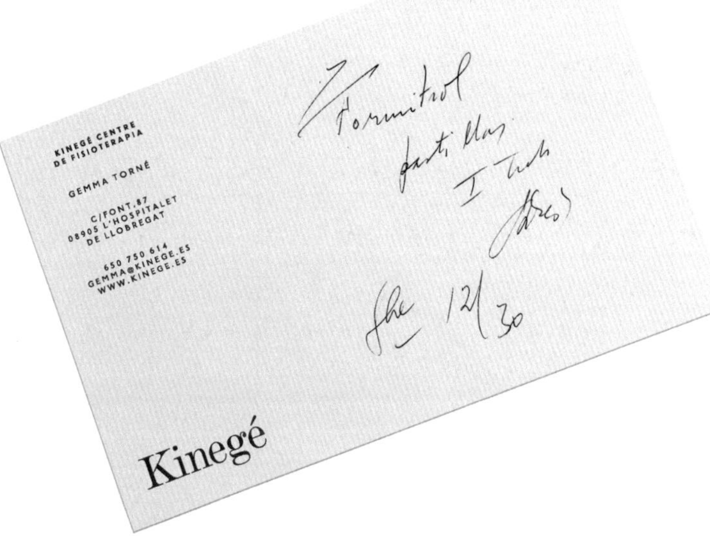

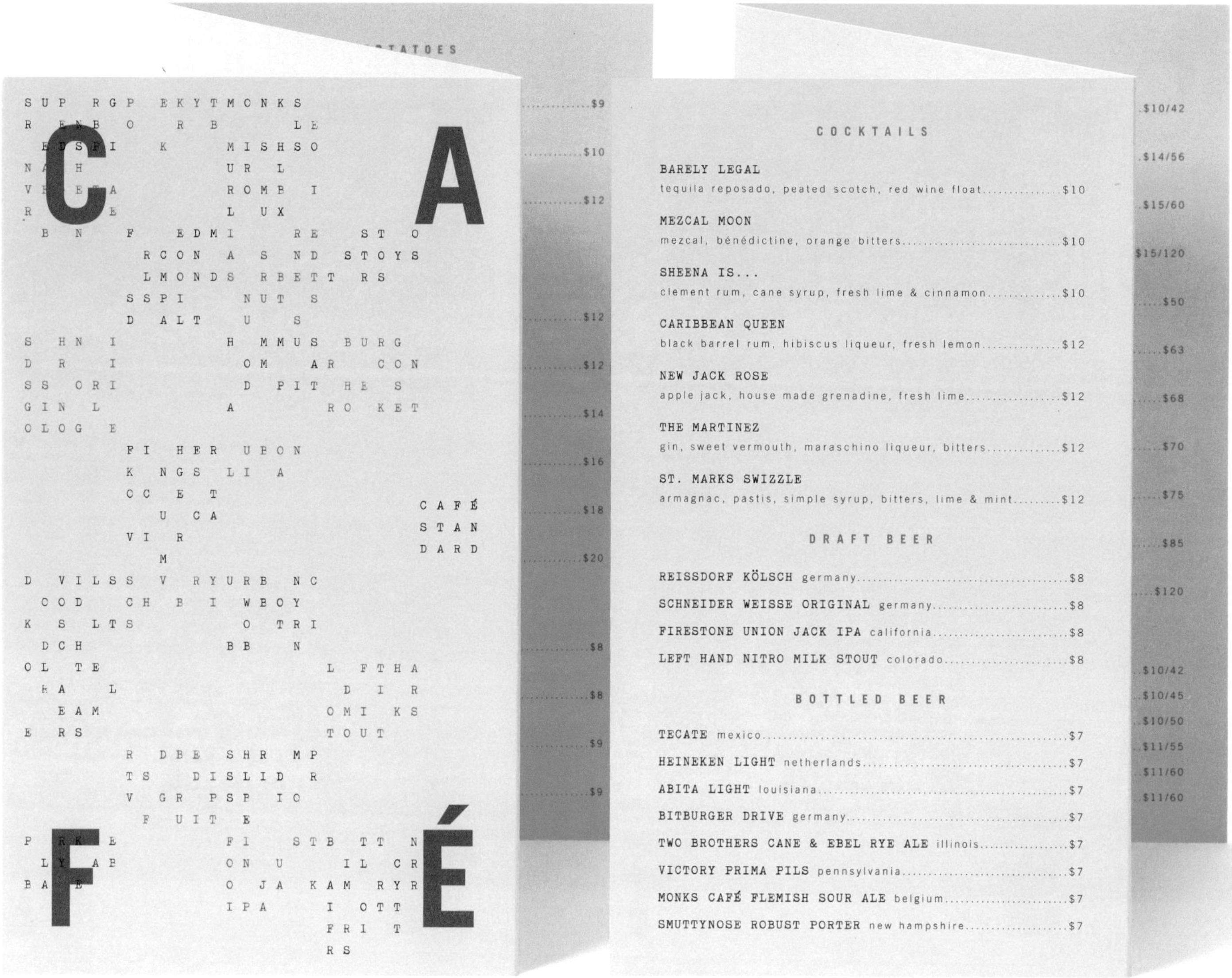

COCKTAILS

BARELY LEGAL
tequila reposado, peated scotch, red wine float.............. $10

MEZCAL MOON
mezcal, bénédictine, orange bitters.............................. $10

SHEENA IS...
clement rum, cane syrup, fresh lime & cinnamon............. $10

CARIBBEAN QUEEN
black barrel rum, hibiscus liqueur, fresh lemon.............. $12

NEW JACK ROSE
apple jack, house made grenadine, fresh lime.................. $12

THE MARTINEZ
gin, sweet vermouth, maraschino liqueur, bitters............. $12

ST. MARKS SWIZZLE
armagnac, pastis, simple syrup, bitters, lime & mint......... $12

DRAFT BEER

REISSDORF KÖLSCH germany.. $8
SCHNEIDER WEISSE ORIGINAL germany........................... $8
FIRESTONE UNION JACK IPA california........................... $8
LEFT HAND NITRO MILK STOUT colorado.......................... $8

BOTTLED BEER

TECATE mexico.. $7
HEINEKEN LIGHT netherlands.. $7
ABITA LIGHT louisiana... $7
BITBURGER DRIVE germany.. $7
TWO BROTHERS CANE & EBEL RYE ALE illinois.................. $7
VICTORY PRIMA PILS pennsylvania..................................... $7
MONKS CAFÉ FLEMISH SOUR ALE belgium........................ $7
SMUTTYNOSE ROBUST PORTER new hampshire.................... $7

Café Standard

COFFEE SHOP & BAR

New York, NY, USA, *by Triboro*

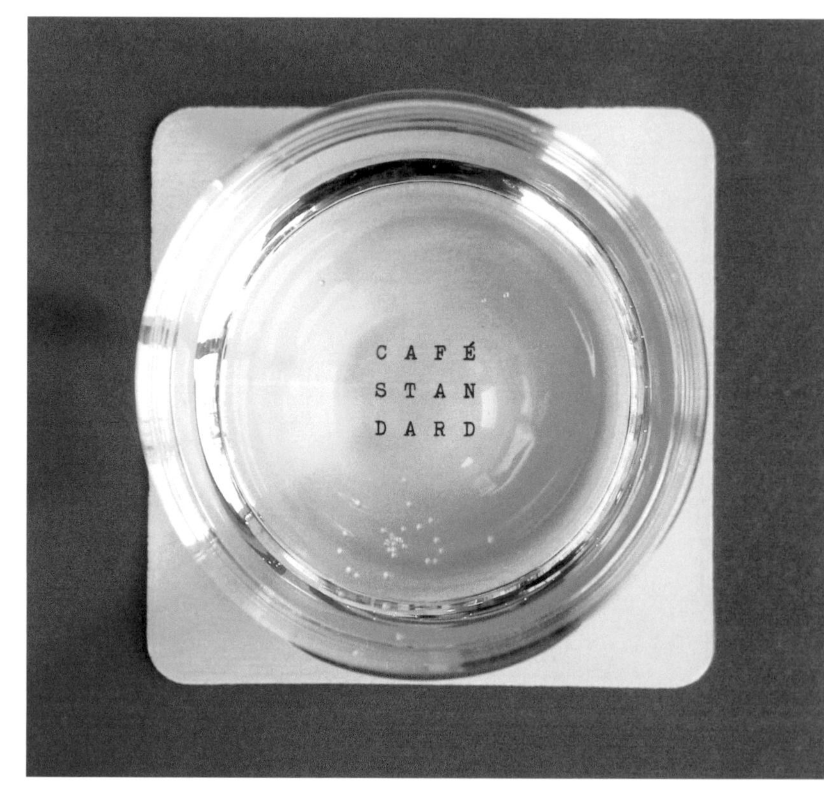

WITH ITS LOCATION STEEPED IN LEGEND, CAFÉ STANDARD'S GASTRO BRAND STRIVES TO SET STANDARDS IN STYLE AND BRING BACK A BIT OF THE BEAT GENERATION.

Located on New York's legendary wery street, the Standard Hotel's st Village branch has become a me away from home for a variety regular visitors, and its vibrant fé provides Village residents with a neighborhood hotspot. Combining the charm of a simple street eatery with the electricity of a bustling bar, Café Standard's identity ties in with the iconic Standard Hotel style. Besides, its brand by Triboro is tightly anchored with the Bowery's past, bringing in a taste of the Beat Generation's pulsating poetic atmosphere. The communication concept consists of two parts: the word C A F É placed in the corners of all applications, and additional typographic content typed out on an old typewriter that prompted the designers to play with words along the lines of concrete poetry.

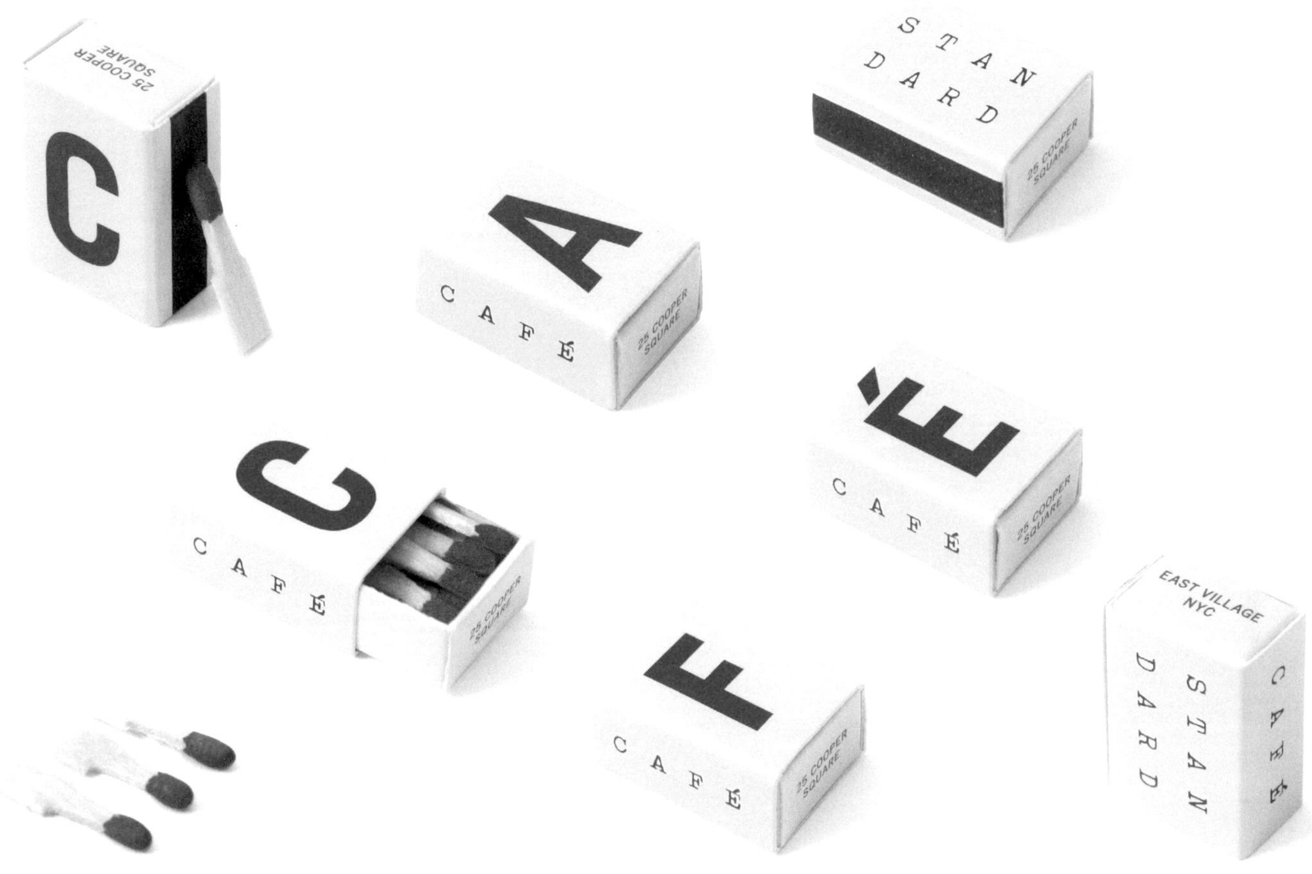

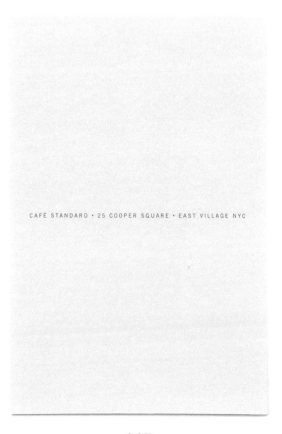

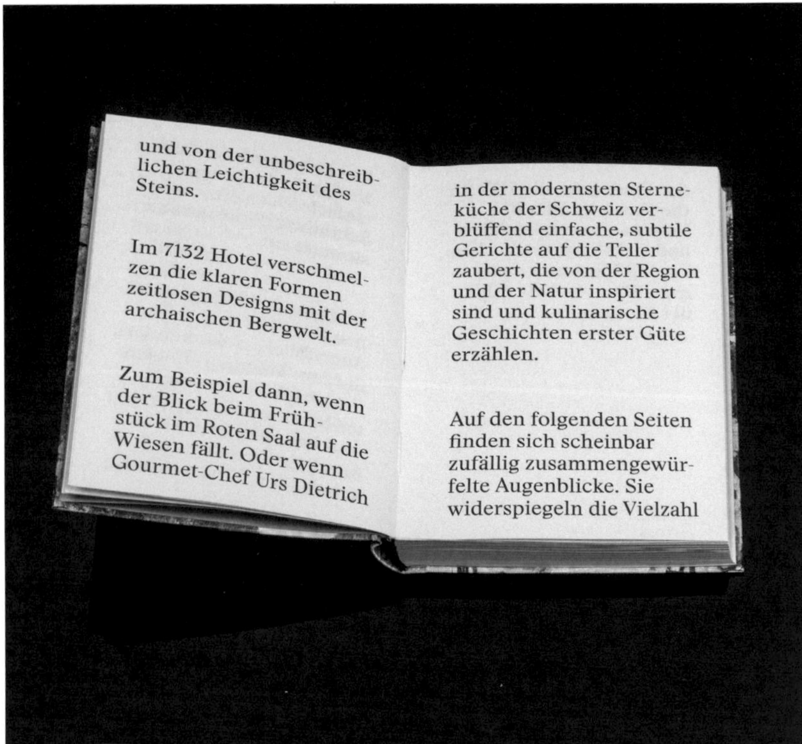

und von der unbeschreiblichen Leichtigkeit des Steins.

Im 7132 Hotel verschmelzen die klaren Formen zeitlosen Designs mit der archaischen Bergwelt.

Zum Beispiel dann, wenn der Blick beim Frühstück im Roten Saal auf die Wiesen fällt. Oder wenn Gourmet-Chef Urs Dietrich

in der modernsten Sterneküche der Schweiz verblüffend einfache, subtile Gerichte auf die Teller zaubert, die von der Region und der Natur inspiriert sind und kulinarische Geschichten erster Güte erzählen.

Auf den folgenden Seiten finden sich scheinbar zufällig zusammengewürfelte Augenblicke. Sie widerspiegeln die Vielzahl

7132

HOTEL & THERMAL SPA

Vals, Switzerland, *by Raffinerie AG für Gestaltung*

MUCH MORE THAN A MERE NUMBER: 7132 COUNTERS TAWDRY MASS TOURISM WITH SUPERB STYLE AND A MONUMENTAL THERMAL SPA.

Notwithstanding its impersonal name, the hotel 7132 takes a personalized and holistic approach to tourism. Reciting the postal code of its picturesque place, the number rather refers to the touristic values of the Vals Valley, a region rich in thermal springs. One of them is attached to the hotel, housed in an incredible structure by Swiss architect Peter Zumthor. A tribute to the archaic world of the Vals Valley, he has stacked 60,000 slabs of Vals quartzite into a splendid thermal spa. Seeking to establish a brand that would befit both the hotel's sophisticated architectural ambience and its scenic surroundings, while catering to an upmarket clientele, the 7132 AG approached Raffinerie AG für Gestaltung, who arrived at a corporate identity concept combining the edgy character of the Vals quartzite with suave, international charm.

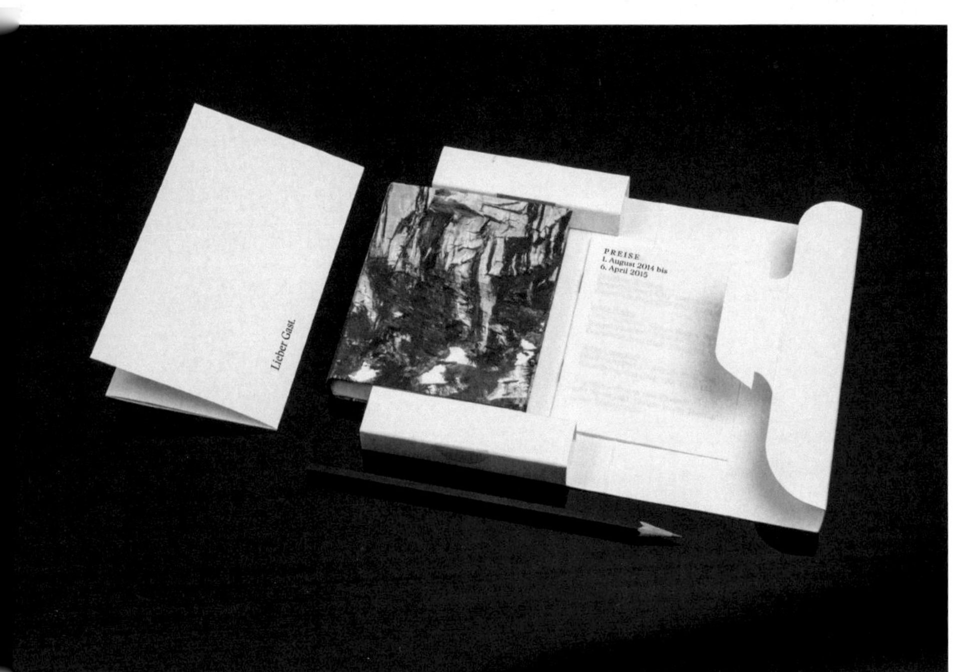

7132

7132 HOTEL 7132 VALS

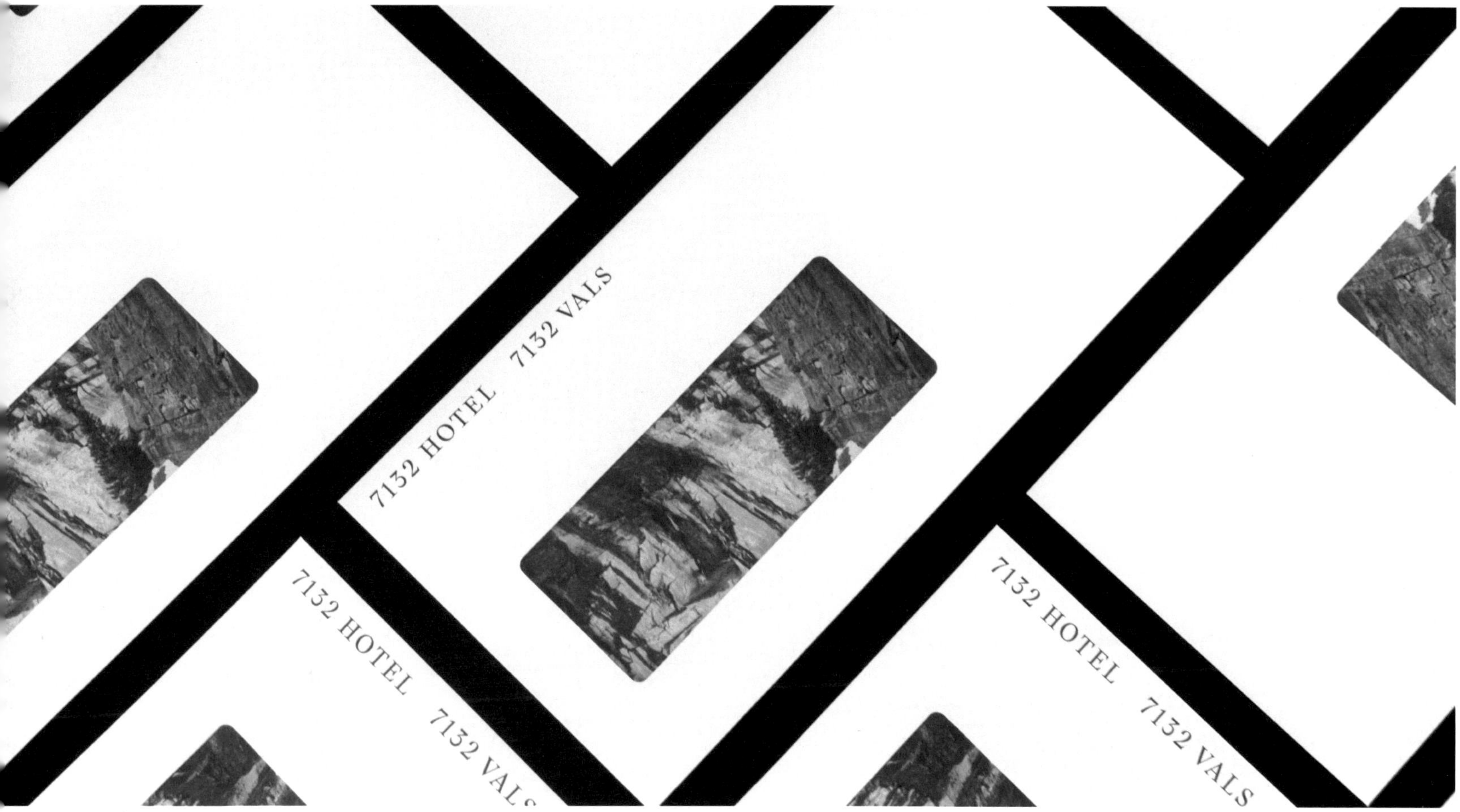

ManuTeeFaktur

TEA MAKER

Berlin, Germany, *by Manu Kumar*

BRINGING MEMORIES OF FAR-OFF MARKETS, NOMADIC TENTS, AND TRADITIONAL TEA ROOMS BACK TO BERLIN, MANU KUMAR OPENED HIS OWN TEA MANUFACTORY IN MELDED KREUZBERG. FOR THE BRAND, HE GOT BY WITH A LITTLE HELP FROM HIS FRIENDS.

Having tasted traditional tea on his travels, Manu Kumar found himself ıssing comparable blends back home in Berlin and founded ManuTeeFaktur, authentic tea atelier tucked away in a clandestine commercial backyard. lmut Stummer, a commercial copywriter and longtime friend, came up with the ɔniker, combining the founder's first name Manu with tea and his traditional take it. He also helped get the phrasing right to print the business' background story on the bottles—or rather, onto their functional labels, designed by befriended creative director Michael Schickinger of Lambs and Lions. Like the making of their tea, ManuTeeFaktur's labels and cartons are rolled, glued, and stamped by hand. Besides flavored fruit and herbal blends sold in select cafés across the city or directly from the Kreuzberg tasting room and production plant, ManuTeeFaktur's selection comprises chilled ice teas for the summer that come in reusable milk bottles.

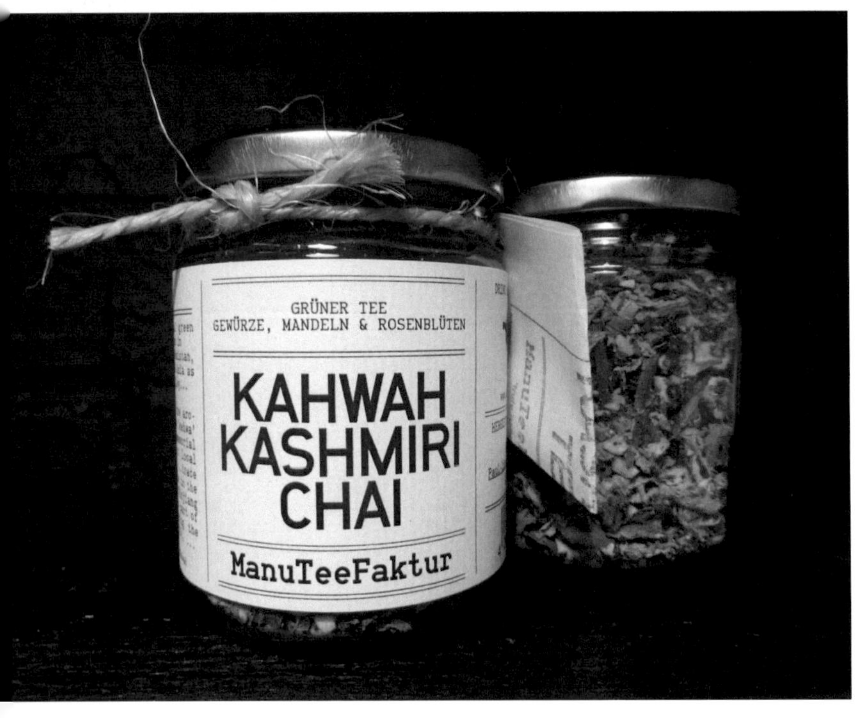
GRÜNER TEE
GEWÜRZE, MANDELN & ROSENBLÜTEN
KAHWAH
KASHMIRI
CHAI
ManuTeeFaktur

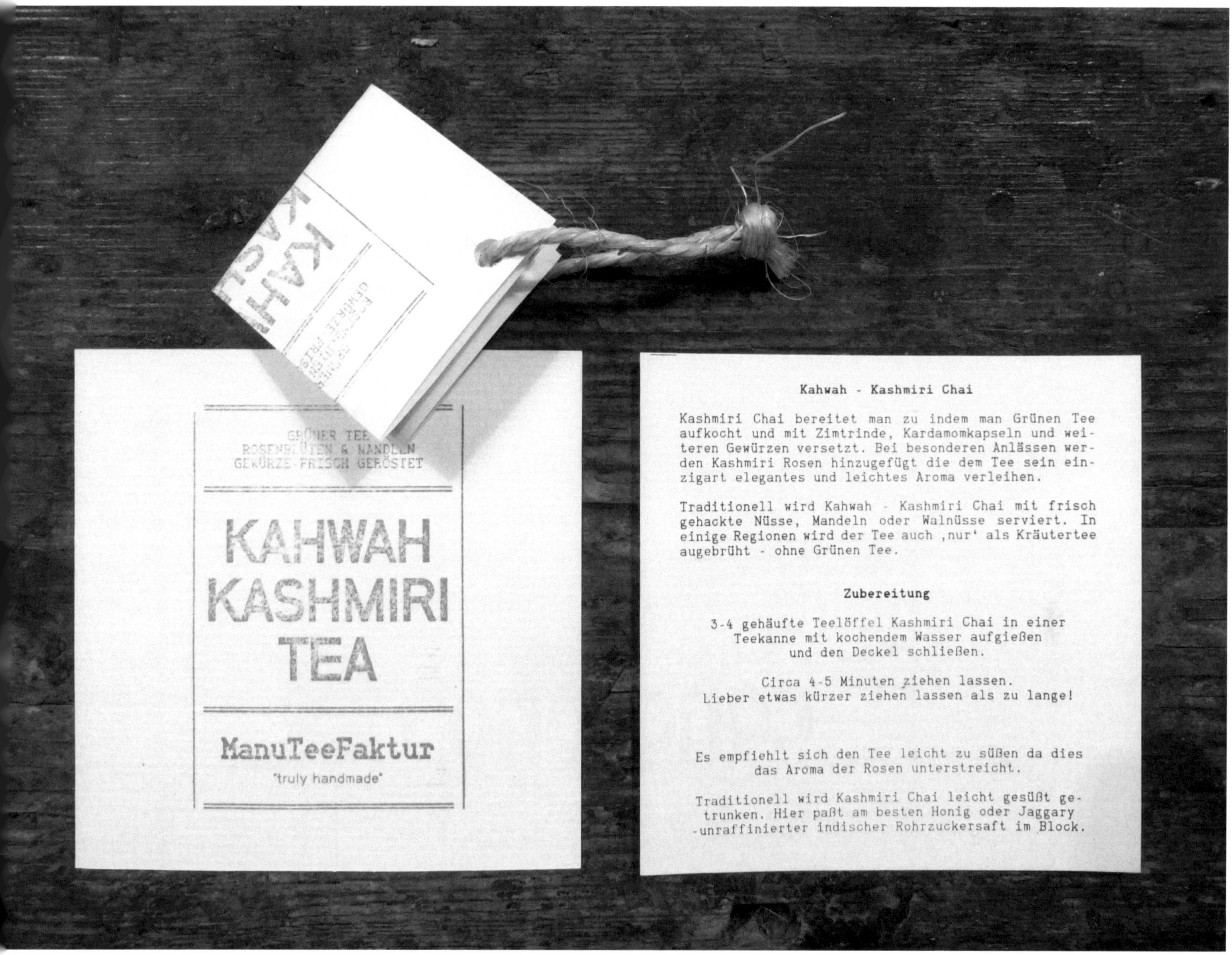

GRÜNER TEE
ROSENBLÜTEN & MANDELN
GEWÜRZE FRISCH GERÖSTET

KAHWAH
KASHMIRI
TEA

ManuTeeFaktur
"truly handmade"

Kahwah - Kashmiri Chai

Kashmiri Chai bereitet man zu indem man Grünen Tee aufkocht und mit Zimtrinde, Kardamomkapseln und weiteren Gewürzen versetzt. Bei besonderen Anlässen werden Kashmiri Rosen hinzugefügt die dem Tee sein einzigart elegantes und leichtes Aroma verleihen.

Traditionell wird Kahwah - Kashmiri Chai mit frisch gehackte Nüsse, Mandeln oder Walnüsse serviert. In einige Regionen wird der Tee auch ‚nur' als Kräutertee augebrüht - ohne Grünen Tee.

Zubereitung

3-4 gehäufte Teelöffel Kashmiri Chai in einer Teekanne mit kochendem Wasser aufgießen und den Deckel schließen.

Circa 4-5 Minuten ziehen lassen.
Lieber etwas kürzer ziehen lassen als zu lange!

Es empfiehlt sich den Tee leicht zu süßen da dies das Aroma der Rosen unterstreicht.

Traditionell wird Kashmiri Chai leicht gesüßt getrunken. Hier paßt am besten Honig oder Jaggary -unraffinierter indischer Rohrzuckersaft im Block.

Optimo Hats

HAT MAKER

Chicago, IL, USA, *by Knoed*

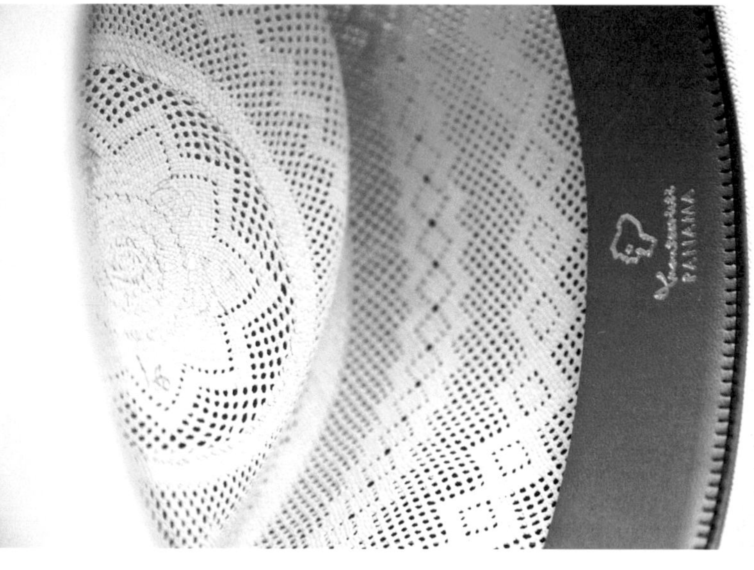

A HANGOVER FROM THE OLD TIMES, OPTIMO HATS HOLD ONTO THE TRADITION OF CUSTOM HATS AND HIGH-QUALITY CRAFTSMANSHIP.

Chicago-based custom hatter Optimo Hats Co. appears as a bastion of a bygone age and a perishing branch of business. The company's success story began with a series of unfinished Panama straw hats that Optimo Hat Co. owner Graham Thompson brought back home from a trip to Hawaii. As those hats still needed to be blocked, he brought them to master hatter Johnny Tyus, who quickly became his mentor, and whose workshop he would take over in 1995. Since then, Thompson and his team have hand-produced bespoke headpieces from the finest fur-felt and similarly high-end materials, all carefully sourced and mostly imported from Portugal. Customizing exquisite cuts for each and every customer, the business is much celebrated by both Chicago locals and celebrities—many Optimo hats have even made it into movies. In good time for the hat's comeback into the real world's weekday fashion, Optimo have hooked up with Knoed to refine their identity. The designers developed new hat-box packaging as well as a range of print and online materials, and continue to maintain the brand.

OPTIMO
FINE HATS

CHICAGO, ILLINOIS 606
HANDLE YOUR HAT GENTLY
BY THE BRIM, DO NOT PINCH THE CROWN
SET YOUR HAT ON FLAT SURFACES
BRIM-UP, TO MAINTAIN ITS SHAPE
IF YOUR HAT GETS WET
LET IT AIR-DRY NATURALLY

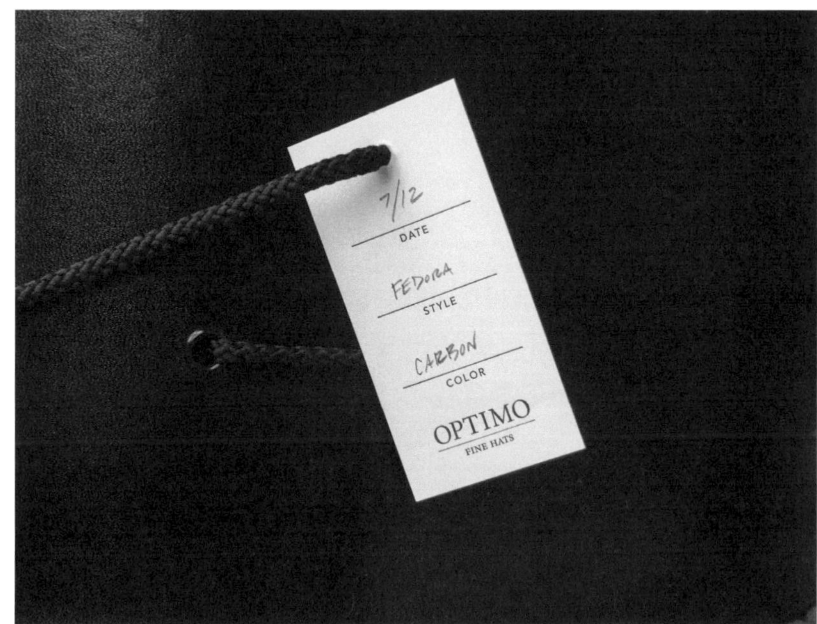
7/12
DATE
FEDORA
STYLE
CARBON
COLOR
OPTIMO
FINE HATS

OPTIMO
FINE HATS
OPTIMO
from the
HATTER'S BENCH
THE OPTIMO MILAN STRAW
Bringing Back A Legend
IN THIS ISSUE
OTHER ISSUES
DOWNLOAD
HISTORY OF THE NAME MILAN

OPTIMO
FINE HATS
HANDLE YOUR HAT GENTLY
BY THE BRIM, DO NOT PINCH THE CROWN
SET YOUR HAT ON FLAT SURFACES
BRIM-UP, TO MAINTAIN ITS SHAPE
IF YOUR HAT GETS WET
LET IT AIR-DRY NATURALLY
FORM YOUR HAT GENTLY BACK INTO SHAPE
IF IT IS CRUSHED
PLACE YOUR HAT IN THIS BOX
FOR LONG-TERM STORAGE
STORE YOUR HAT
IN A COOL, DRY ENVIRONMENT
USE A LINT ROLLER
TO GENTLY REMOVE DUST AND DEBRIS
SEND YOUR HAT BACK TO OPTIMO ANNUALLY
FOR EXPERT HAT CLEANING AND RENOVATION
OPTIMO
FINE HATS
DATE
STYLE
COLOR
OPTIMO
FINE HATS
OPTIMO
FINE HATS
GRAHAM THOMPSON
OPTIMOHATS.COM

ICE CREAM & WAFFLE BAR

3ruges, Belgium, by Skinn Branding Agency

PREPPY ICE CREAM PARLOR OYYA PEPS UP OLD BRUGE'S PICTURESQUE PEDESTRIAN PRECINCT.

Based in the historic city center of Bruges, the Oyya bar serves chilly ·e cream, frozen yogurt, and milkshakes contrasted with classic, warm ·elgian waffles. While the latter are freshly baked in front of the customers' yes while they wait, Oyya's ice cream is prepared on a daily basis, with otating flavors such as chocolate cookie, bounty, or classy crème brûlée, ulled from the fixed set of 28 options in the chef's recipe book. The designers t Skinn were consulted to elaborate on the complete branding concept for)yya, and arrived at a thrifty typographic solution of soft appeal. Clear and onsistently used across stickers, cone sleeves, signage, and the sales team's ttire, the unagitated logo lettering unifies all of Oyya's communications.

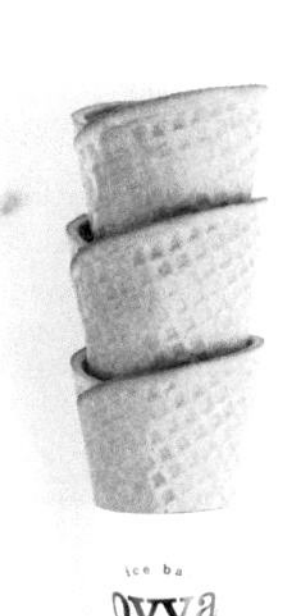

ice bar
oyya®

Noordzandstraat N° 01
8000 Brugge
t: +32 (0)50 333 213
e: info@oyya.be
www.oyya.be

ice bar
oyya

Wildkop is a specialty store set up by Ann De Wilde and Christophe De Muynck, a duo whose shared passion for well-decorated Mediterranean dishes resulted in a promising retail approach. With a product range spanning all sorts of eating equipment from spices and traditional tableware to table linens and cookbooks, Wildkop propagates a holistic perspective towards culinary pleasure and authentic cookery through and through. Branding specialists Skinn served the shop with a savory logo, labels, stationery, and sophisticated packaging solutions for the Wildkop product line.

Wildkop

DELICATESSEN

Nieuwpoort, Belgium
by Skinn Branding Agency

WILDKOP RETAILS MEDITERRANEAN MUNCHIES AND MORE, ALL WRAPPED WITH WONDERFULLY UNRUFFLED GRAPHICS.

WILDKOP
SPECERIJEN & CO.

WILDKOP
SPECERIJEN & CO.
NIEUWPOORT

WILDKOP

Chelsea
Farmers
Club

Berlin Schlüterstraße 50 T 030 8872 7474 **Düsseldorf** Kasernenstraße 23 T 0211 1684 457
info@chelseafarmersclub.de www.chelseafarmersclub.de

Chelsea Farmers Club

GARMENTS & GATHERINGS

Berlin and Duesseldorf, Germany, *by Studio Mahr*

WARENGUTSCHEIN

Euro

Für ein wundervolles Einkaufsvergnügen.

Inklusive sehr viel Gin & mehr oder weniger passablen Witzen.

Berlin, den

Chelsea Farmers Club

Landwirtschaft braucht jeder

"BRITISH FORMAL DRESS, BAGGAGE & GIN": CHELSEA FARMERS CLUB DELIVERS BLACK BRITISH THREE-PIECE SUITS, CLASSY COMMODITIES, AND A DEADPAN SENSE OF SATIRE.

Established in 2005 in Berlin, Chelsea Farmers Club supplies German anglophiles with a selection of traditional British garments and accessories—wearable commodities, rather than fashion. Its founder, Hamburg-born Christoph Tophinke, sets great store by that fact. Catering to fine drinks, sophisticated chatter, concerts, and other frameworks for social gathering, he considers CFC first and foremost a club, its concept a coincidence and some sort of a joke. Jolly it is, as are its communications. Designed by Studio Mahr with the mission to befit both CFC's classy clothing and its medley club culture, they combine the serious looks of a classic gentlemen's outfitter with tipsy taste and pub philosophical phrasings.

DER FERNSEHSMOKING

DAME IM PELZ

100 THINGS YOU'VE NEVER XXXED BEFORE

NEVER HEARD THINGS LIKE THAT BEFORE. NEVER LOVED AN ANGEL BEFORE. NEVER ATE AN EYE BEFORE. NEVER CONSTRUCTED THE BOMB BEFORE. NEVER LAUGHED WITH A BROKEN HEART BEFORE. NEVER SAW A THREE-LEGGED MONSTER BEFORE. NEVER MET THE KING BEFORE. NEVER PLAYED A BOND GIRL BEFORE. NEVER WROTE A HIT BEFORE. NEVER WORE UGLY SHOES BEFORE. NEVER EMAILED GOD BEFORE. NEVER READ 100 THINGS I'VE NEVER DONE BEFORE. BEFORE. NEVER DRUNK TOO LITTLE BEFORE. NEVER BEEN TOO NICE BEFORE. **NEVER BEEN NAKED TO THE OFFICE BEFORE.** NEVER BROKE A PROMISE BEFORE. NEVER STOPPED THINKING DIRTY THINGS BEFORE. NEVER KISSED THE POPE BEFORE. NEVER SAID NEVER BEFORE. NEVER LANDED A 747 BEFORE. NEVER FOUGHT A DRAGON BEFORE. NEVER TWITTERED GOETHE'S FAUST BEFORE. NEVER STUDIED ROCKET SCIENCE BEFORE. NEVER KNEW WHERE ALL THE FLOWERS HAVE GONE BEFORE. NEVER LIKED MY OWN STATUS BEFORE. NEVER WALKED ON THE MOON BEFORE. NEVER TALKED TO AN OLD FURRY WOMAN BEFORE. **NEVER HUNG THE DJ BEFORE.** NEVER LISTENED TO THE FOG BEFORE. NEVER NOTICED STICKY NOTES BEFORE. NEVER SWITCHED TO PLAN Z BEFORE. NEVER DISRESPECTED FATHER NATURE BEFORE. NEVER FOOLED A FOOL WHO FOOLS A FOOL BEFORE. NEVER CRIED TO CELINE DION BEFORE. NEVER CHANGED A WINNING TEAM BEFORE. NEVER SLEPT TOO LONG BEFORE. NEVER MET AN ALIEN BEFORE. NEVER LEARNED ESPERANTO BEFORE. NEVER BELIEVED IN NUMBERS BEFORE. NEVER FELT LIKE FELT BEFORE. NEVER DREAMT OF SAUSSAGES BEFORE. **NEVER FINISHED A DIET BEFORE.** NEVER INVENTED THE LIGHTBULB BEFORE. NEVER HAD A BEARD LIKE ZZ-TOP BEFORE. **NEVER OVERTOOK MY OWN SHADOW BEFORE.** NEVER TRANSPLANTED A HEART BEFORE. NEVER LAUGHED DURING A FUNERAL BEFORE. NEVER SHOOK, NOT STIRRED BEFORE. NEVER STALKED AN EXFRIEND ON FACEBOOK BEFORE. NEVER LIED ABOUT STALKING EXFRIENDS ON FACEBOOK BEFORE. NEVER BEEN TO JAIL BEFORE. NEVER HARRIED AND SALLIED BEFORE. NEVER RATED MY POO BEFORE. NEVER REACHED THE MILLION BEFORE. NEVER REACHED THE IMPOSSIBLE BEFORE. NEVER YOGAED MY ASS OFF BEFORE. **NEVER KNEW THE WAY TO SAN JOSÉ BEFORE.** NEVER UNDERSTOOD VEGANS BEFORE. NEVER CRIED SOMEONE A RIVER BEFORE. NEVER WITNESSED A CAT-GANGBANG BEFORE. NEVER COLLECTED SOUNDS BEFORE. NEVER WOKE UP IN A TREE BEFORE. NEVER IMAGINED THAT WORK COULD BE RELAXING BEFORE. NEVER HAD THE ONE BIG IDEA BEFORE. NEVER BEEN PRESIDENT BEFORE. NEVER BOUGHT EMOTIONS BEFORE. NEVER TRIPPED OVER MY EGO BEFORE. NEVER BEEN BORED BY MY SOUL BEFORE. NEVER BEEN SO CLOSE BEFORE. NEVER KNEW THE DIFFERENCE BETWEEN „A BING" AND „THE BING". NEVER KILLED MY FEARS BEFORE. NEVER WASTED TOO MANY TEARS BEFORE. NEVER PRETENDED TO DO NOTHING BEFORE. NEVER DELIVERED AN EMAIL PERSONALLY BEFORE. NEVER WANTED TO HURT SOMEONE BEFORE. NEVER OFFENDED THE BOSS BEFORE. NEVER FELL IN LOVE WITH RAIN BEFORE. NEVER CALLED JESUS FROM MY IPHONE BEFORE. NEVER MADE A POTATO MASH-WAR BEFORE. NEVER BEHAVED BEFORE. NEVER SEEN WITH EARS BEFORE. BEFORE. NEVER CHANGED OSAMA WITH OBAMA BEFORE. NEVER GOT CURED BY THE CURE BEFORE. NEVER BOY-GEORGE-MICHAEL-JACKSON-BROWNED SO MUCH BEFORE. NEVER LOREM IPSUM DOLORSIT AMET BEFORE. NEVER HIJACKED A HITCHHIKER BEFORE. **NEVER NEVERED SO MUCH BEFORE.** NEVER LOOPED A LOOP BEFORE. NEVER COMMITED A CRIME BEFORE. NEVER BOUNCED TO THE STARS BEFORE. NEVER INTRODUCED MYSELF WITH MR. KUDDELDADDELDU BEFORE. NEVER WAPBAMBOOGIED TO BEETHOVEN BEFORE. NEVER PAID FOR FEELING OLD BEFORE. NEVER FOUND TWO AND A HALF MEN FUNNY BEFORE. NEVER VISITED A MITTERALTERLICH SPECTACULUM BEFORE. NEVER DRESSED LIKE MISS GAGA BEFORE. NEVER USED THE WORD „GOSH" IN A MEETING BEFORE. NEVER SURPRISED A PRISONER BEFORE. NEVER HAD AN OPINION BEFORE. NEVER TRIED VIAGRA BEFORE. NEVER UNDERSTOOD THE MEANING OF LIFE BEFORE. **NEVER PROUDLY PRESENTED 100 THINGS BEFORE.**

PHILOSOPH UND ENTSORGER

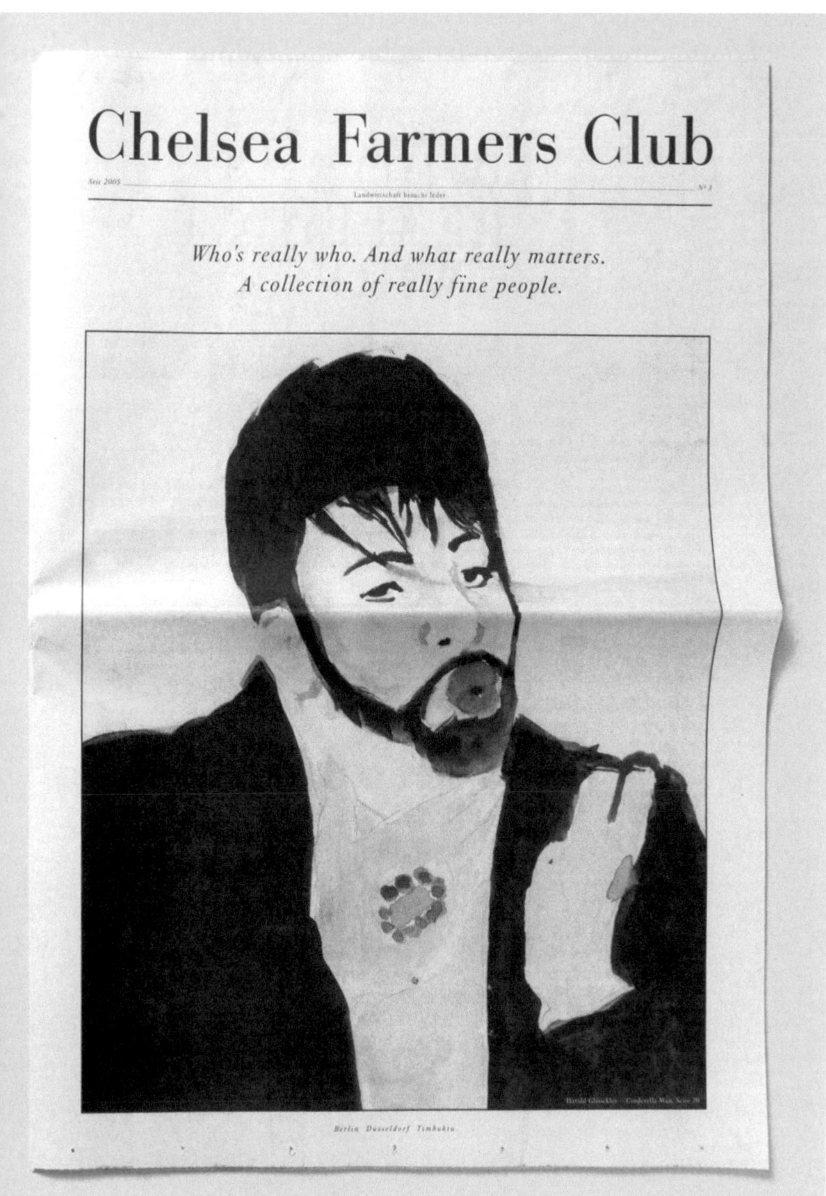
Chelsea Farmers Club
Who's really who. And what really matters.
A collection of really fine people.
Berlin Düsseldorf Timbuktu

Modern
Tea Time:
Gin & Tonic.
FOR THE BEST DRINKS IN THE WORLD, IN THE BEST BARS IN THE WORLD.
DES HERRSCHERS LUSTIGE KLEIDER

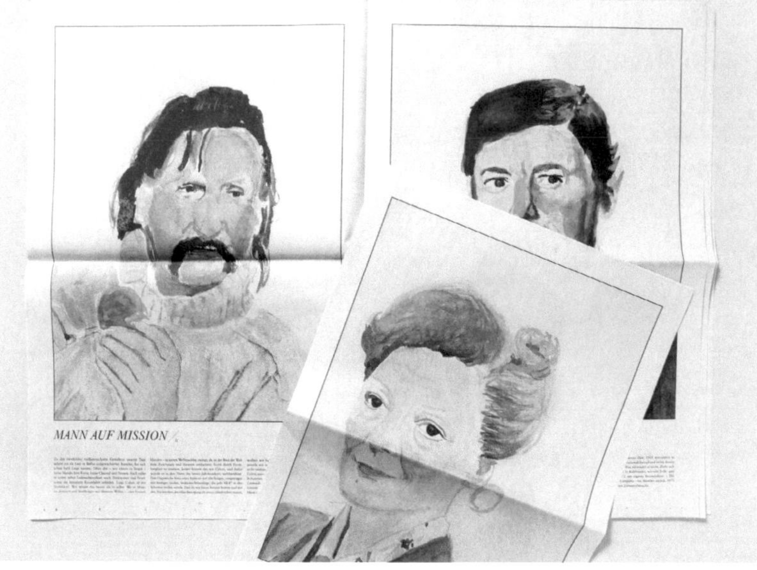
MANN AUF MISSION

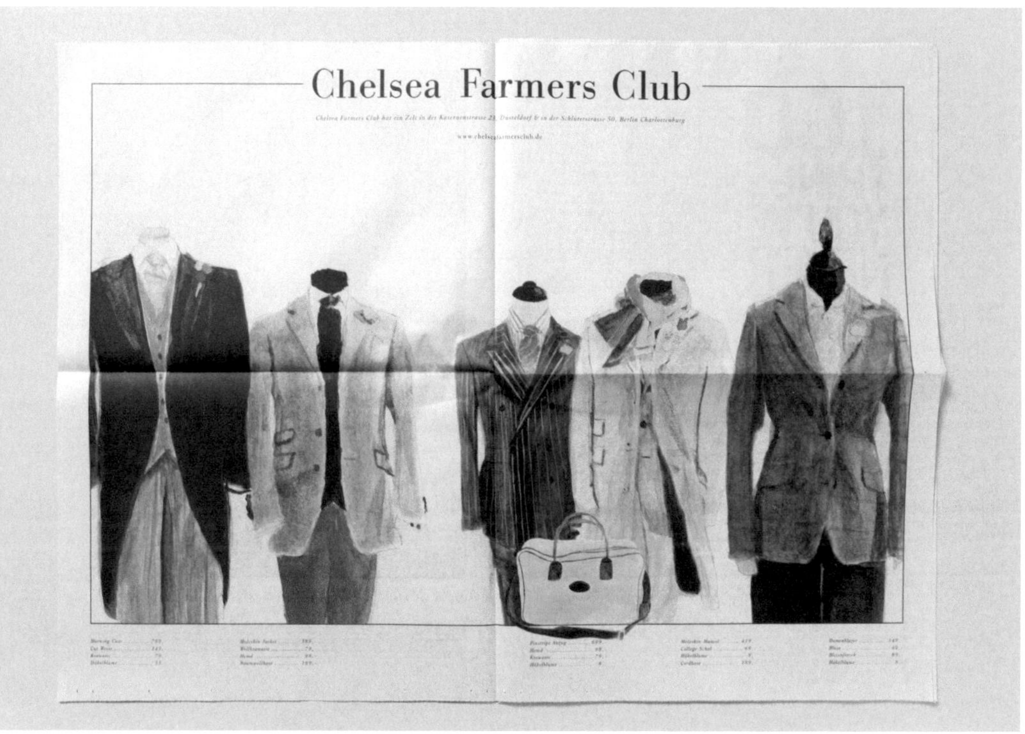
Chelsea Farmers Club

When it's hot
please dress
for the body
you have,
not the body
you want.
Thanks.
Chelsea Farmers Club

Chelsea Farmers Club
MADE IN ENGLAND

Chelsea Farmers Club

Chelsea Farmers Club

GOMPF+
KEHRER
GOMPF+
KEHRER
GOMPF+
KEHRER
GOMPF+KEHRER ALTER SCHLACHTHOF 3 D-76131 KARLSRUHE
Gompf und Kehrer Gbr
Verena Stella Gompf
Cordula Kehrer
USt-IdNr. DE291259128
Alter Schlachthof 3
D-76131 Karlsruhe
+49 721.66 499 743
www.gompf-kehrer.com
info@gompf-kehrer.com
DAB Bank
Bic Code: COBADEHD055
IBAN: DE89 7012 0400 8382 9170 06

Gompf + Kehrer

HOME ACCESSORIES

Karlsruhe, Germany
by Veronika Salzseiler

CONTEMPORARY AND COOPERATIVE: VERONIKA SALZSEILER PRODUCED GOOD-TEMPERED GRAPHICS FOR PRODUCT DESIGNERS GOMPF + KEHRER.

After various positions at home and abroad, product designers Verena Stella Gompf and Cordula Kehrer have settled into their studio in Karlsruhe to work as a team. As Gompf + Kehrer, they dedicate themselves to the design of simplistic home accessories with stories tucked away under smoothly structured surfaces. Their Bow Bins, for example, upcycle unwanted materials, reminding us of developing countries' limited means. Veronika Salzseiler's graphics follow Gompf + Kehrer's fondness for fair trade with thrifty typography and lots of love for fine details.

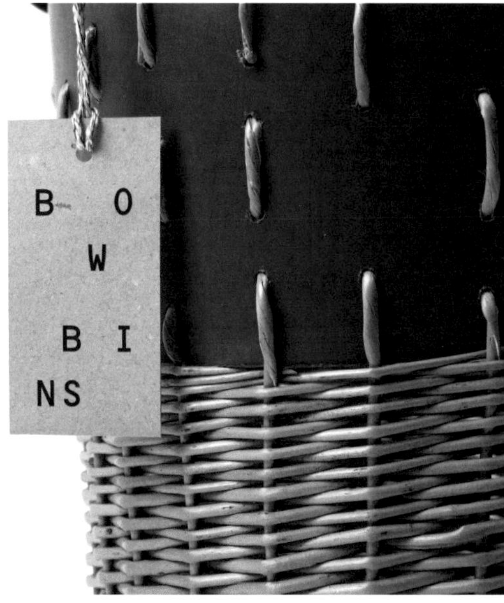

Jay Bennett

ELECTRICIAN

Cornwall, UK, *by Afterhours*

HIGH VOLTAGE MEETS HEAVY METAL: CORNISH ELECTRICIAN JAY BENNETT CHALLENGES HIS COMPETITORS WITH A CORPORATE BRAND OF ELECTRIFYING IMPACT.

English electrician Jay Bennett endeavored to oost his business with a low-cost, yet flashy corporate nage. He assigned the task to Afterhours, who developed budget-conscious branding concept based on a central J-like electrical bolt motif. The stationery is printed digitally on sugar paper stock for a raw, stripped-back aesthetic. Matchbook business cards promote Bennett's services by means of a simple phrase: "Need a light, Boy?" To top off the electrician's self-promotional toolkit, a playful pastiche of a promo music t-shirt is produced annually, announcing his tour of work venues around Devon and Cornwall.

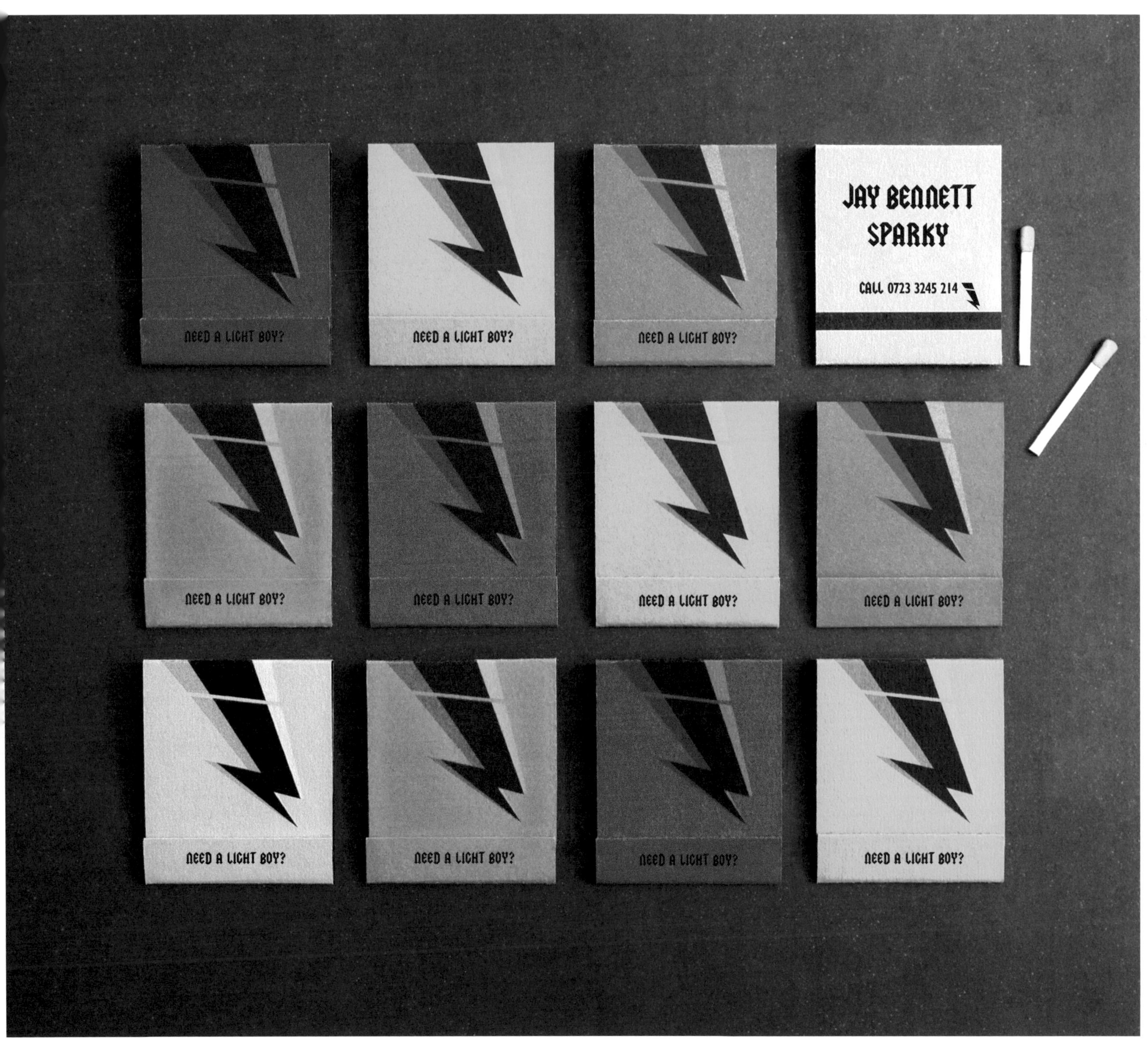

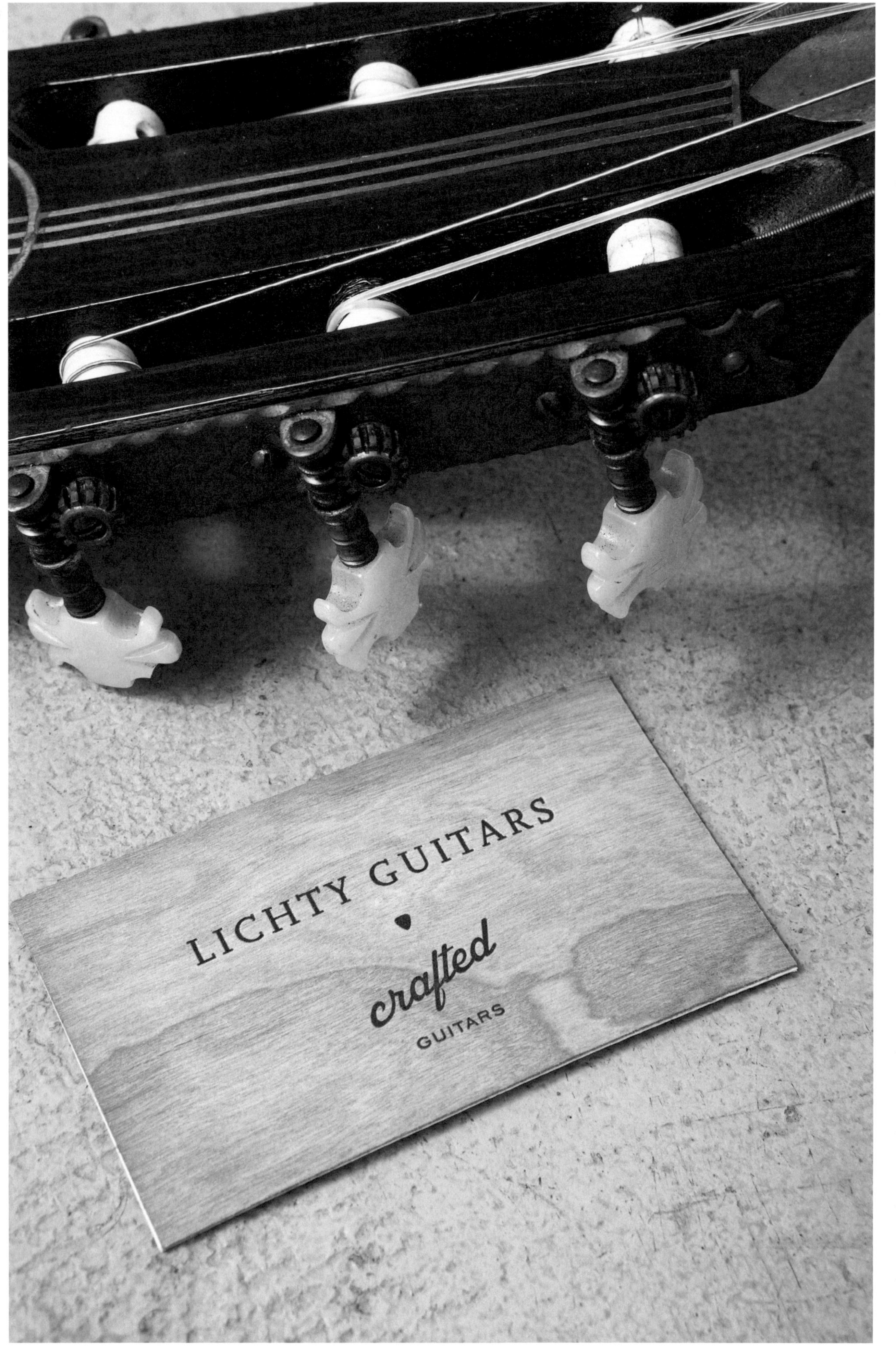

Lichty Guitars

LUTHIER

Tryon, NC, USA
by Stitch Design Co.

JAY LICHTY WAS BUILDING HOMES AS A CONSTRUCTION CONTRACTOR WHEN HE BEGAN HOME-BUILDING UKULELES FOR FUN. ONE CAREFULLY CRAFTED INSTRUMENT LED TO ANOTHER, AND EVENTUALLY TO A CHANGE OF INDUSTRY ALTOGETHER.

Homebuilder Luthier Jay Lichty began making ukuleles when work became scarce in his sector. His expertise grew as he attended guitar-building workshops conducted by established custom builders like Wayne Henderson and Charles Fox, and in 2009 Lichty closed down his construction company to get Lichty Guitars going. After only a year, world-touring musicians lined up for a custom-made Lichty. While Jay Lichty works in the shop, his wife Corrie Woods works on getting the word out, managing all marketing aspects. To refresh the company's corporate image, the couple commissioned Stitch Design Co., who came up with a set of stationery showing the same astounding attention to detail that goes into each of Lichty's handcrafted guitars.

GIFT CERTICATE
FOR AN ARTISAN CRAFTED INSTRUMENT BUILT
BY NORTH CAROLINA
luthier
JAY LICHTY
GUITARS

LICHTY GUITARS
crafted
INSTRUMENT GENERAL CARE CARD
take care of your instrument
IT WILL PROVIDE A LIFETIME OF PLAY AND PLEASURE.
TIPS FOR CARE:
the basics

GIFT CERTICATE
JAY LICHTY
LICHTY GUITARS
crafted
LICHTY GUITARS WARRANTY
WE WANT YOU TO ENJOY A LIFETIME OF PLAY FROM YOUR LICHTY HANDCRAFTED INSTRUMENT. THEREFORE THE MATERIALS AND WORKMANSHIP ARE GUARANTEED FOR THE LIFE OF THE LUTHIER.
APPROVAL PERIOD
LIMITED LIFETIME WARRANTY
crafted
LICHTY GUITARS

Goodhood

FASHION & LIFESTYLE STORE

London, UK, *by Goodhood Creative*

Kyle Stewart and Jo Sindle had both worked for denim labels before they founded their select fashion boutique Goodhood. Started as a self-initiated, self-funded project to curate clothing collections, the store soon developed into a renowned retail business with worldwide web distribution.
It has since been expanded from fashion to lifestyle and living goods, and, more recently, from its humble home-base in a Hoxton backstreet to a 3,000-square-foot flagship store close-by. Communicating exclusively in black, white, and gray, their brand, developed by affiliate design agency Goodhood Creative, underlines the store's understated yet still superb style, and a business ethos based on ideas of independence and exclusivity. Goodhood store's fifth anniversary was accompanied by a capsule collection comprising a selection of bespoke garments and goods in the Goodhood brand colors. The collection came with custom swing tags and labeling featurin the Goodhood store's fifth anniversary motif, a pattern of palm trees and pyramids that Goodhood Creative conceived for the celebration.

BLACK AND WHITE BRAND. STYLISH TROUSERS AND SHIRTS. PALM TREES AND PYRAMIDS. CELEBRATING THE GOODHOOD STORE'S FIFTH ANNIVERSARY, AFFILIATE AGENCY GOODHOOD CREATIVE TRANSLATED THEIR IDEA OF GOODHOOD TO A GRAPHIC PATTERN.

GUTSCHEIN
GUTSCHEIN
FRISEUR
ALEX & ANTJE
030.70 24 82 1
B
10999
L
WWW.ALEXUNDANTJE.
MEISTER
FRAENKE
-UFER •28
GUTSCHEIN

Alex & Antje

HAIR SALON

Berlin, Germany, *by 44flavours*

ALEX & ANTJE CELEBRATE THE HAIR CUTTER'S CRAFT WITH GRITTY GRAPHICS BY 44FLAVOURS.

Alex & Antje is a Berlin-based barbershop operated by Alexander Peikert and Antje Kullmann. Creatively ambitious, the two shunned an off-the-shelf salon, and, with the help of their friend Christian Hebbe, developed an offbeat DIY interior instead. The salon's corporate identity was designed by the befriended creatives from 44flavours, who claim that Alex & Antje are certified first-league when it comes to chopping wigs. They chose some woodcut-inspired type to celebrate their friends' fondness for the traditional aspects of their craft.

Oribe

HAIR PRODUCTS

New York, NY, USA, *by Buero New York*

Famed for having obscured some top models' faces with unbridled hunks of hair, Cuban-born American hairstylist Oribe had long been a star in the fashion scene when he founded his eponymous product line. It all started back in 1994 with the first styling product, launched in celebration of Oribe's new salon: a colored pomade inspired by the two-toned hair of comic book heroes, with packaging design direction by Karl Lagerfeld. Now, combining over 30 years of styling heritage at the top of the editorial and salon worlds with traditional craftsmanship and cutting-edge innovation, Oribe stands among the industry's most recognized hairstyle brands. Buero New York were entrusted to fit Oribe with a visual identity that would represent that prestige and reflect the fusion of heritage and modernity that the product line stands for.

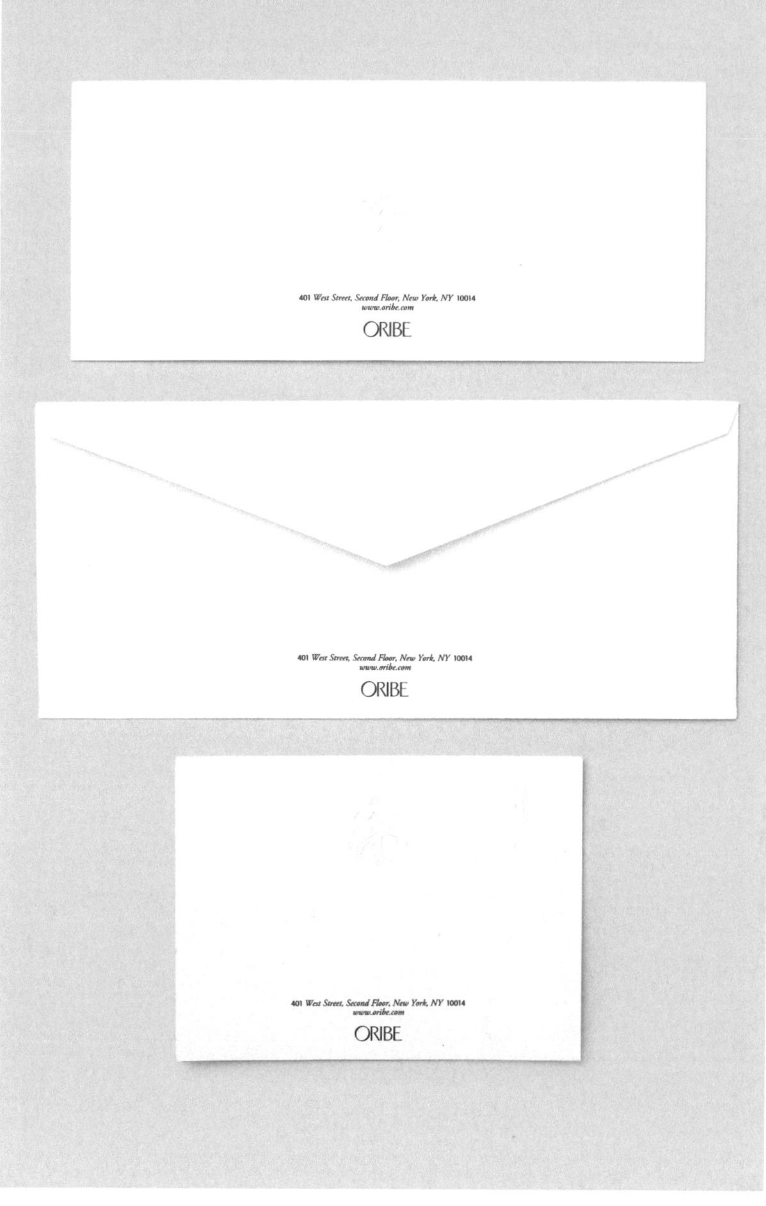

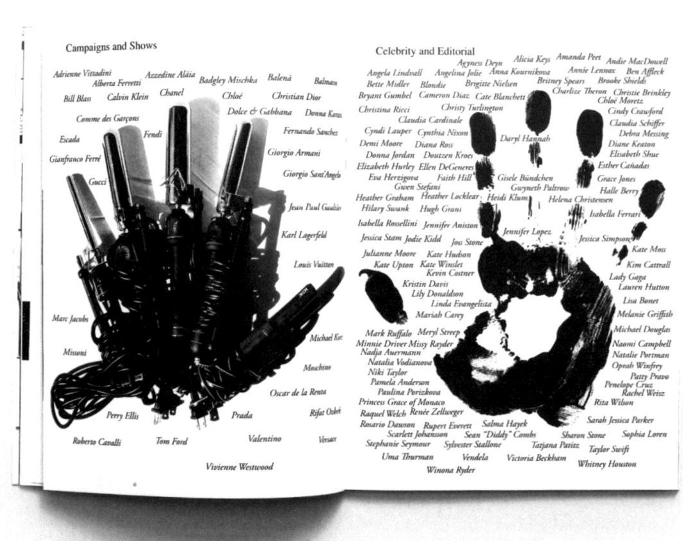

BAD HAIR DAYS SEEM NUMBERED THANKS TO A BAD BOY FROM CUBA,
WHO BECAME ONE OF THE MOST SOUGHT-AFTER BEAUTY ARTISANS. THANKS TO BUERO NEW YORK,
HIS BRAND IDENTITY SITS IN NO WAY INFERIOR TO ORIBE-CARED HAIR.

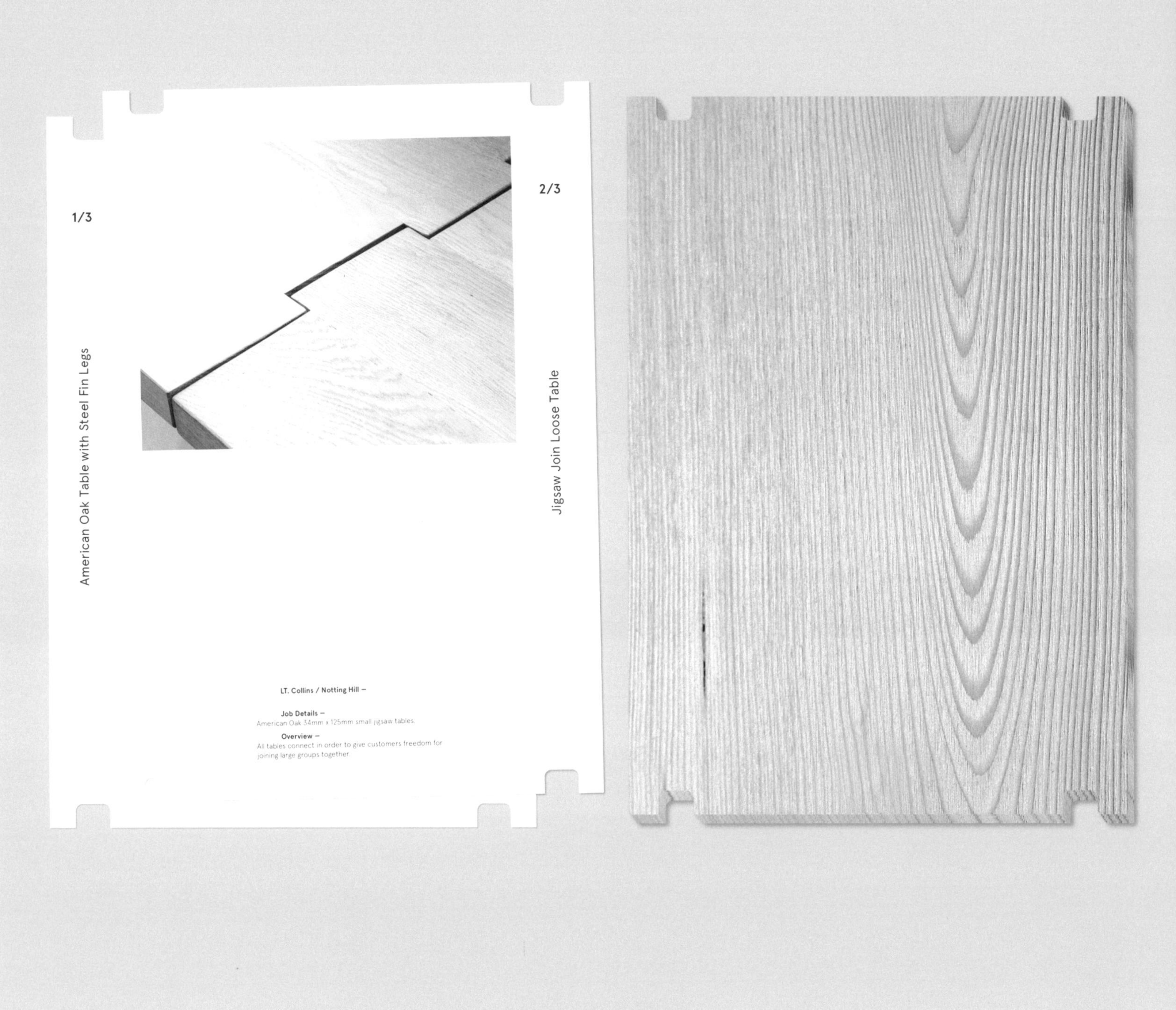

1/3
2/3
American Oak Table with Steel Fin Legs
Jigsaw Join Loose Table
LT. Collins / Notting Hill –
Job Details –
American Oak 34mm x 125mm small jigsaw tables.
Overview –
All tables connect in order to give customers freedom for joining large groups together.

AP-DB

FURNITURE DESIGN & MANUFACTURER

Melbourne, Australia, *by Studio SP-GD*

AP-DB is Melbourne furniture maker Ari Prasetya. Studio SP-GD fitted his firm with a superb set of corporate collateral to support the minimalist style of his manufactures. Since many of Prasetya's projects are inspired by Danish modernism, the designers decided to keep the pallet clean and civil like the streets of Copenhagen. They worked with a lot of white space and combined it with wooden surfaces, like the cut larch plate lock system they had custom-made for the presentation folder. Some strikingly set type symbolizes AP-DB's experimental approach.

CLEVERLY SUCCINCT: A NO-FUSS NO-FRILLS APPROACH TO CORPORATE BRANDING MIRRORS AP-DB'S CLEAN-LINED FURNITURE.

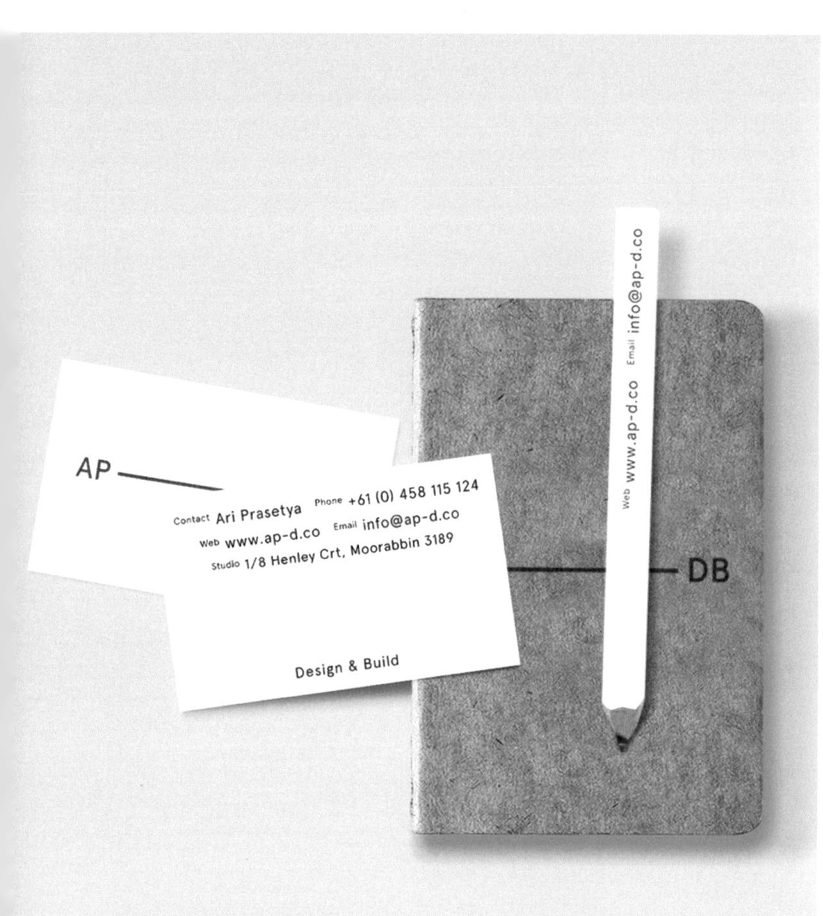

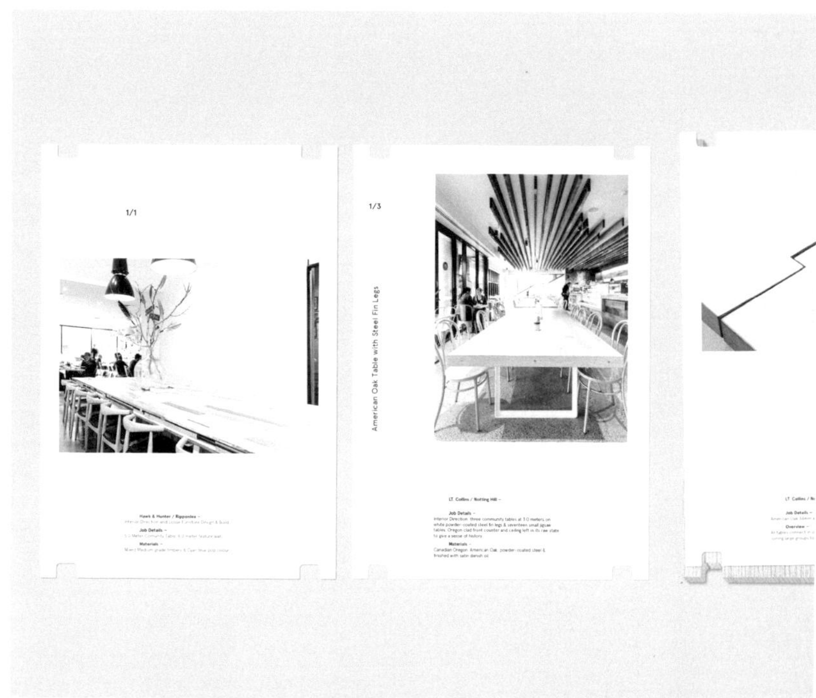

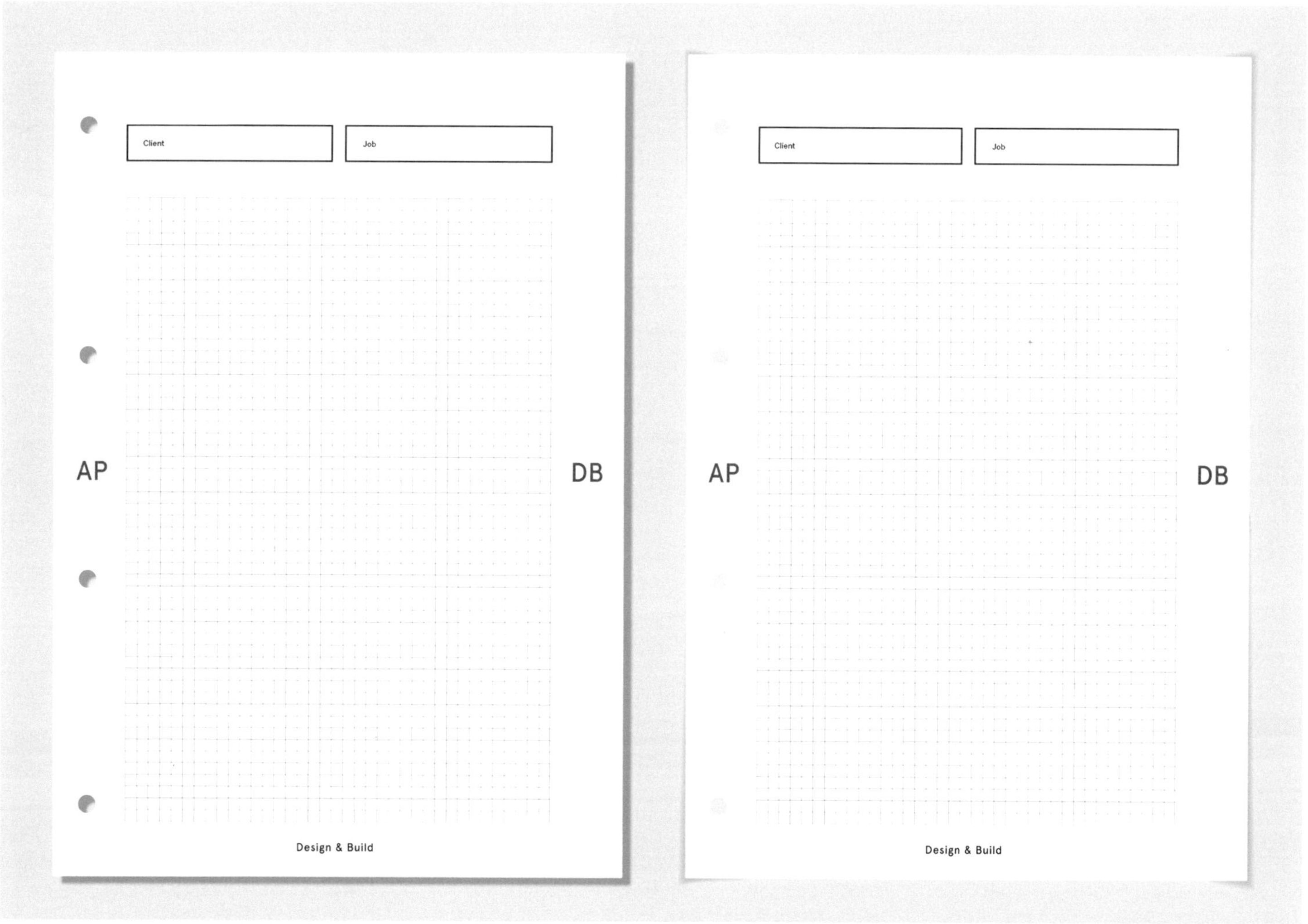

Client
Job
AP
DB
Design & Build

Client
Job
AP
DB
Design & Build

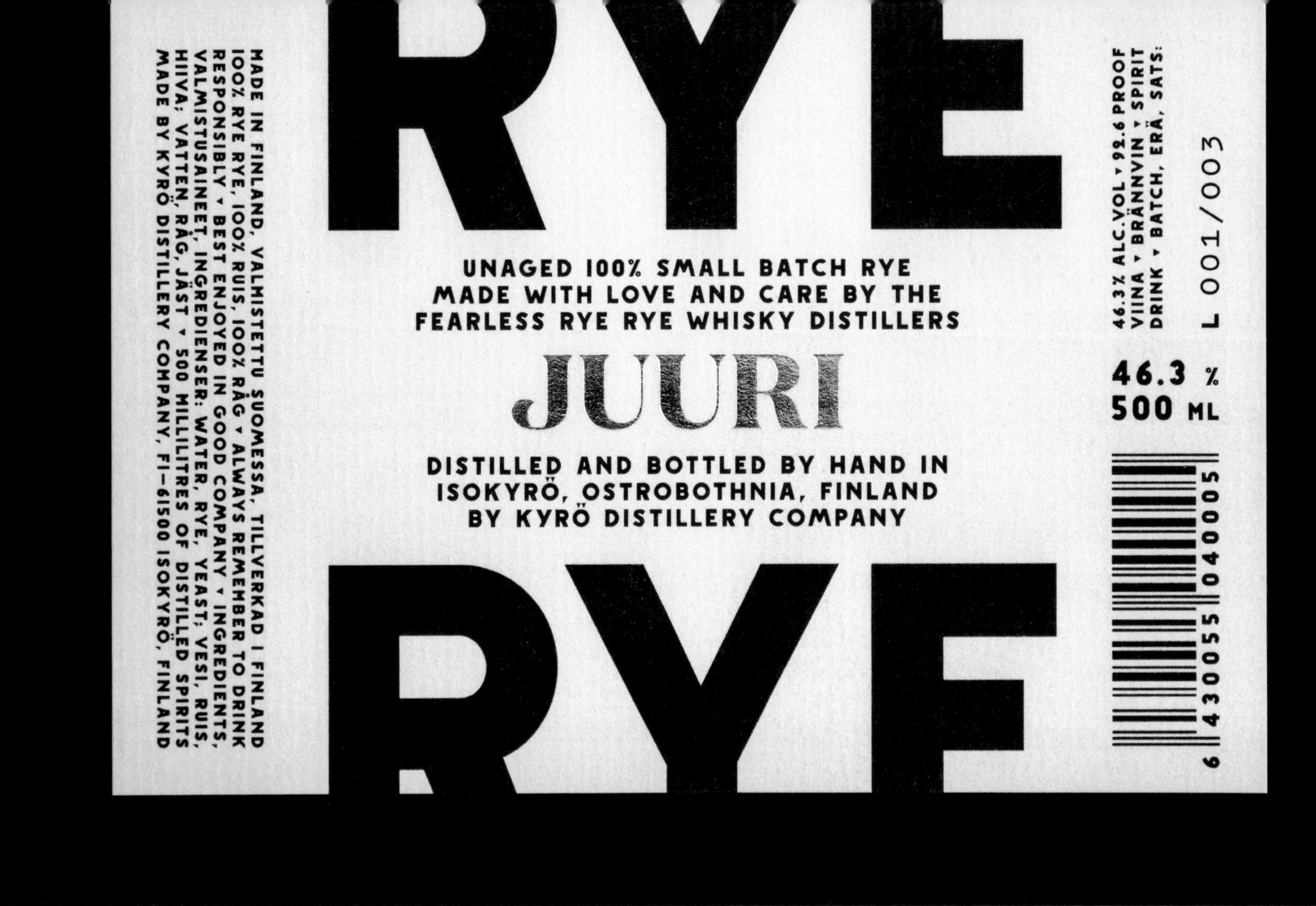

Kyrö

WHISKEY DISTILLERY

Isokyrö, Finland, *by Werklig*

THE STORY OF KYRÖ'S FOUNDATION IS SUPER FINNISH, NAMELY SET IN A SAUNA. THE COMPANY SEAL IS INFUSED WITH LOCAL HERITAGE TOO, RECREATING THE CITY OF ISOKYRÖ'S COAT OF ARMS, A BEAR HUGGING A TREE, AND REPLACING THE TREE WITH A BOTTLE.

It was during the start of summer 2012 that five sweaty Finns sat in a sauna, speaking about savoring whiskey in good company, and wondering why there was no good company to refine savory rye whiskey in their country. Their first test batch from 100 percent malted rye mash was produced around a year later, and in 2013 they picked the perfect home for their project: the long disused Kyrönmaa dairy factory. It dates back to 1908 and is located on a historic site of Isokyrö, in the heartlands of Finland's Ostrobothnia, where the remains of a hundred human sacrifices from 500 BC were once found, and where several battles and rebellions raged in the centuries that followed. When the five young entrepreneurs first entered the local pub of this peculiar place, people thought they were a band. They say that they feel a bit like one, and landed their first hit with a brilliant branding concept by Werklig. The identity is infused with Nordic heritage and based on a custom typeface called "Napue Sans," drawing inspiration from old Napue battle memorial monument engravings that can be found next to the distillery building. Basically black and white, with only slight silver and golden accents, the design direction for the distillery is stylish yet sober enough to stand the test of time: its initial products called "Juuri" (rye) and "Napue" (gin) are already in production, the first batch of matured whiskey won't be available before 2017.

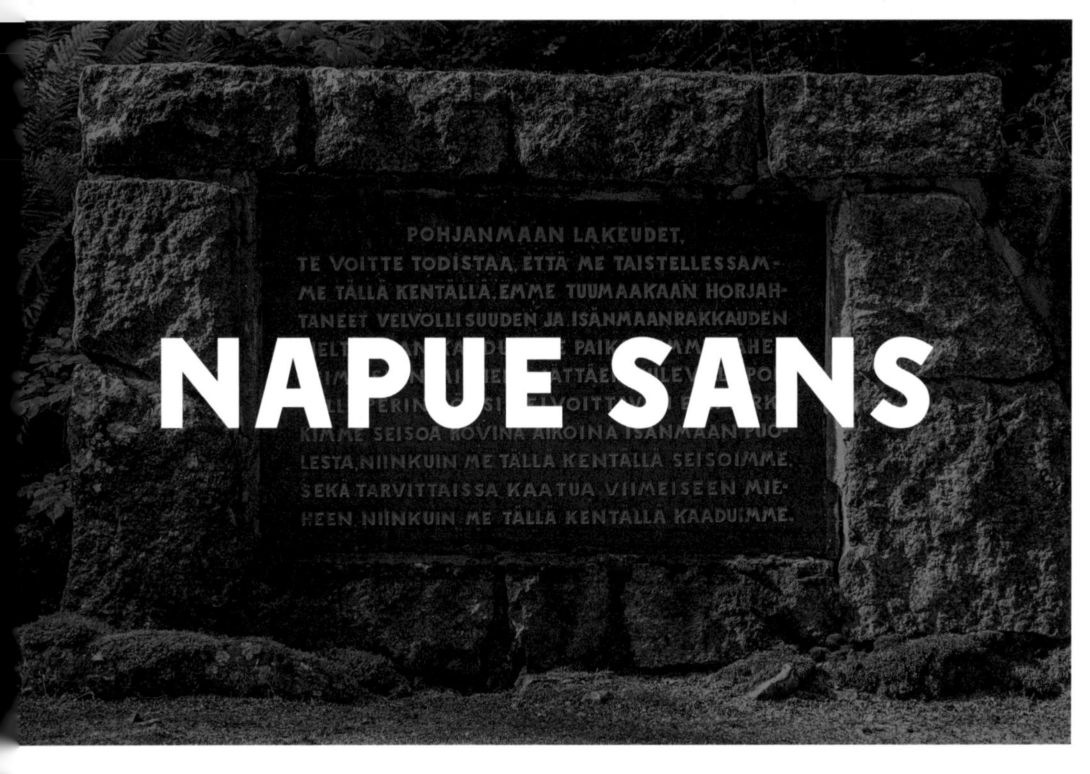

ABCCDEFGGHIJK
LMMNOOPQRST
UVWXYYZÅÄÖ
12345678900
!?@:;.,*£¥$€%+&
OF AT .COM .FI TO

ISOKYRÖ

FIN
OKYRŐ
RŐ
ERY
NY

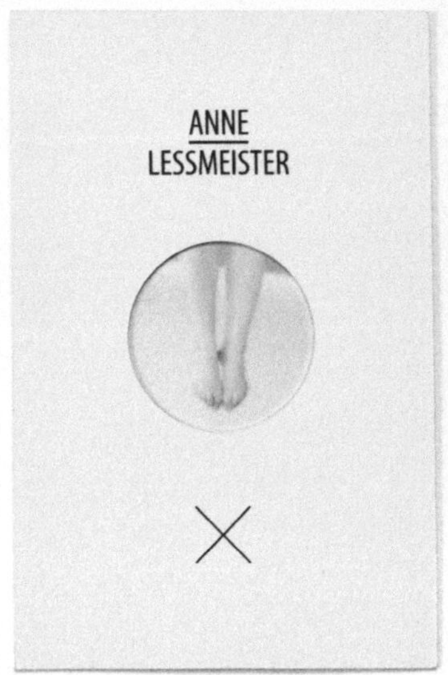

Anne Lessmeister

ACTRESS

Baden-Baden, Germany
by Perezramerstorfer Design

Competition is brutal in the performing arts business, which is why actress Anne Lessmeister was looking for promotional materials that ensure a lot of attention. She assigned the task to Perezramerstorfer Design, who provided her with a very personal solution of carefully crafted cards. Knowing that Lessmeister would not need large amounts of business cards, the designers decided to go for a small handmade set, and pasted in photo prints portraying the actress herself in various poses.
With a series of animated gifs based on the same photos, they transported the theme to Lessmeister's new website.

ACTRESS ANNE LESSMEISTER LOVES PHOTO BOOTHS, AND HAS CREATED SMALL PERFORMANCES SHOOTING PHOTOS OF HERSELF. PEREZRAMERSTORFER PROVIDED HER WITH A SET OF BUSINESS CARDS BASED ON HER PASSION.

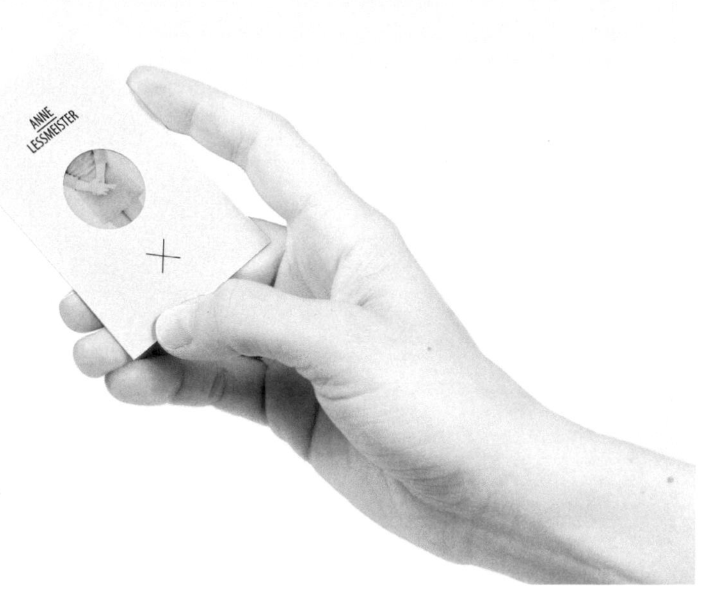

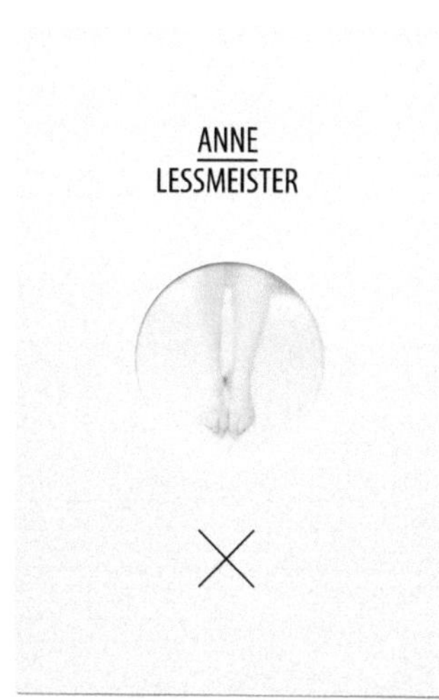

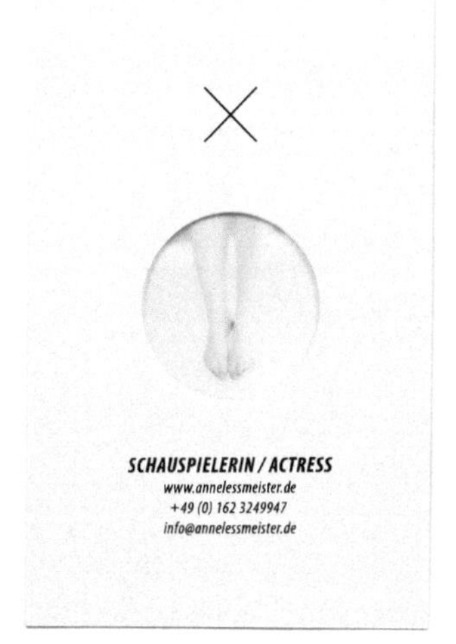

Index

DAVID BÜSSER & PATRIK FERRARELLI

www.davidbuesser.com

Annette Hamburger

CLIENT: Annette Hamburger
DESIGNER: David Büsser & Patrik Ferrarelli
PHOTOGRAPHER CREDITS: David Büsser
PP. 32—33

DDMMYY

www.ddmmyy.com

Triumph & Disaster

CLIENT: Triumph & Disaster
DESIGNER: DDMMYY
PHOTOGRAPHER CREDITS: Kelvin Soh
PP. 122—125

DENNIS ADELMANN

www.dennisadelmann.de

Wanderlust

CLIENT: Wanderlust
DESIGNER: Dennis Adelmann, David Heinze
PHOTOGRAPHER CREDITS: Dennis Adelmann, David Heinze
PP. 178—179

DESIGN STUDIO OF BOTH

www.designstudioofboth.com

Kinegé

CLIENT: Centre de Fisioteràpia Kinegé
DESIGNER: Àxel Durana
PHOTOGRAPHER CREDITS: Design Studio of Both
PP. 204—205

DEUTSCHE & JAPANER

www.deutscheundjapaner.com

SPEICHER7

CLIENT: Speicher7 Hotel
DESIGNER: Deutsche & Japaner
PHOTOGRAPHER CREDITS: severafrahm.com, Mario Mata Parducci, Nico Krijno
PP. 68–71

DIOTOYS

WWW.DIOTOYS.COM

Diotoys

CLIENT: Diotoys
DESIGNER: Réka Diósi
PHOTOGRAPHER CREDITS: Tamás Egry,
Toy design: Imre Diósi
PP. 180—183

DOT DASH

www.thisisdotdash.com

Fatties

CLIENT: Fatties
DESIGNER: Laura Walpole, Justin Hallstrom
PHOTOGRAPHER CREDITS: Jessica Nerstrand
Image Credits: Dot Dash
PP. 44—45

ELVIRE DELANOTE

www.elviredelanote.be

Supersaga

CLIENT: Supersaga
DESIGNER: Elvire Delanote
PHOTOGRAPHER CREDITS: Elvire Delanote
PP. 116—117

ESKIMO DESIGN

www.eskimodesign.ru

Shave & Blade

CLIENT: Shave & Blade
DESIGNER: Pavel Emelyanov
PHOTOGRAPHER CREDITS: Andrey Pleshkov
ADDITIONAL CREDITS:
Manager: Denis Gluschenko
Illustrator: Valeriy Golubzov
PP. 34—39

FLORENTINE KITCHEN KNIVES

www.florentinekitchenknives.com

Florentine Kitchen Knives

CLIENT: Florentine Kitchen Knives
DESIGNER: Branding: Ran Shauli
Industrial design: Tomer Botner
PHOTOGRAPHER CREDITS: Aya Wind
PP. 132—135

FOREIGN POLICY DESIGN GROUP

www.foreignpolicydesign.com

Hay Market

CLIENT: Hong Kong Jockey Club
DESIGNER: Foreign Policy Design Group
PHOTOGRAPHER CREDITS: Jovian Lim
PP. 78—81

FRANK LEDER

www.frank-leder.com

Frank Leder / Tradition

CLIENT: Frank Leder
DESIGNER: Frank Leder
PHOTOGRAPHER CREDITS: Achim Hatzius, Frank Leder, Hirohito Okayasu
PP. 130—131

FRIENDSHIP HAMBURG

www.friendship-hamburg.com

Försterei Reinbek

CLIENT: Försterei Reinbek
DESIGNER: Friendship Hamburg
PHOTOGRAPHER CREDITS: Marco Hess
Art Direction: Marco Hess & Nina Brandt
PP. 46—47

Dachdeckmeister Garling

CLIENT: Dachdeckmeister Garling
DESIGNER: Friendship Hamburg
PHOTOGRAPHER CREDITS: Marco Hess
Art Direction: Marco Hess & Nina Brand
PP. 48—49

FULLFILL

www.fullfillisme.com

Onni Flower Market

CLIENT: Onni Flower Market
DESIGNER: FullFill
PHOTOGRAPHER CREDITS: FullFill
PP. 40—41

GLASFURD & WALKER

www.glasfurdandwalker.com

Rain Or Shine

CLIENT: Rain Or Shine
DESIGNER: Glasfurd & Walker
PHOTOGRAPHER CREDITS: Glasfurd & Walker
PP. 74—75

GOOD DESIGN COMPANY

www.gooddesigncompany.com

THE

CLIENT: THE Co,.Ltd.
DESIGNER: Good Design Company
PHOTOGRAPHER CREDITS: Kiyoshi Obara
Product design: Keita Suzuki
Package design: good design company
CD: Manabu Mizuno
PP. 146—147

motta

CLIENT: Nakagawa Masashichi Shoten Co., Ltd.
DESIGNER: Good Design Company
PHOTOGRAPHER CREDITS: Good Design Company
PP. 148—149

Shimogamosaryo

CLIENT: Shimogamosaryo
DESIGNER: Good Design Company
PHOTOGRAPHER CREDITS: Good Design Company
PP. 152—153

GOODHOOD CREATIVE

www.goodhoodcreative.com

Goodhood

CLIENT: Goodhood Store
DESIGNER: Goodhood Creative
PHOTOGRAPHER CREDITS: Goodhood Creative
PP. 236 — 237

JONATHAN S. GARRETT

www.jonogarrett.com

Frida von Fuchs

CLIENT: Frida von Fuchs
DESIGNER: Jono Garrett
PHOTOGRAPHER CREDITS: Jono Garrett
Project Management: Femke Peter & Ben Bencivinni
PP. 52 — 53

HAW-LIN SERVICES

www.haw-lin-services.com

PB 0110

CLIENT: PB 0110, Philipp Bree
PHOTOGRAPHER CREDITS: Haw-lin Services
PP. 98 — 101

Kostas Murkudis

CLIENT: Kostas Murkudis
PHOTOGRAPHER CREDITS: Jonas Lindström, Haw-lin Services
PP. 102 — 103

Marsano Berlin

CLIENT: Marsano Berlin
DESIGNER: Haw-lin Services
PHOTOGRAPHER CREDITS: Haw-lin Services
PP. 194 — 195

HELLOME

www.tillwiedeck.com

Marsano Berlin

CLIENT: Marsano Berlin
DESIGNER: HelloMe
PHOTOGRAPHER CREDITS: HelloMe
PP. 192 — 193

HEYDAYS

www.heydays.no

Skovin Gulv

CLIENT: Skovin Gulv
DESIGNER: Heydays
PHOTOGRAPHER CREDITS: Heydays
PP. 42 — 43

KNOED CREATIVE

www.knoed.com

Outpost General Store

CLIENT: Outpost General Store
DESIGNER: Kim Knoll
PHOTOGRAPHER CREDITS: Knoed Creative
PP. 114 — 115

British American Household Staffing

CLIENT: British American Household Staffing
DESIGNER: Knoed Creatives
PHOTOGRAPHER CREDITS: Knoed Creative
PP. 138 — 139

Optimo Hats

CLIENT: Optimo Hats
DESIGNER: Knoed Creative
PHOTOGRAPHER CREDITS: Chris Lake, Tadd Myers (courtesy of AmericanCraftsmanProject.com), Knoed Creative
PP. 214 — 217

LA TORTILLERÍA

www.latortilleria.com

Tamarindo

CLIENT: Ruben Gil D. and Gretta R. Valdés
DESIGNER: La Tortillería
PHOTOGRAPHER CREDITS: CAROGA and La Tortillería

LABOUR & WAIT

www.labourandwait.co.uk

Labour and Wait

CLIENT: Labour and Wait
DESIGNER: Labour and Wait
PHOTOGRAPHER CREDITS: Andrew Moran, Labour and Wait
Design: Simon Watkins, Rachel Wythe-Moran, Richard Sanderson
PP. 136 — 137

LOTTA NIEMINEN

www.lottanieminen.com

Paintbox

CLIENT: Paintbox
DESIGNER: Lotta Nieminen
PHOTOGRAPHER CREDITS: Jamie Nelson
PP. 184 — 187

MADE THOUGHT

www.madethought.com

G . F Smith

CLIENT: G . F Smith
DESIGNER: Made Thought
PHOTOGRAPHER CREDITS: Made Thought
PP. 96 — 97

MANUTEEFAKTUR

www.manuteefaktur.com

ManuTeeFaktur

DESIGNER: Manu Kumar
PHOTOGRAPHER CREDITS: Manu Kumar, Ira Hadžić, Marco Baass, Felix Broede
PP. 210 — 213

MARK BROOKS

www.markbrooksgraphikdesign.com

Magro Cardona

CLIENT: Irene Magro & Ana Cardona
DESIGNER: Mark Brooks
PHOTOGRAPHER CREDITS: Jorge de Bobadilla & Mark Brooks
PP. 174—175

MERCHANT & MILLS

www.merchantandmills.com

Merchant & Mills

CLIENT: Merchant & Mills
DESIGNER: Roderick Field
PHOTOGRAPHER CREDITS: Roderick Field, Creative Director at Merchant & Mills
PP. 166 — 167

MEMELA

www.memela.mx

Barbierattoo

CLIENT: The Creative Co
DESIGNER: Memela
PHOTOGRAPHER CREDITS: David Sayeg & Wen Ramos
Concept & Art direction: Memela, Nick Cabrera
Account Manager: Jorge Lazcano
PP. 188 — 191

MICHAEL THORSBY

www.michaelthorsby.com

At Les

CLIENT: At Les
DESIGNER: Michael Thorsby
PHOTOGRAPHER CREDITS: Michael Thorsby
PP. 76—77

MOODLEY BRAND IDENTITY

www.moodley.at

Am Dorfplatz 8

CLIENT: Bettina Stoisser-Hubmann
DESIGNER: Mike Fuisz, Natascha Triebl, Stefan Unger
PHOTOGRAPHER CREDITS: Michael Königshofer
PP. 16 — 17

Martina Sperl

CLIENT: Martina Sperl
DESIGNER: Mike Fuisz, Sabine Kernbichler
PHOTOGRAPHER CREDITS: Michael Königshofer
PP. 18 — 19

Leading Search Partners

CLIENT: Leading Search Partners
DESIGNER: Mike Fuisz, Nicole Lugitsch
PHOTOGRAPHER CREDITS: Marion Luttenberger
Illustration: Malgorzata Bieroza bieroza.pl
PP. 20 — 21

NICHOLAS CHRISTOWITZ

www.nicholaschristowitz.com

ANVIL

CLIENT: Anvil
DESIGNER: Nicholas Christowitz
PHOTOGRAPHER CREDITS: Nicholas Christowitz, Craig Morrison
PP. 66 — 67

NOISE 13

www.noise13.com

Ziesche

CLIENT: Sherri Ziesche
DESIGNER: Ben Wong
PHOTOGRAPHER CREDITS: Noise 13
Creative Director: Dava Guthmiller
PP. 168 — 169

NONUSUAL

www.nonusual.com

Gropes

CLIENT: Nonusual
DESIGNER: Akira Chatani
PHOTOGRAPHER CREDITS: Akira Chantani, Yu Fujiwara
PP. 54 — 57

OK-RM

www.ok-rm.co.uk

Foundwell

CLIENT: Foundwell
DESIGNER: OK-RM
PHOTOGRAPHER CREDITS: OK-RM, Matthieu Lavanchy
PP. 140 — 141

Black Isle Bakery

CLIENT: Black Isle Bakery
DESIGNER: OK-RM
PHOTOGRAPHER CREDITS: OK-RM, Lena C. Emery
PP. 142 — 145

P.A.R

www.p-a-r.net/lapatente.html

La Patente

CLIENT: La Patente
DESIGNER: P.A.R
PHOTOGRAPHER CREDITS: P.A.R
Illustration: Pol Montserrat
PP. 64 — 65

PARIS+HENDZEL CO.

www.parishendzel.co

Paris+Hendzel Handcrafted Goods

DESIGNER: Lukasz Hendzel, Paris+Hendzel Studio
PHOTOGRAPHER CREDITS: Paris+Hendzel Studio
PP. 154 — 157

PEREZRAMER-STORFER

www.perezramerstorfer.com

Anne Lessmeister

CLIENT: Anne Lessmeister
DESIGNER: perezramerstorfer design & creative studio
PHOTOGRAPHER CREDITS: Rodrigo Pérez
PP. 248 — 249

PLAU

www.plau.co/en

Andaluz Audiovisual

CLIENT: Andaluz Audiovisual
DESIGNER: Plau, Designers: Eduardo Mattos, Gustavo Saiani, Luisa Borja, Caio Vaccaro, Lucas Campoi
PHOTOGRAPHER CREDITS: Eduardo Mattos
PP. 50 — 51

POHJALA BEER

www.pohjalabeer.com

Põhjala Beer

DESIGNER: Marke Saaremets
PHOTOGRAPHER CREDITS: Põhjala
Image Credits: Renee Altrov www.reneealtrov.tumblr.com
PP. 118 — 119

RAFFINERIE AG

www.raffinerie.com

7132

CLIENT: 7132 AG
DESIGNER: Raffinerie AG für Gestaltung
PHOTOGRAPHER CREDITS: Gianni Pisano
PP. 208 — 209

RE-PUBLIC

www.re-public.com

Ipsen & Co

CLIENT: Ipsen & Co
DESIGNER: Søren Severin
ADDITIONAL CREDITS: Thomas Bræstrup
PP. 58 — 59

RED ANTLER LLC

www.redantler.com

Casper

CLIENT: Casper
DESIGNER: Red Antler
PHOTOGRAPHER CREDITS: Henry Hargreaves
PP. 128 — 129

SAVVY STUDIO

www.savvy-studio.net

Casa Virginia

CLIENT: Mónica Patiño
DESIGNER: Eduardo Heréndez
PHOTOGRAPHER CREDITS: Alejandro Cartagena
PP. 92 — 93

Par La Roy

CLIENT: Par La Roy
DESIGNER: Eduardo Heréndez
PHOTOGRAPHER CREDITS: Alejandro Cartagena
Additional Credits: Emilio Álvarez
PP. 94 — 95

SAY WHAT STUDIO

www.saywhat-studio.com

Apartment A

CLIENT: Apartment A
DESIGNER: Say What Studio
PHOTOGRAPHER CREDITS: Say What Studio
PP. 158 — 161

SKINN BRANDING AGENCY

www.skinn.be

Oyya – ice bar

CLIENT: oyya – ice bar
DESIGNER: Kurt De Vlieghere, Matty Bossouw
PHOTOGRAPHER CREDITS: Skinn Branding Agency, Eddy Paesschezoone
PP. 218 — 219

Wildkop

CLIENT: Wildkop
DESIGNER: Kurt De Vlieghere, Gert Cornelis
PHOTOGRAPHER CREDITS: Skinn Branding Agency, Hannes Verstraete
PP. 220 — 221

STAHL R

www.stahl-r.com

Folkdays

CLIENT: Folkdays
DESIGNER: Stahl R
PHOTOGRAPHER CREDITS: Stahl R
PP. 126 — 127

STITCH DESIGN CO.

www.stitchdesignco.com

Lichty Guitars

CLIENT: Jay Lichty
DESIGNER: Courtney Rowson, Amy Pastre
PHOTOGRAPHER CREDITS: Sully Sullivan
PP. 232 — 235

STUDIO BEIGE

www.studiobeige.nl

GIMSEL Supermarket

CLIENT: Gimsel Supermarket
DESIGNER: Masja van Deursen and Silvia Vergeer
PHOTOGRAPHER CREDITS: Jan Bijl, Leontien Herkelman
Text: Hanne Marckmann
PP. 120 — 121

STUDIO MAHR

www.studiomahr.de

Chelsea Farmers Club

CLIENT: Chelsea Farmers Club
DESIGNER: Lena Mahr
PHOTOGRAPHER CREDITS: Lena Mahr, Christoph Tophinke
PP. 222—227

STUDIO NEWWORK

www.studionewwork.com

BESPOKE

CLIENT: Bespoke
DESIGNER: Studio Newwork (Ryotatsu Tanaka, Ryo Kumazaki, Hitomi Ishigaki)
PHOTOGRAPHER CREDITS: Studio Newwork
PP. 176—177

STUDIOAHAMED

www.studioahamed.com

Puree Organics

CLIENT: Puree Organics
DESIGNER: Sophia Ahamed, Studioahamed
PHOTOGRAPHER CREDITS: Studioahamed
PP. 150—151

STUDIO SP—GD

www.sp-gd.com

AP-DB

CLIENT: AP-DB
DESIGNER: Studio SP-GD
PHOTOGRAPHER CREDITS: Mara Tonetti
PP. 242—243

THE PRESSERY

www.thepressery.co.uk

The Pressery

CLIENT: The Pressery
DESIGNER: Tim Jarvis (Profission)
PHOTOGRAPHER CREDITS: The Pressery, Tim Jarvis, Tomas Jivanda, Michael Thomas Jones
PP. 82—83

TRIBORO DESIGN

www.triborodesign.com

Café Standard

CLIENT: André Balazs Properties
DESIGNER: Triboro (Stefanie Weigler, David Heasty)
PHOTOGRAPHER CREDITS: Triboro
PP. 206—207

V

VERONIKA SALZSEILER

wwww.veronikasalzseiler.de

Gompf + Kehrer

CLIENT: Gompf + Kehrer
DESIGNER: Veronika Salzseiler
PHOTOGRAPHER CREDITS: Veronika Salzseiler
PP. 228—229

VINCENT MEERTENS

www.vincentmeertens.com

Strietman

CLIENT: Strietman
DESIGNER: Vincent Meertens
PHOTOGRAPHER CREDITS: Vincent Meertens/ES3, Wouter Strietman
PP. 162—163

WEISS-HEITEN

www.weiss-heiten.com

Rzany&Hund dermatologists

CLIENT: Rzany&Hund private practice
DESIGNER: Weiss-heiten
PHOTOGRAPHER CREDITS: Christian Beutler
PP. 86—89

WERKLIG

www.werklig.com

Kyrö Distillery Company

CLIENT: Kyrö Distillery Company
DESIGNER: Werklig
PHOTOGRAPHER CREDITS: Kimmo Syväri & Werklig
PP. 244—247

WIDE AND NARROW

www.wideandnarrow.co.th

4/52

CLIENT: Fourth of Fifty Second
DESIGNER: Poomruethai Suebsantiwongse, Kanwee Harichanwong, Jakkrapat Oupkham
PHOTOGRAPHER CREDITS: Wide and Narrow Co., Ltd
PP. 84—85

WINTER SESSION

www.winter-session.com

Winter Session

CLIENT: Winter Session
DESIGNER: Nathan Michael
PHOTOGRAPHER CREDITS: Winter Session, Nathan Michael, Ross Evertson
PP. 202—203

YUKIKO

www.y-u-k-i-k-o.com

Walt Hats

CLIENT: Walt Hats
DESIGNER: YUKIKO
PHOTOGRAPHER CREDITS: Eva Napp
PP. 72—73

Start Me Up!

This book was conceived, edited, and designed by **Gestalten.**

Edited by Robert Klanten and Anna Sinofzik
Preface and texts by Anna Sinofzik

Cover design by George Popov
Cover photography by Anagrama, Caroga
Layout and design by George Popov
Typefaces: Grilli Type Sectra Fine by Marc Kappeler, Dominik Huber, and Noël Leu; Grilli Type Haptik by Reto Moser and Tobias Rechsteiner

Copy-editing by Noelia Hobeika
Proofreading by Rachel Sampson

Printed by Nino Druck GmbH, Neustadt/Weinstraße
Made in Germany

Published by Gestalten, Berlin 2015
ISBN 978-3-89955-556-1
3rd printing, 2017

For more information, and to order books, please visit www.gestalten.com.

Bibliographic information published by the Deutsche Nationalbibliothek.
The Deutsche Nationalbibliothek lists this publication in the Deutsche Nationalbibliografie; detailed bibliographic data are available online at http://dnb.d-nb.de.

None of the content in this book was published in exchange for payment by commercial parties or designers; Gestalten selected all included work based solely on its artistic merit.

This book was printed on paper certified according to the standard of FSC®.